AF473966

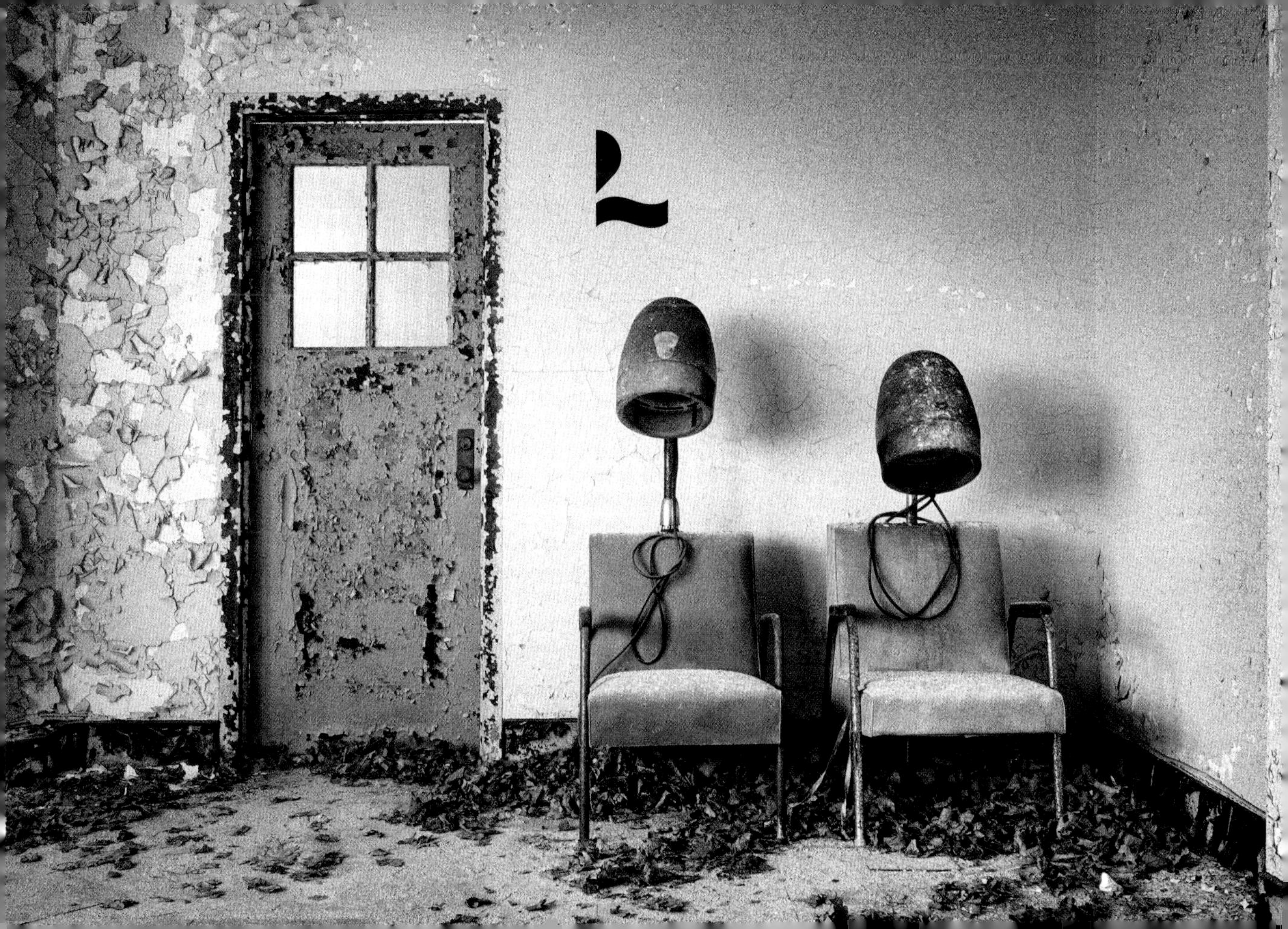
2

HENK VAN RENSBERGEN

ABANDONED PLACES

Lannoo

P1: New Jersey State Lunatic Asylum, USA, 2004

PREFACE

HENK VAN RENSBERGEN

We had been sneaking around the villa in the dunes for days. Was anyone still living there? Some of the windows had been broken and the front door was wide open, but when we peered into the villa we saw furniture, crockery in the cupboards and the remains of food on the table. Taking that step through the front door seemed like the most challenging feat, but our excitement only increased as we ventured further in. We walked past the coats on the coat stand and into the living room.

The stairs creaked as we climbed them. Suddenly, we heard stumbling. In the half-darkness there was total panic, as everyone tried to run for the front door at the same time, and there, in the daylight, we recognized the boys we had played with the previous day on the beach.

It felt as though the summer holidays would never end. We got to know every nook and cranny of the ghost villa. There was an ancient black and white TV, which exploded with a loud bang, sending a cloud of dust into the room. We played hide and seek in the upstairs bedrooms and came upon an old clock that still worked. A year later, the villa had disappeared and the year after that, new apartments had risen up in its place.

I bought my first camera in 1984, when I was 16. I made a habit of taking my camera with me on visits to new abandoned buildings I discovered. In those early years, I had a fascination for all things industrial. Once I got my driving license, I could travel further afield to seek out places such as Charleroi, Anderlues, Tertre, Ghent or Zeebrugge, and of course, the Buda

Marly factory by the canal in Brussels.

In the early 1990s, I built a website, which was fairly unique at the time. I called it Industrial Art, a rather silly name that I soon replaced with www.abandoned-places.com. Later I developed another website - www.henkvanrensbergen.com. Press interest started growing, and sometimes, when a building was to be demolished, I was asked to be interviewed. Eventually, the number of visitors to my website peaked, and slowly, a network of urban explorers began to develop. We exchanged information and occasionally met up. These early friendships are still alive today, and they have left me with many fond and often exciting memories. For me, the challenge in photography was not simply to record what was there to see, but to reproduce the atmosphere: the tension, the complexity, the philosophical questions, the emotions and the surprises these places would have in store.

I regularly revisited the same places, befriended the local iron thieves, and saw how factories were slowly looted and finally razed to the ground.

My flying career enabled me to explore abandoned places abroad. I visited most European countries, travelled to Japan, Sri Lanka, Mexico, Brazil, Africa and the United States, to name a few. I met some fantastic people with whom I teamed up to explore. I also like to venture out on my own when it is safe to do so.

Should you ever want to start exploring yourself, think about the following: Take nothing but photos, leave nothing but footsteps. It's never the intention to force open windows or doors and to break in. It is equally important not to invade the privacy of the former residents; call it urban exploration ethics.

The book you're now holding is an update of 'Abandoned Places', the 2016 edition, which included a collection of the best photos. This 2019 book includes new photos and stories from my recent trips to Abkhazia, Croatia, Italy and Portugal. Enjoy! ◆

Carlo Rizzoli's post, Belgium, 1996

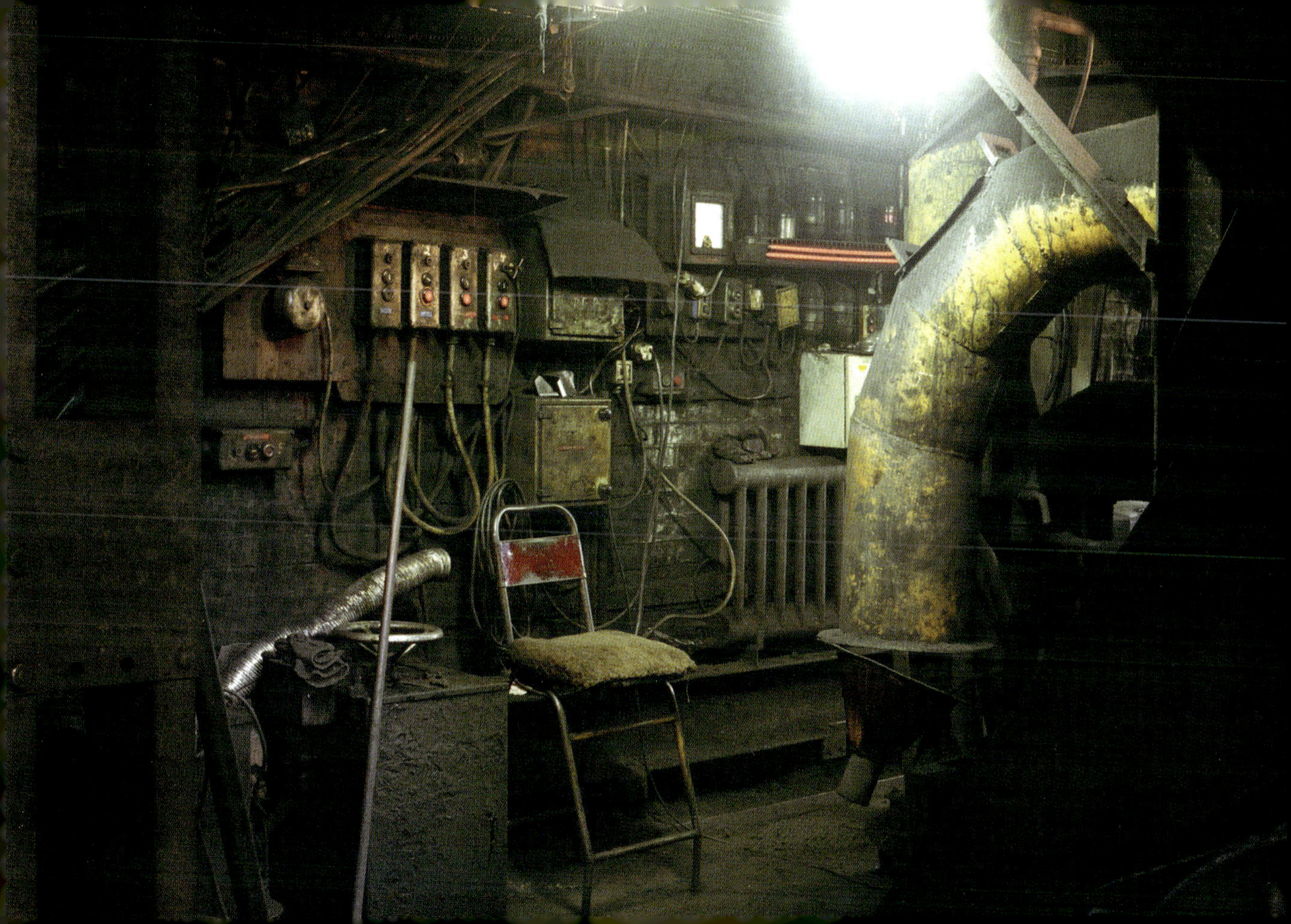

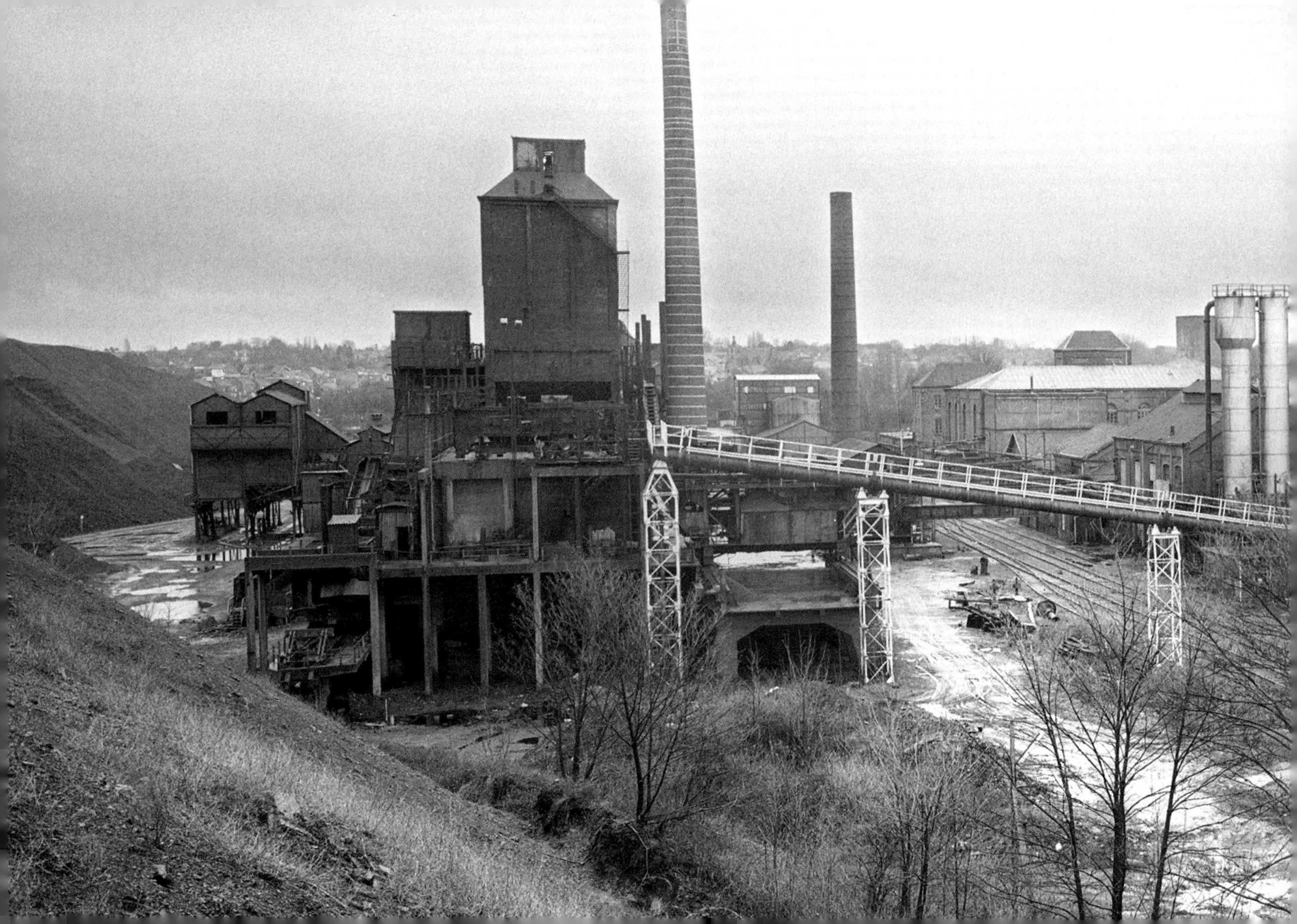

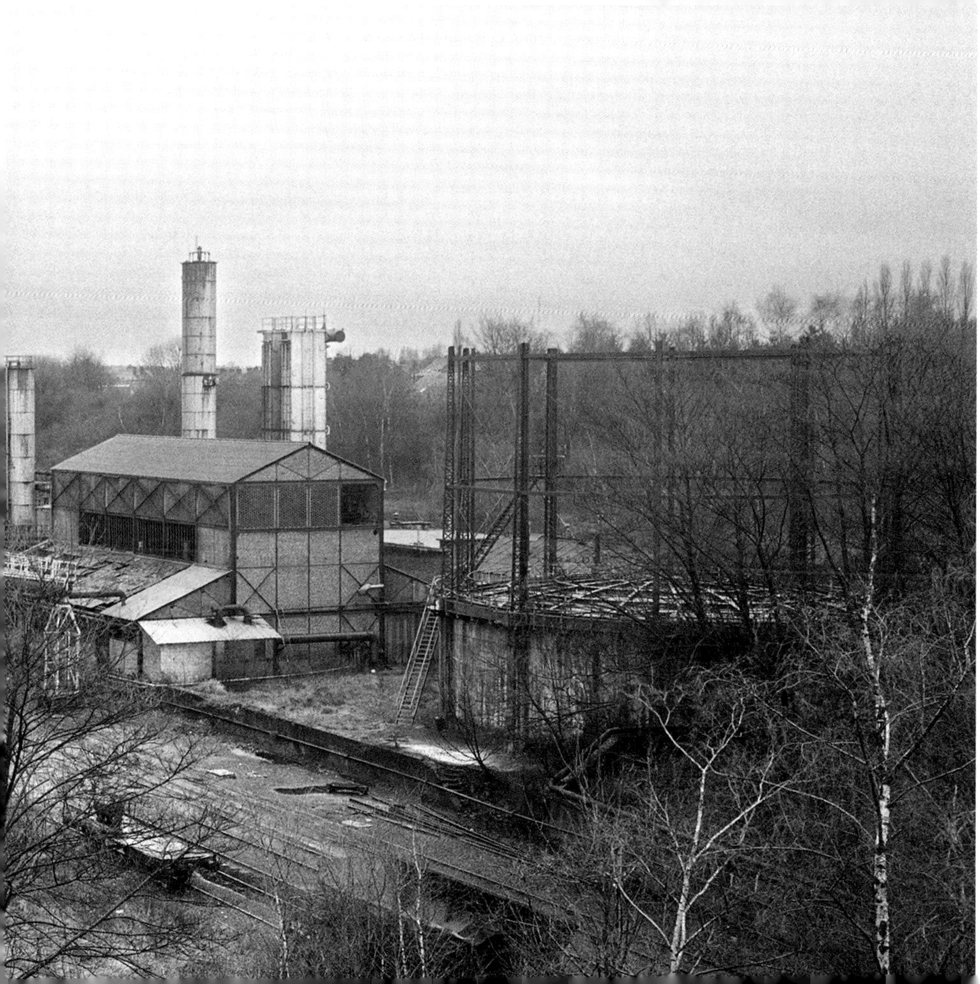

9 Anderlues, Belgium, 2002

10 Centrales Electriques des Flandres, Belgium, 2009

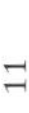

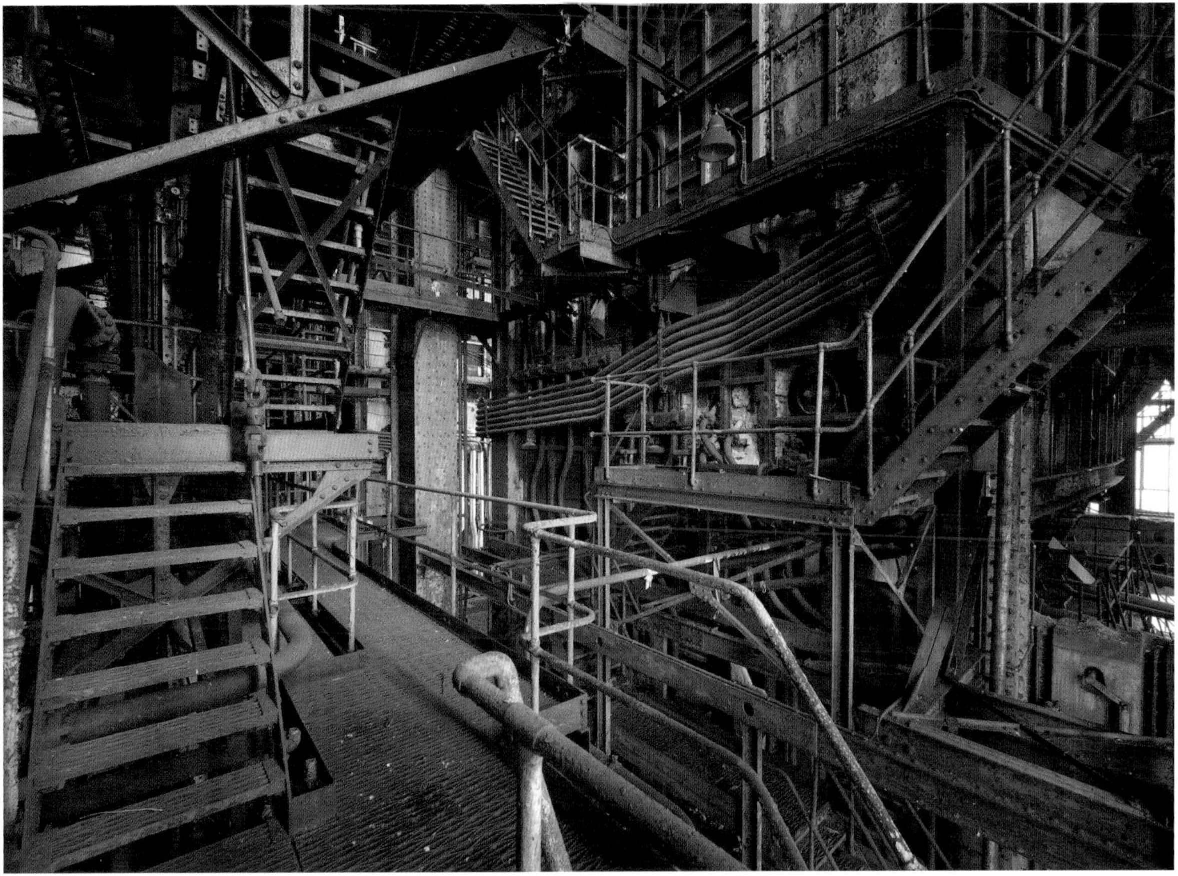

11 Centrales Electriques des Flandres, Belgium, 2009

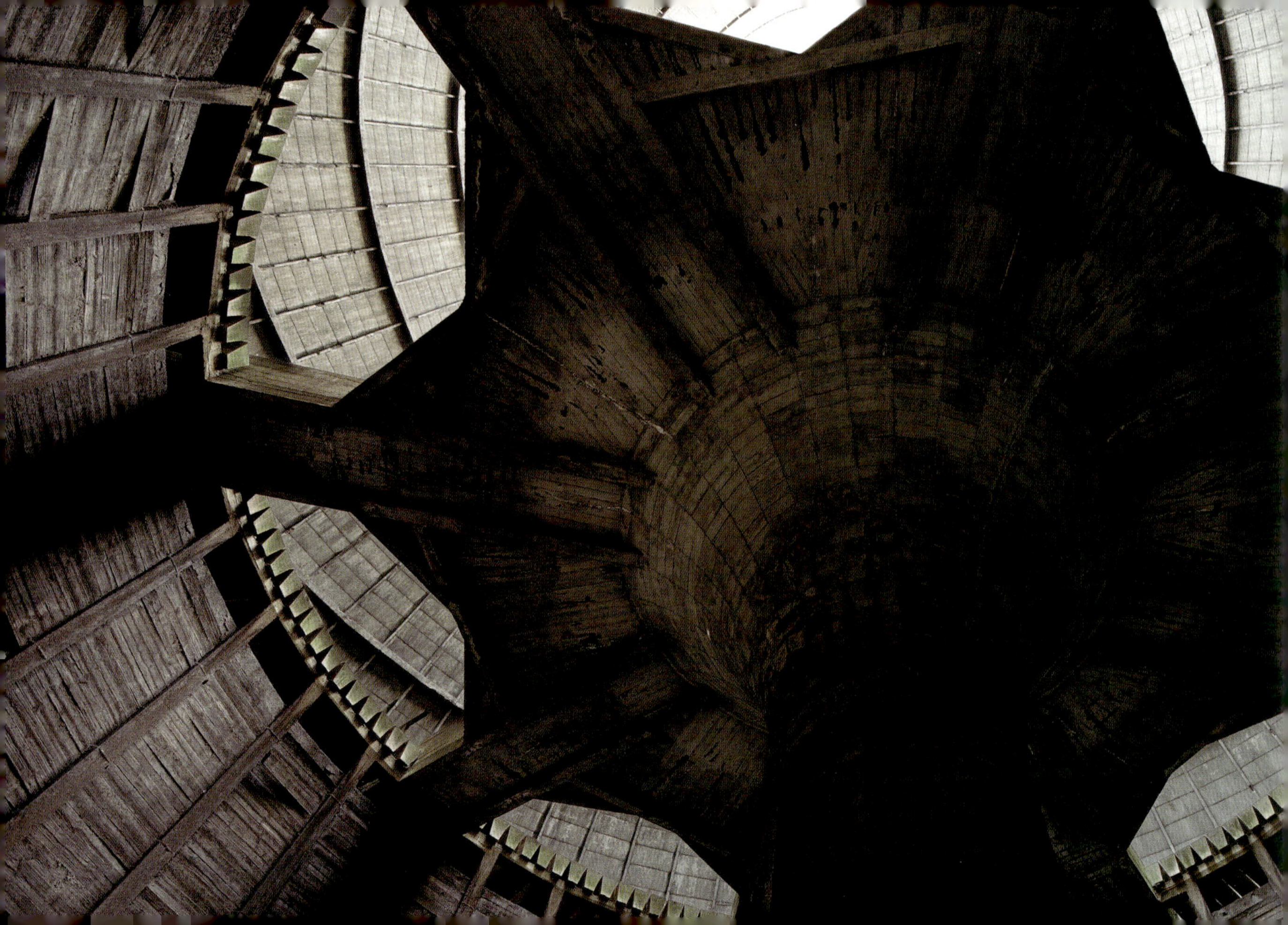

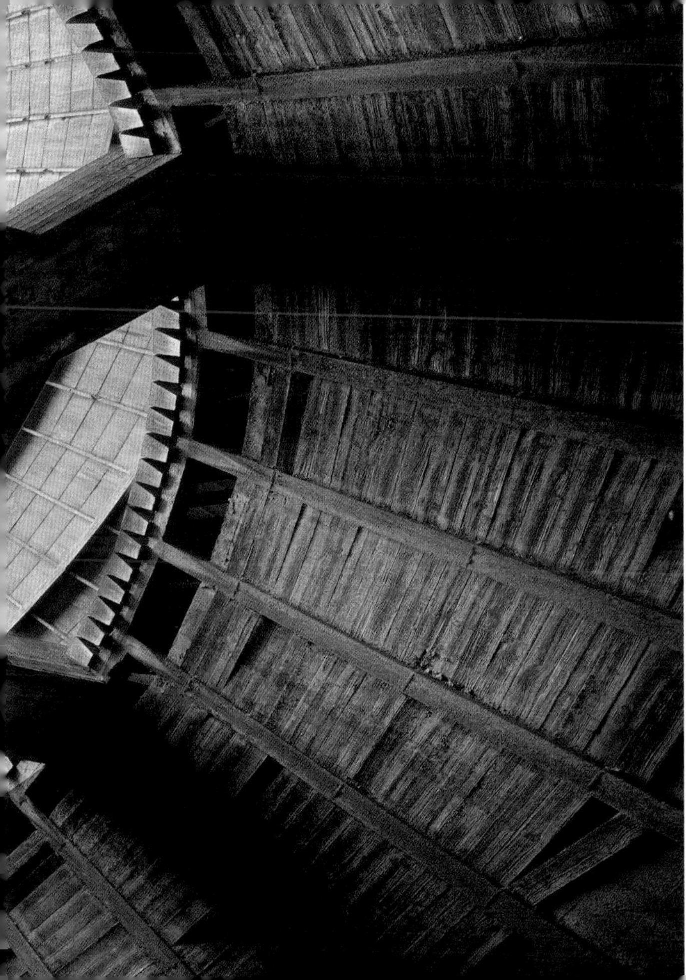

◁ POWERPLANT IM

BELGIUM, 2014

Pays Noir, Black Country, is the region around Charleroi, named so for the presence of coal-mines and heavy steel industry. Even though most of the factories have been closed since the 1950s, the landscape remains dotted with spoil tips and old industrial buildings.

This gigantic cooling tower is just one of many abandoned buildings that dot the gloomy skyline of Charleroi.

Built in 1921 and shut down in 2007, this coal-burning electric power station was responsible for 10% of the CO_2 produced throughout the entire country.

The interior never was and never is completely silent. Even when the building is properly sealed off, East European copper thieves always find ways to get in. ◆

WARSHIP CEMETERY ▷

FRANCE, 2012

This was a risky expedition. In a wide river that flows into the Atlantic Ocean, there are some ten warships waiting to be dismantled. Chains and gangplanks hold them together. Strong currents follow the rhythms of the tides, and military speedboats carry out regular patrols.

When we began to pump up our rubber boats, we found a hole, bigger than the one that sank the Titanic. Plan C was for me to take all the baggage and for my friend to swim over on an airbed. With four bags, my boat was overloaded, and the lack of space made it hard to row. After pausing at the buoys halfway, we set off on the second stage of our journey. The current was much stronger in the middle of the river. The bags in my boat began to slide and I temporarily lost one of the oars. I started drifting off course and saw the boats disappearing in the darkness. There was one last chance of success, and that was the buoy that held the boats in position. I rowed like a madman and was just able to catch hold of the cable...

Once on board, with knocking knees, we exchanged our trademark grin and cracked open a well-earned can of beer!

That night on the boat was magical. It was raining, and the boats were slippery with oil. The deck was full of young gulls that had never seen human beings before. At daybreak, the entire colony of gulls took off and flew over the boats, calling loudly, their droppings raining down on us. ◆

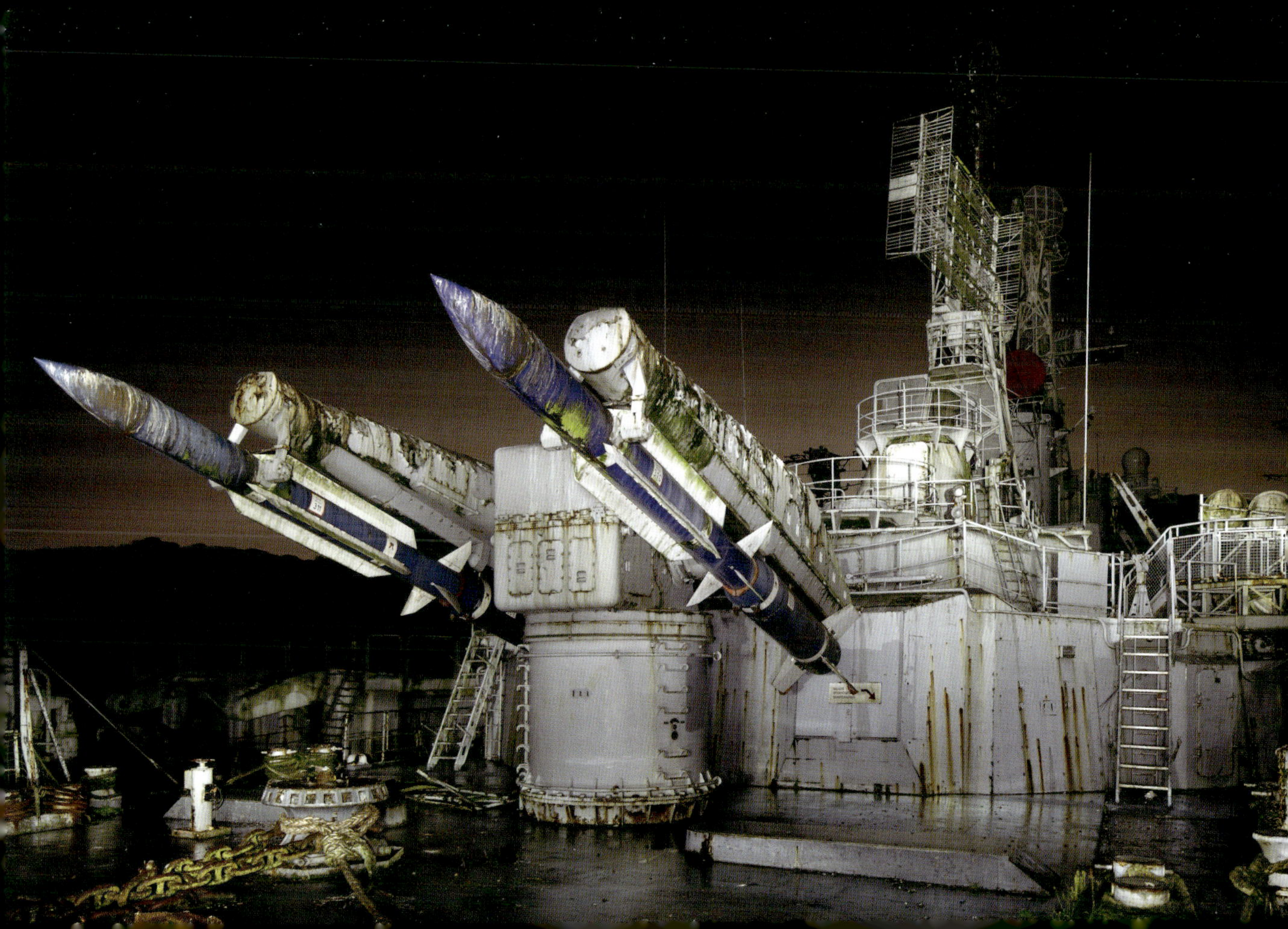

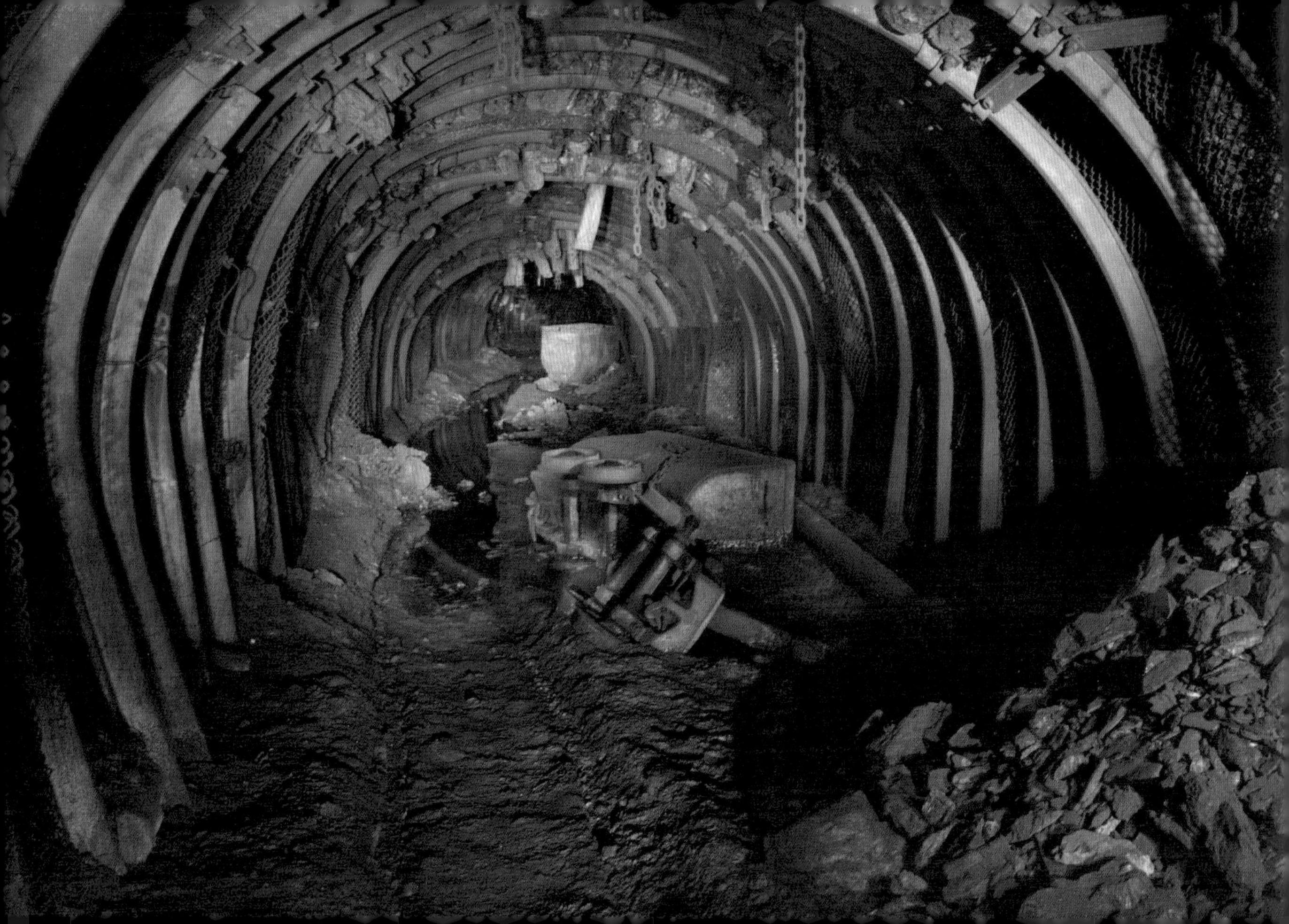

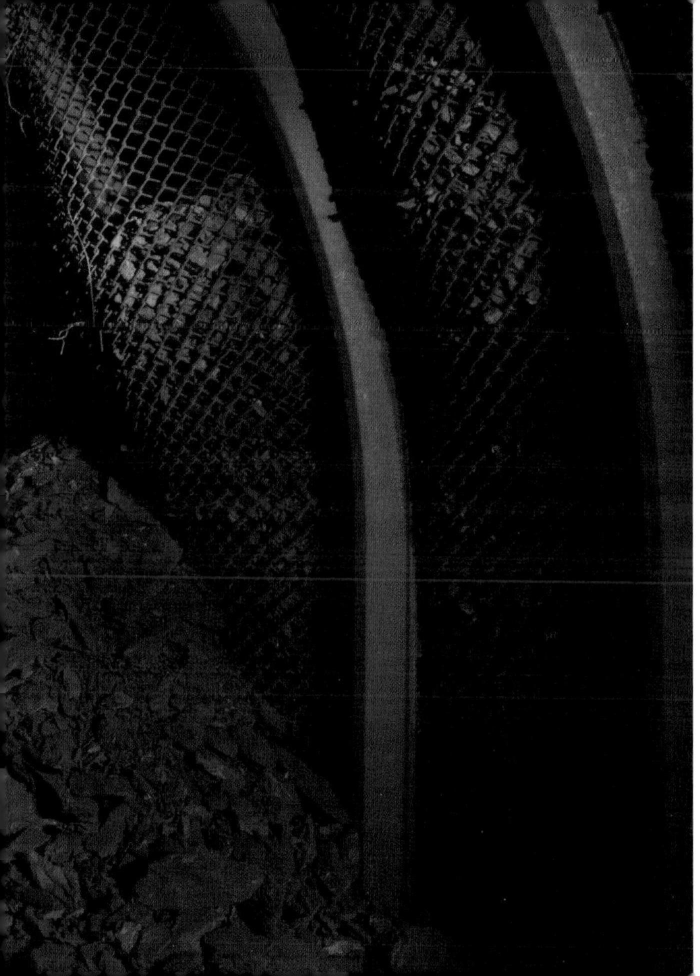

◁ URICANI

ROMANIA, 2015

A thousand metres under the ground, everything hangs by a thread. Pumps operate night and day to keep the water level low, and fans blow fresh air through the mine to remove methane and supply the miners with oxygen. If there is a power outage, the place becomes pitch black, quiet as a mouse and very quickly unliveable. Wearing miner's garb, I walk through the endless passageways of Uricani. There is only one place here where they still excavate; the rest, for the most part, looks like a world that has perished. Besides cockroaches and rats, there is no sign of life. The cockroaches arrive in the mines together with the lumber. The rats are always there, and in passageways where few people venture, they get hungry and aggressive. If you stand still for a minute, they start climbing up your clothes. ◆

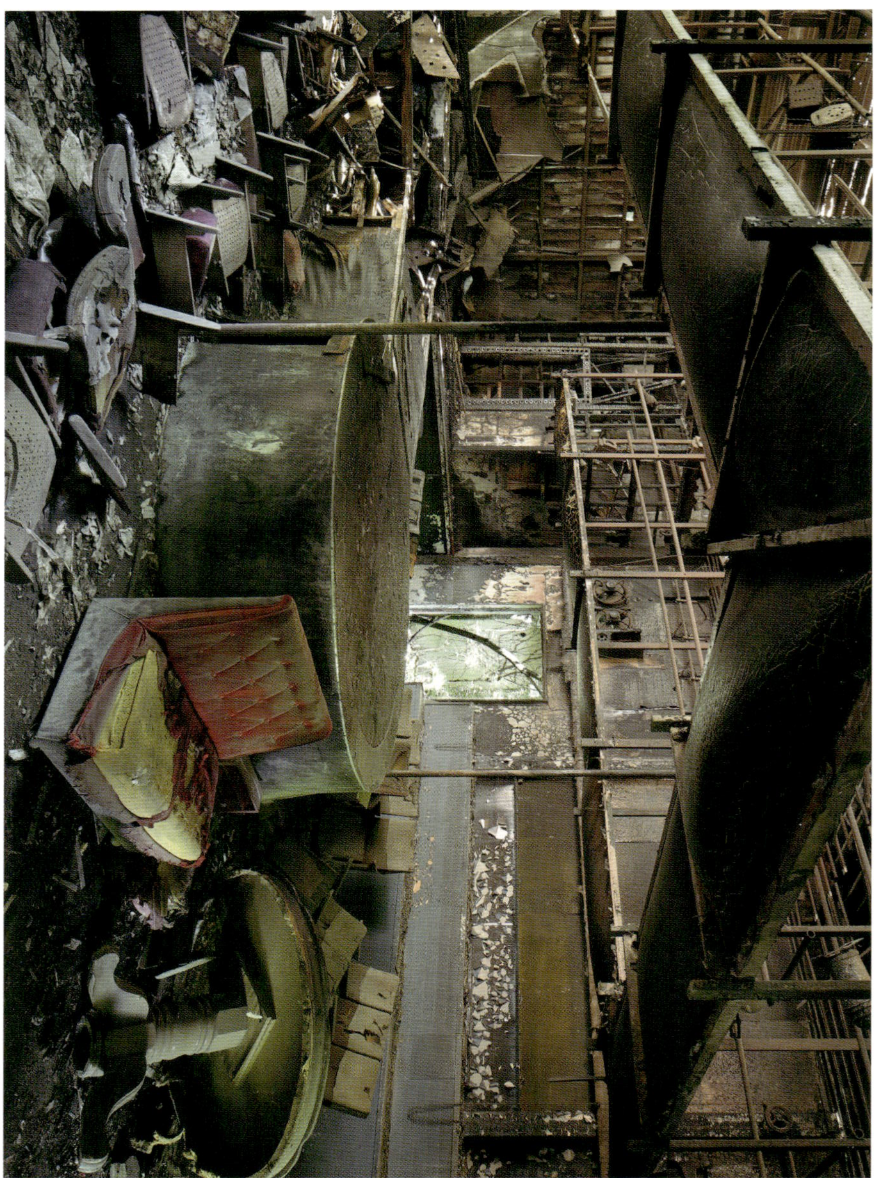

 Akeno Strip Club, Japan, 2013

Akeno Strip Club, Japan, 2013

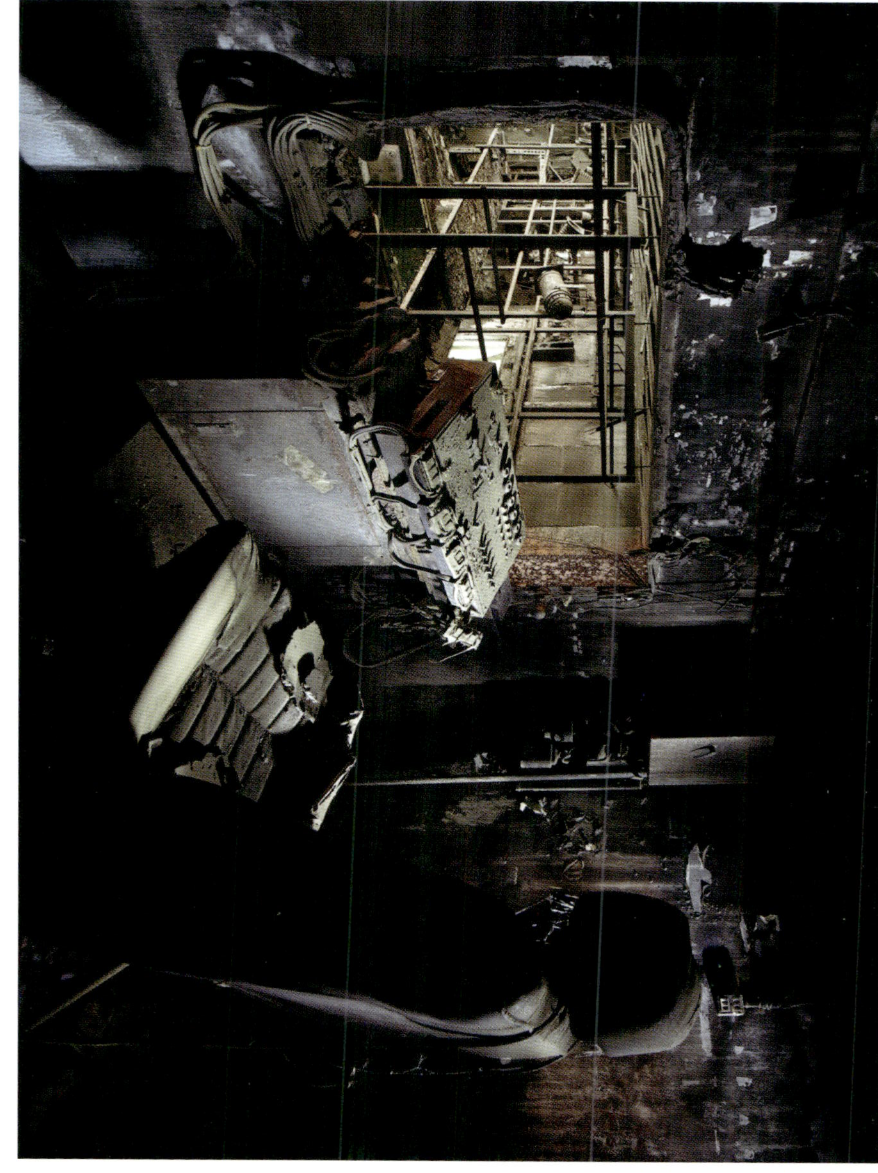

BUZLUDZHA ▷

BULGARIA, 2013

In 1981, the Bulgarian communist regime built a monument on 'Mount Buzludzha', a historic but virtually inaccessible place.

Since 1989, Bulgaria's largest ideological building has stood empty. After the villagers stole the copper roofing, the building decayed even faster.

In the winter, access is restricted to 4 wheel drive vehicles or snow scooters, and for the final kilometer, you need snow shoes. 'Buzludzha' literally means 'icy', and for good reason: it is incredibly cold up there; the icy wind blows right through you. At night, temperatures plummet to way below freezing.

The monument stands inviolable on the barren mountaintop like an alien spaceship. I slipped inside through a crack in the concrete. This was where real challenge greeted me: due to a cycle of thawing and freezing, the floors were like a vast ice rink. Even the stairways were covered with a thick layer of slippery ice, making it literally impossible to climb even a few steps. The worse thing is that there are holes in the concrete everywhere, and if you start to slip, it may be impossible to stop...

The reward for all these risks is the beautiful arena with its mosaics and UFO-like roof.

The missing face on the mosaics-covered wall is that of Todor Zhivkov, Bulgaria's last communist leader who reigned from 1954 until 1989. It's unclear whether unhappy people removed his face, or if he ordered its removal so as to distance himself from the collapsing Soviet regime. ◆

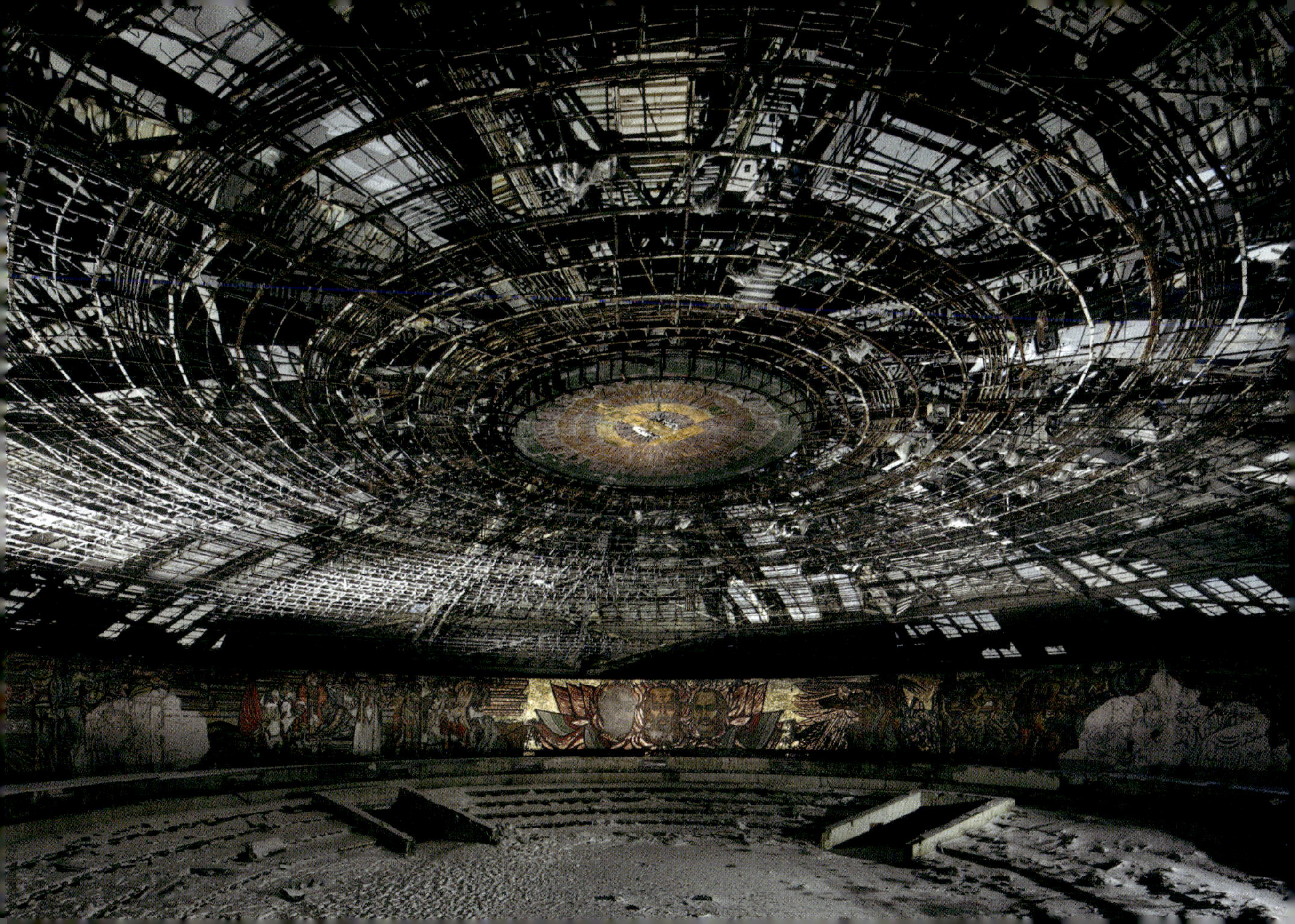

Highland Park, Detroit, 2015

Heinrich Heine, Germany, 2015

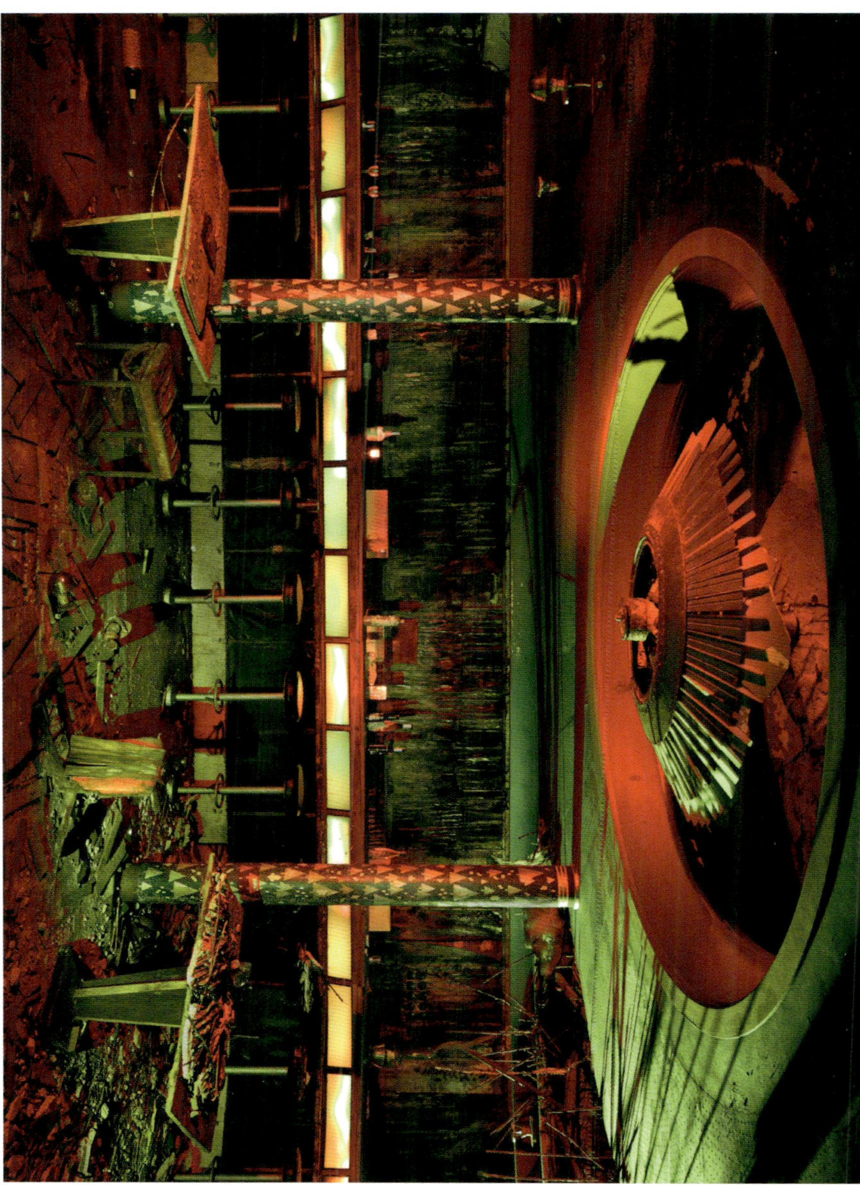

MONTGOMERY MALL

ALABAMA, USA, 2012

This huge mall has been abandoned for some years. Even the larger parking lot was deserted when we arrived... except for one car with two occupants sitting half-hidden in a corner of the parking lot. Tough luck: security!

Almost immediately, they got into action and trailed us. We stopped. They stopped too. We turned left, they too. Right... right. We decided to leave the parking lot, drive around the block and return via the other entrance. But who was standing right there waiting for us? You've got it.

Plan B: talk to them, explain, and hope they might look away while we try and enter the building. We parked our car, got out, walked towards them and watched the hesitant maneuvering of their car. Inside it were two women. We looked at each other: we invitingly, they uncomprehendingly. They reversed, parked again. The older woman explained something to the younger one. They had already forgotten about us.

Such is life when a mother is teaching her daughter to drive. ◆

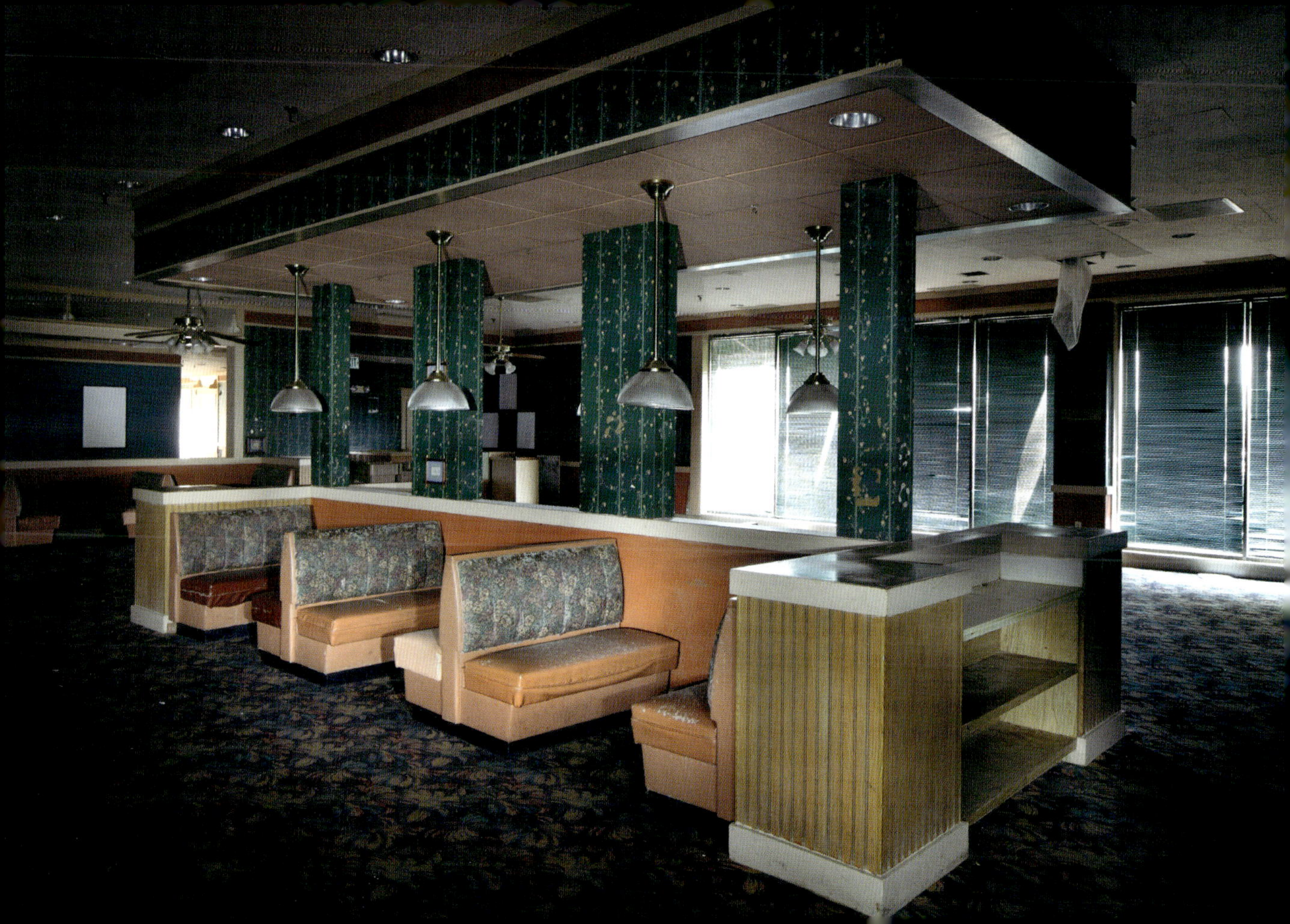

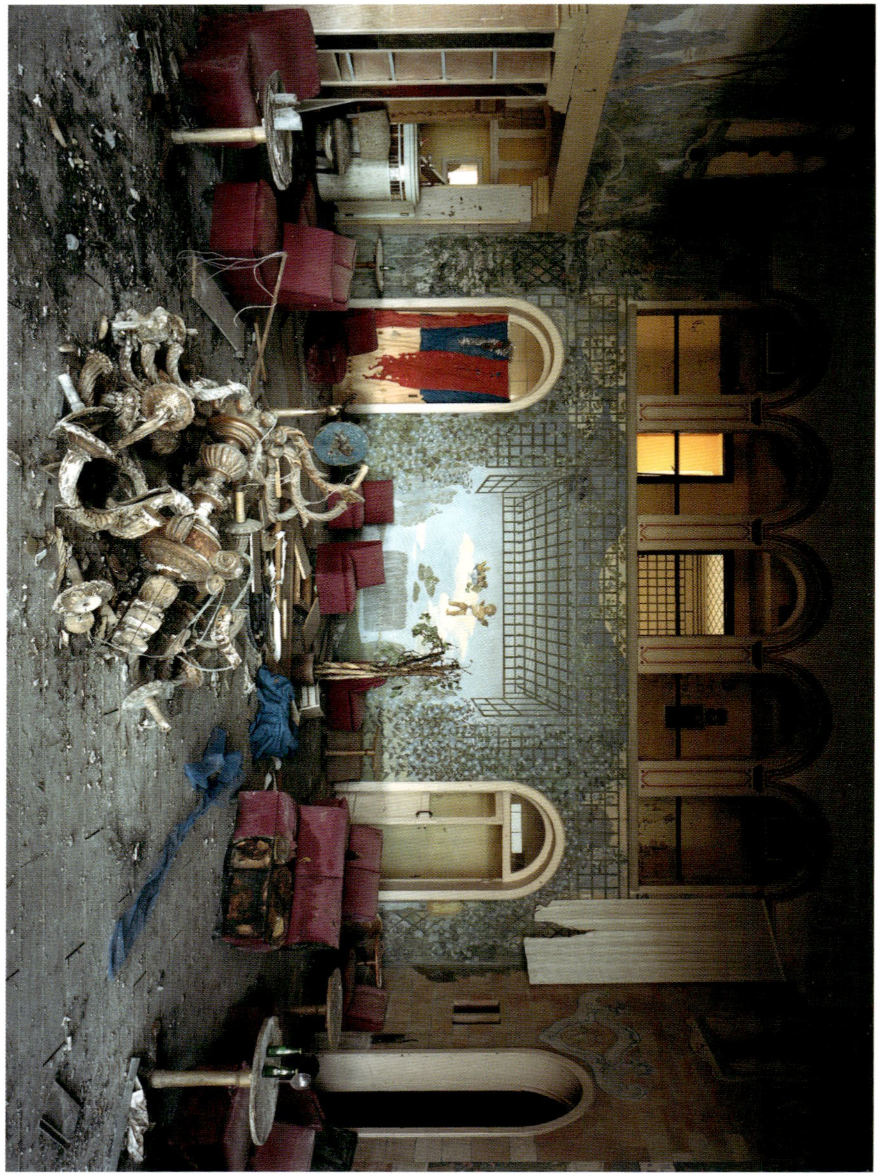

 Disco Mafia, Italy, 2016

Train drivers' resting area, Belgium, 2006

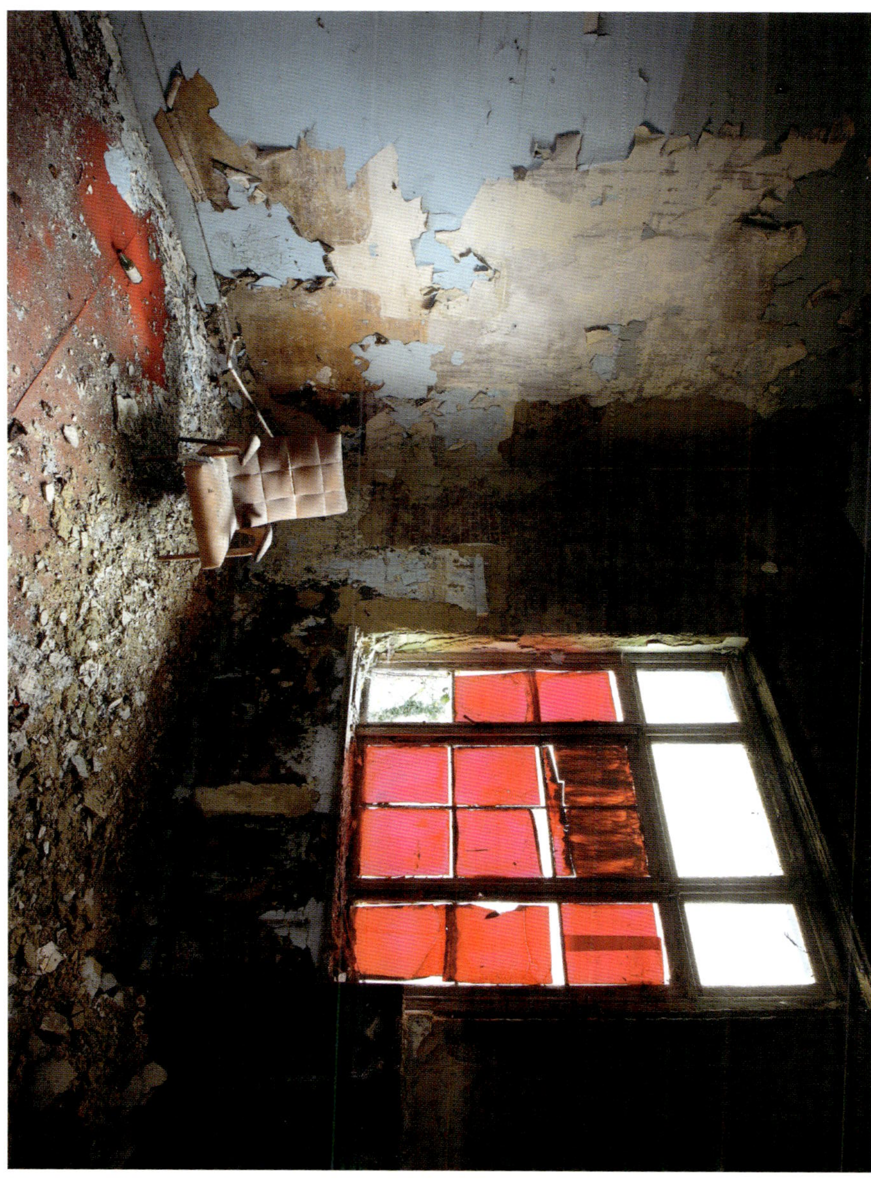

DOME HOUSES ▷

FLORIDA, 2014

I camped on the island, on the beach, just out of reach of the waves and as far as possible from the mangrove forest with its thirsty mosquitoes.

Rumour has it that in better times these extra-terrestrial homes were safeguarded with machine guns. Yet the real enemies of these houses were hurricanes Andrew and Wilma that washed away the shoreline. Ultimately, the sea will swallow the houses, but on this morning, they stood invincibly, yet vulnerable, in the bluish light. ◆

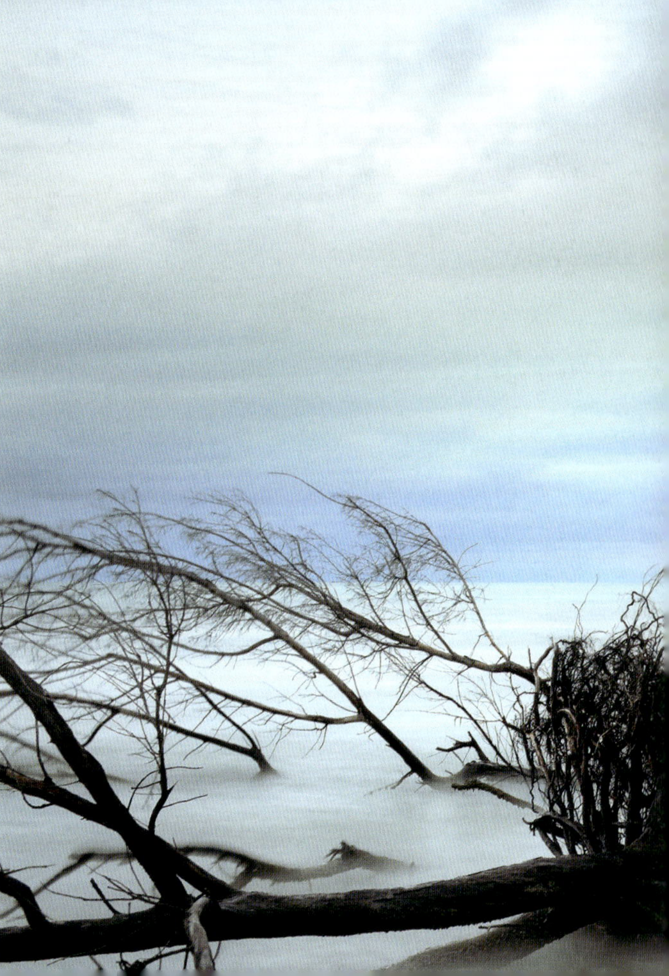

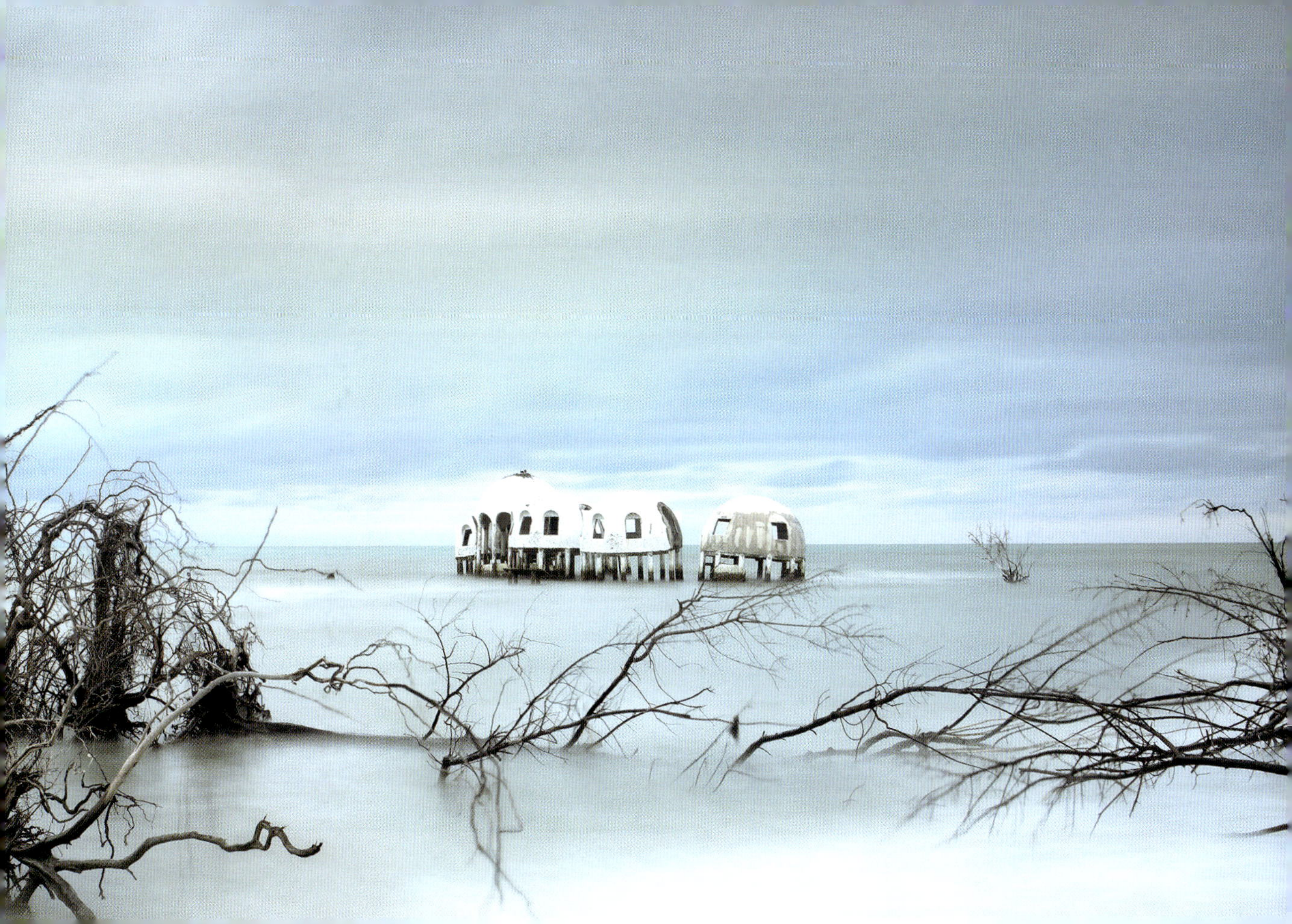

KURIOSHI INN ▷
JAPAN, 2012

KAPPA ONSEN HOTEL P31
JAPAN, 2012

If you manage to fend off the stray dogs that regard this establishment as their territory, the lobby is the first space you come into contact with in this stunning hotel. The view over the ocean is endless and the Seventies atmosphere immediately envelops you.

For me, the lamps in this photo conjure up an image of a cuckoo clock. They have a loop in their cables and hang neatly at the same height. Over the course of time, in the roughly 20 years that this hotel has stood empty, seven of the loops have come loose. About once every three years, one of the lamps drops down a metre with an audible clunk, followed by the metallic sound of the hook. For a minute or two, the lamp will swing to and fro, enjoying its short-lived freedom. It will then return to its motionless state, until the next cuckoo call. I sat for a while, a long while in fact, hoping, in vain, for a tick of the clock.

The monstrous Kappa Onsen Hotel with its labyrinth of corridors, rooms and baths, clings to the steep cliffs of the tempestuous melted-ice river. Park your car in front of the door and come in through the window.

Sit down and close your eyes, smell the air, feel the dust and listen to the silence that tells the story of this mythical hotel. ◆

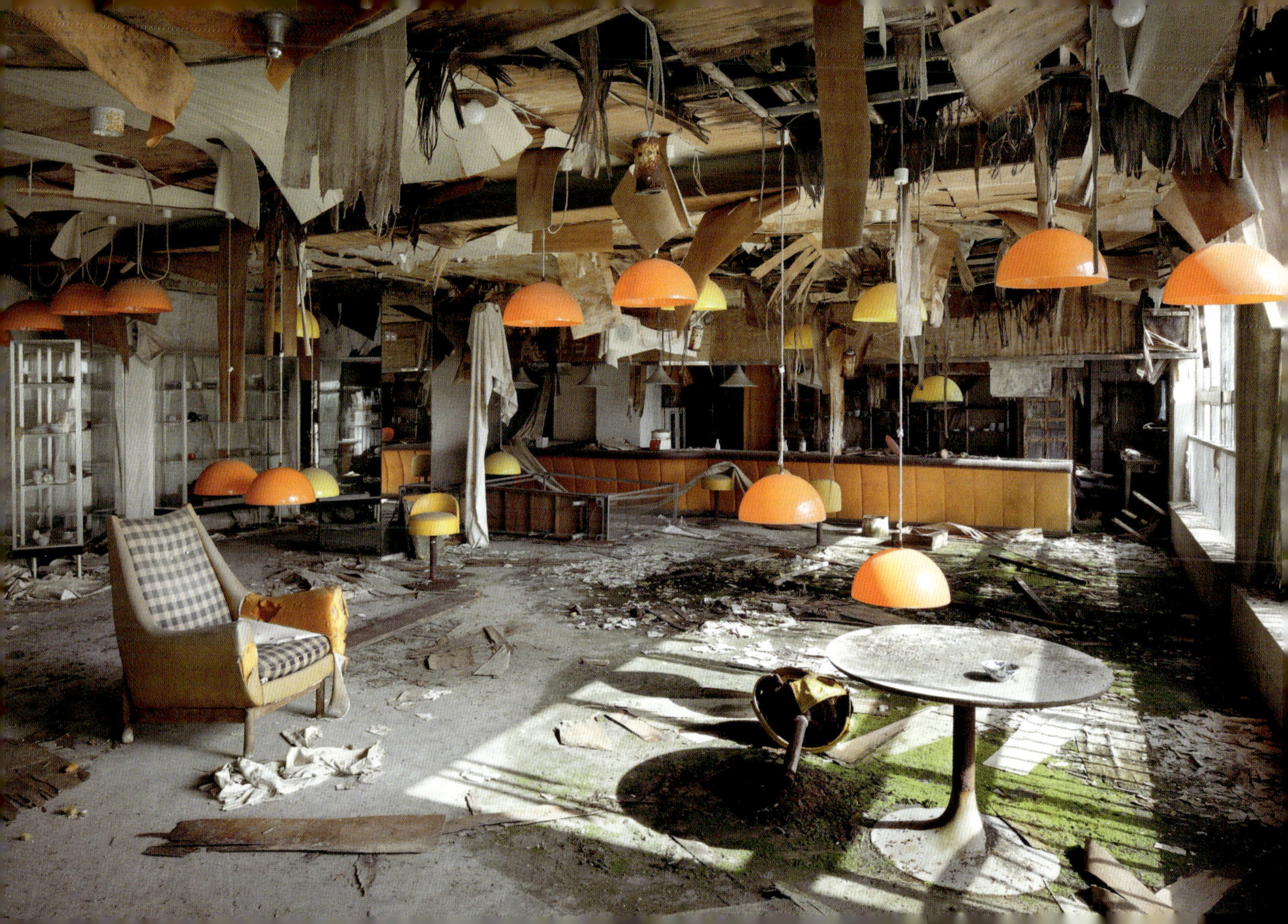

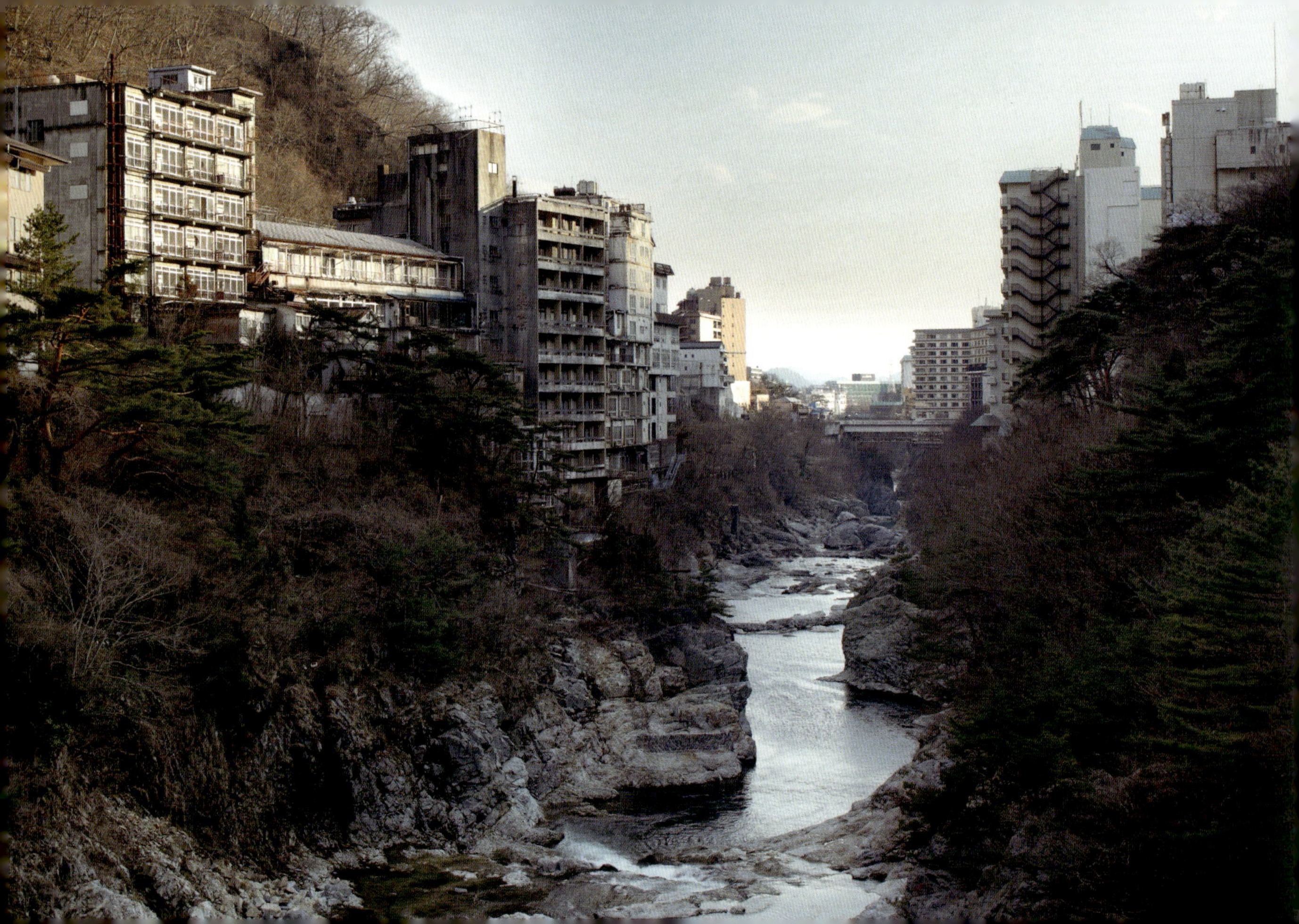

▵ Kappa Onsen, Japan, 2012

▿ Željava airforce base, Croatia, 2018

 △ Shiraishi, Japan, 2012 ▽ Kappa Onsen, Japan, 2012

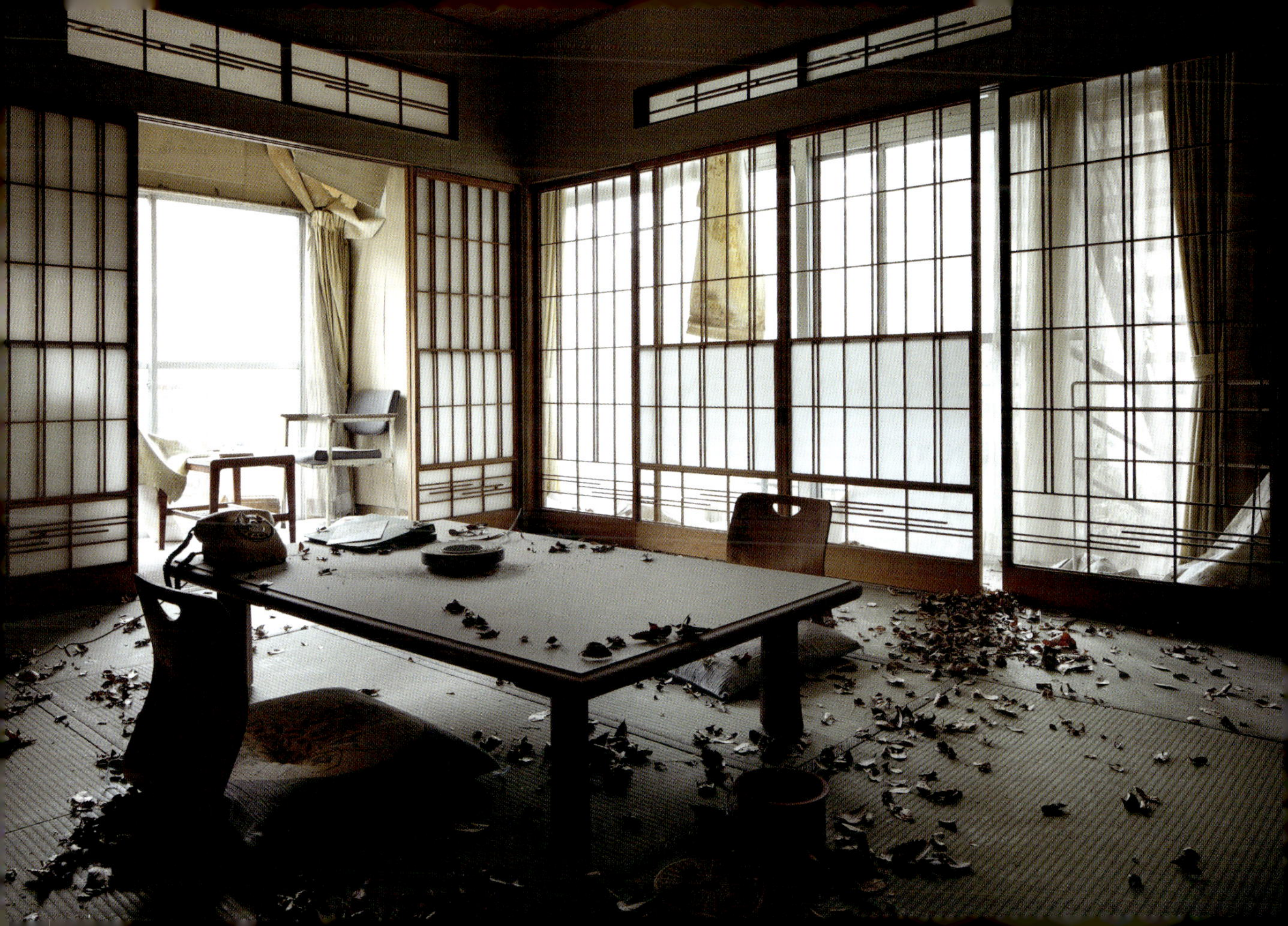

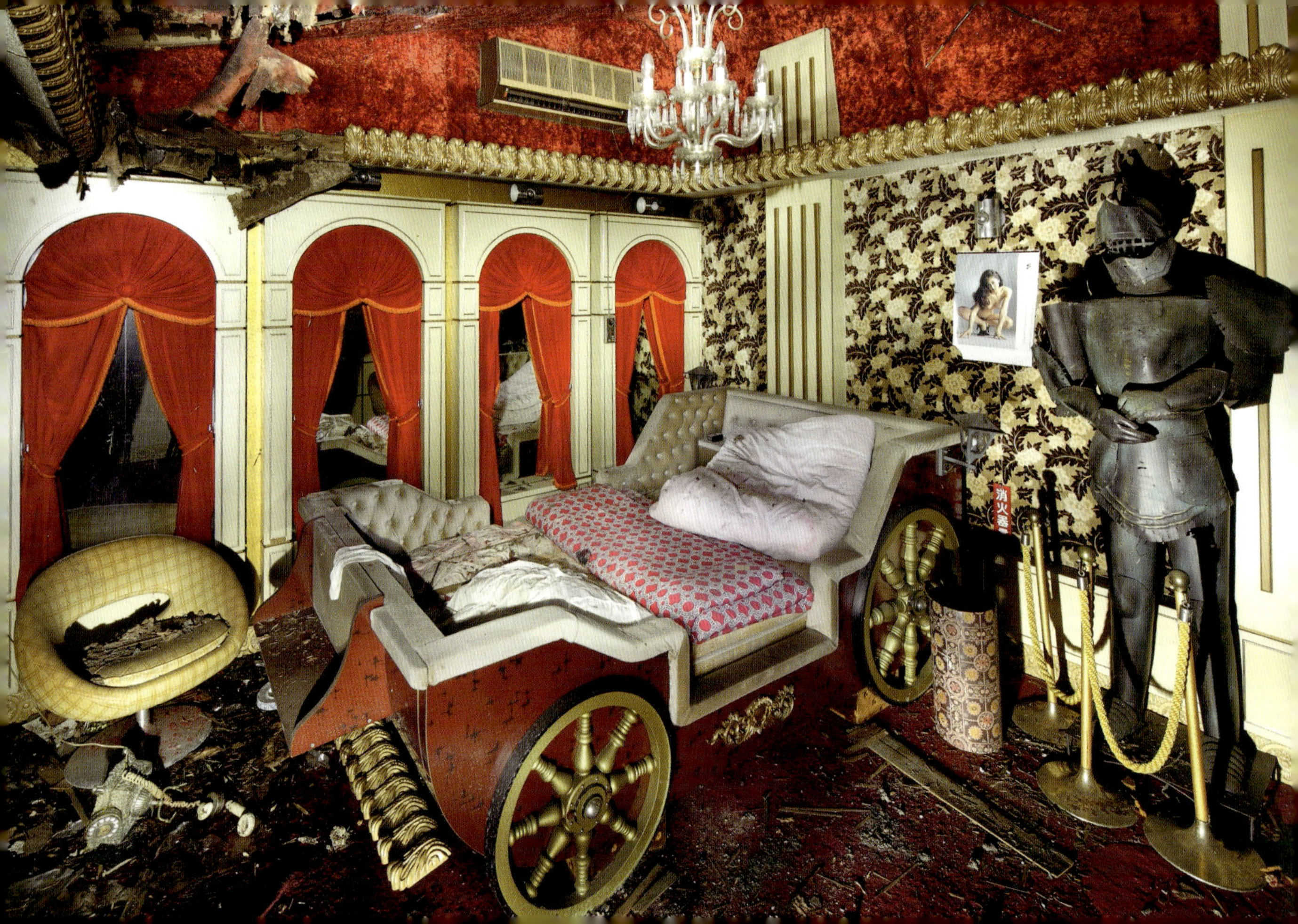
消火器

◁ **FUU MOTEL**
JAPAN, 2012

HOKKAIDO SEX MUSEUM P40
JAPAN, 2014

Some of the most amazing forgotten places lie in ordinary residential neighbourhoods. This 'love hotel' was one of many love nests, a safe little place of respite in the overcrowded city. Its guests were couples, married or not, looking for discretion, as well as those wishing to experience their paid sex in optimal conditions. Guests paid by the hour, for a whole night, or a special day rate for a luxury room with kitschy decoration, fantasy bed, Jacuzzi, TV and karaoke machine. The hasty shedding of clothes, squeaky mattresses and suppressed panting have been replaced with rotten floors and the rustling of mice behind the ceiling decoration. Nevertheless, the place has certainly not lost its charm... or its discretion for that matter.

What does one do after a day of refreshing mountain air and a relaxing hot bath? Drink sake and sing karaoke? Or perhaps visit the Sex Museum to view stuffed animals in Kama Sutra positions?

Better give me that bottle of sake! ◆

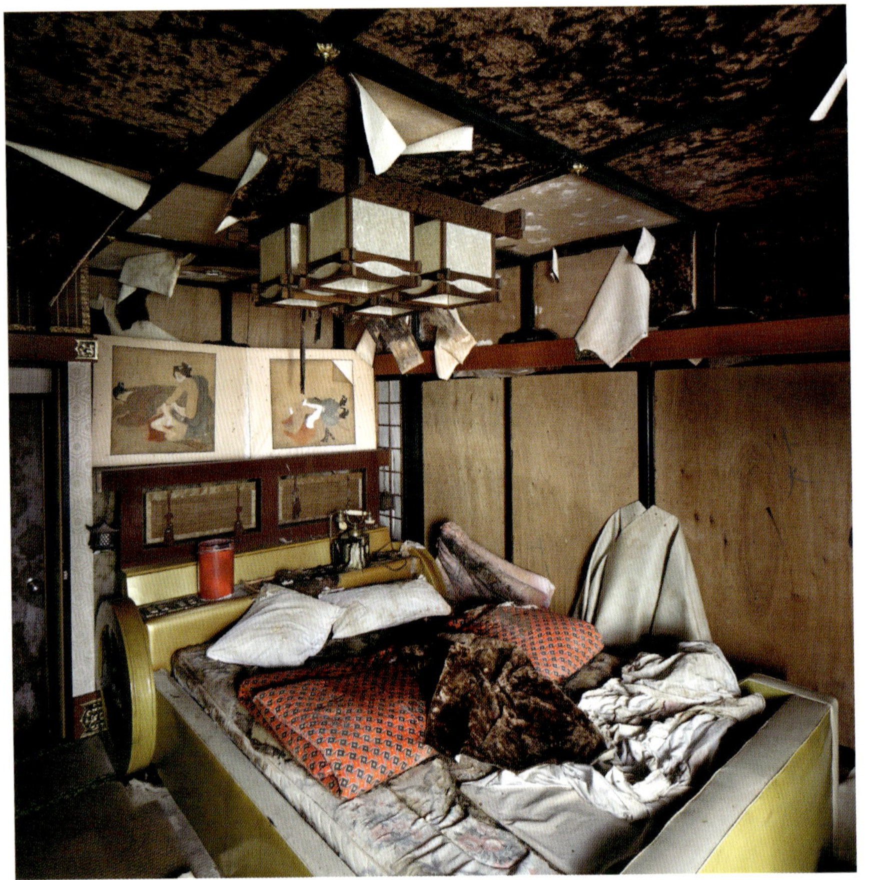

Fuu Motel, Japan, 2012

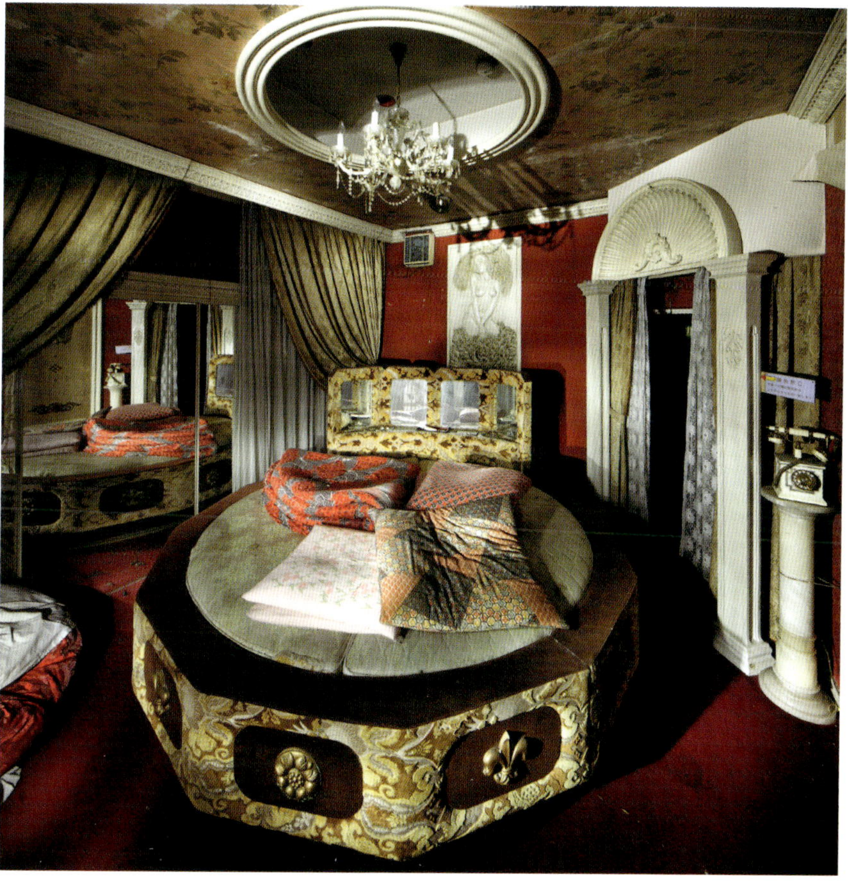

Fuu Motel, Japan, 2012

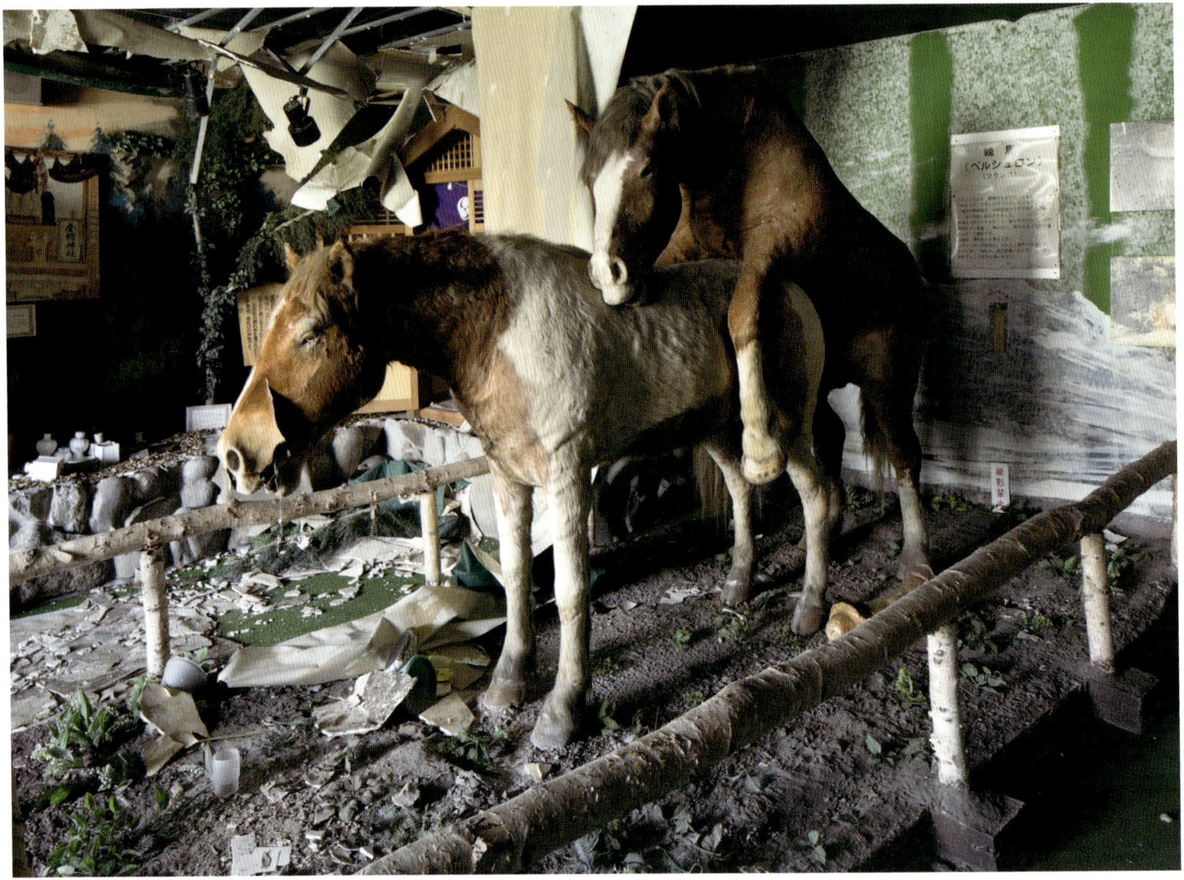

Hokkaido Sex Museum, Japan, 2014

Yubari High, Japan, 2014

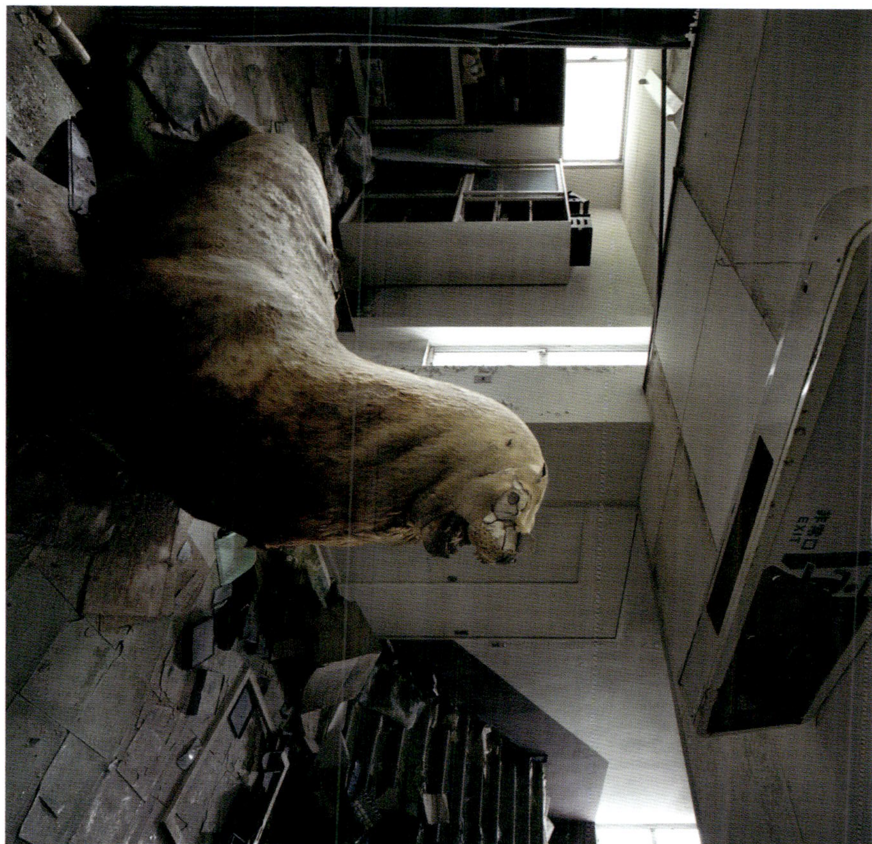

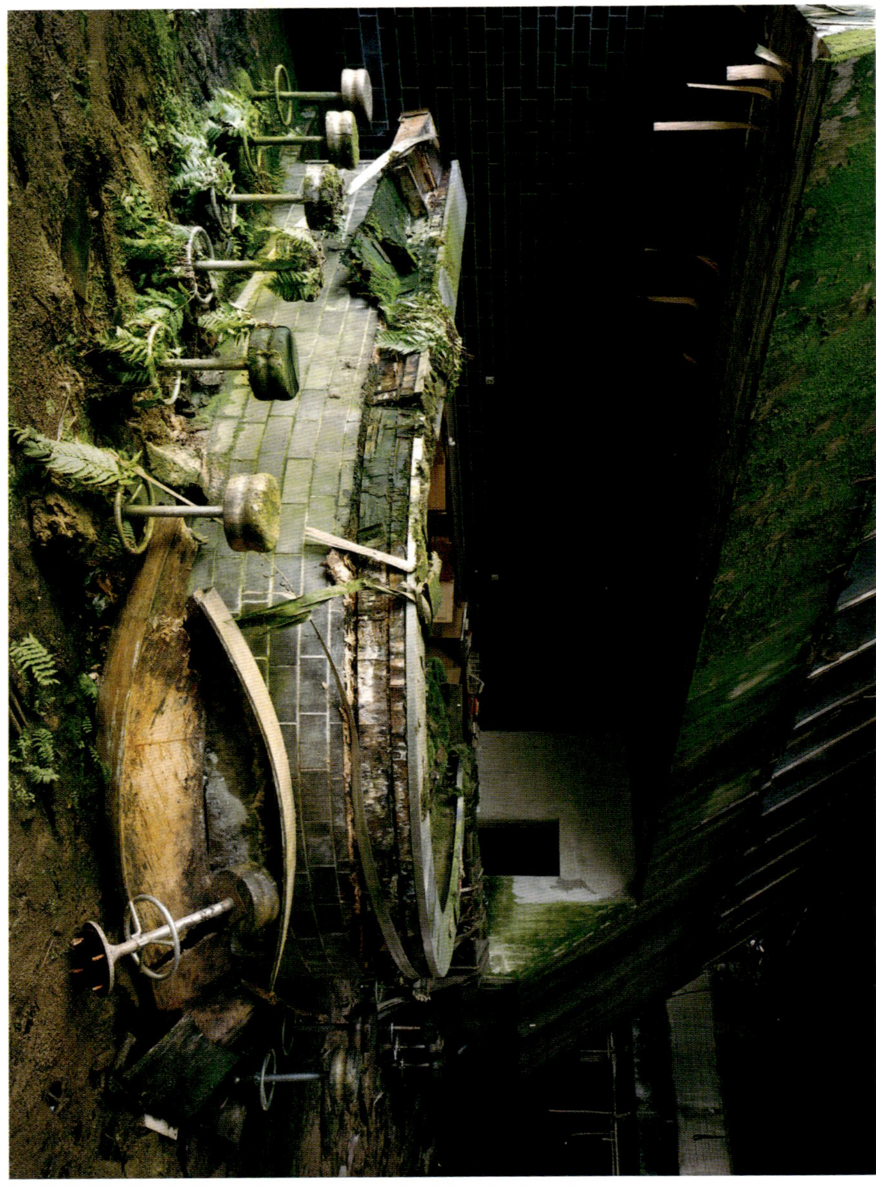

 Tito's School, Croatia, 2018

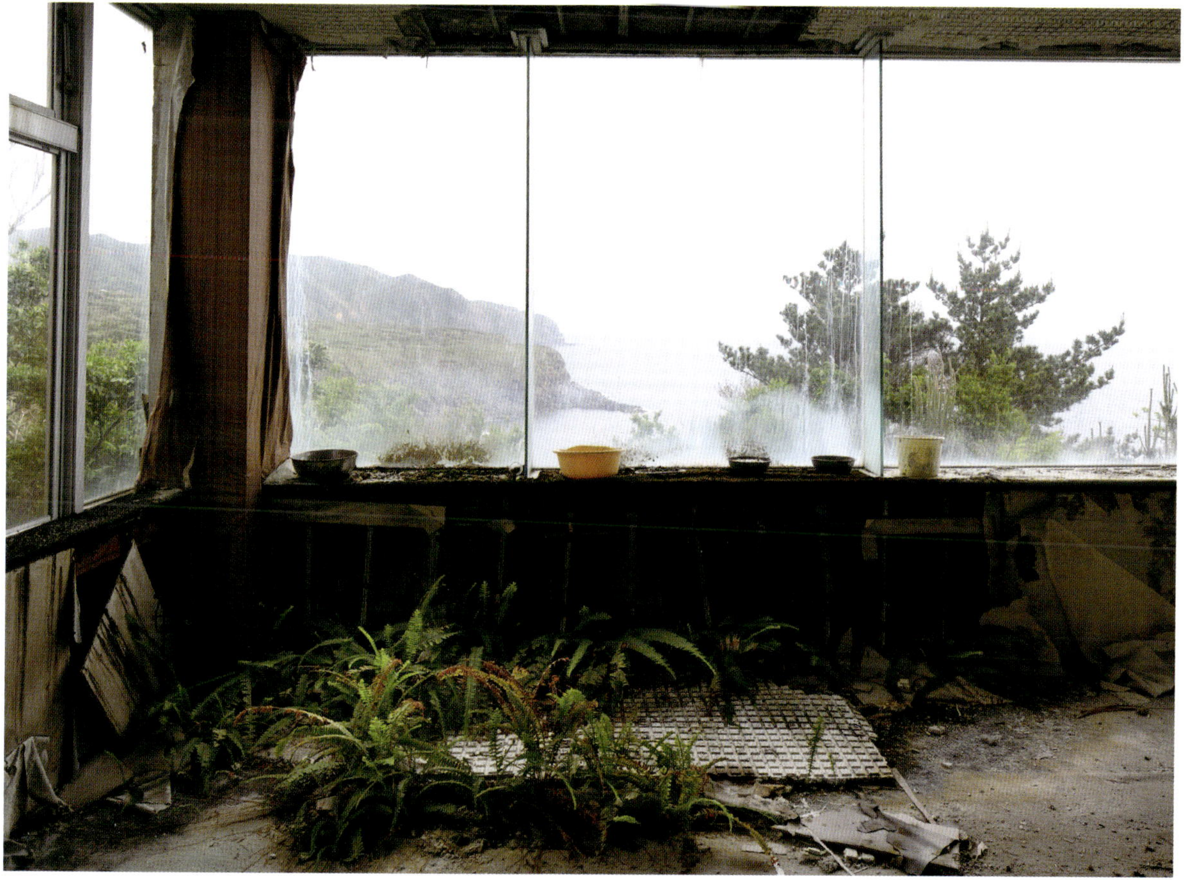

Onsen Ferns, Japan, 2014

Wagakawa Highway, Japan, 2013

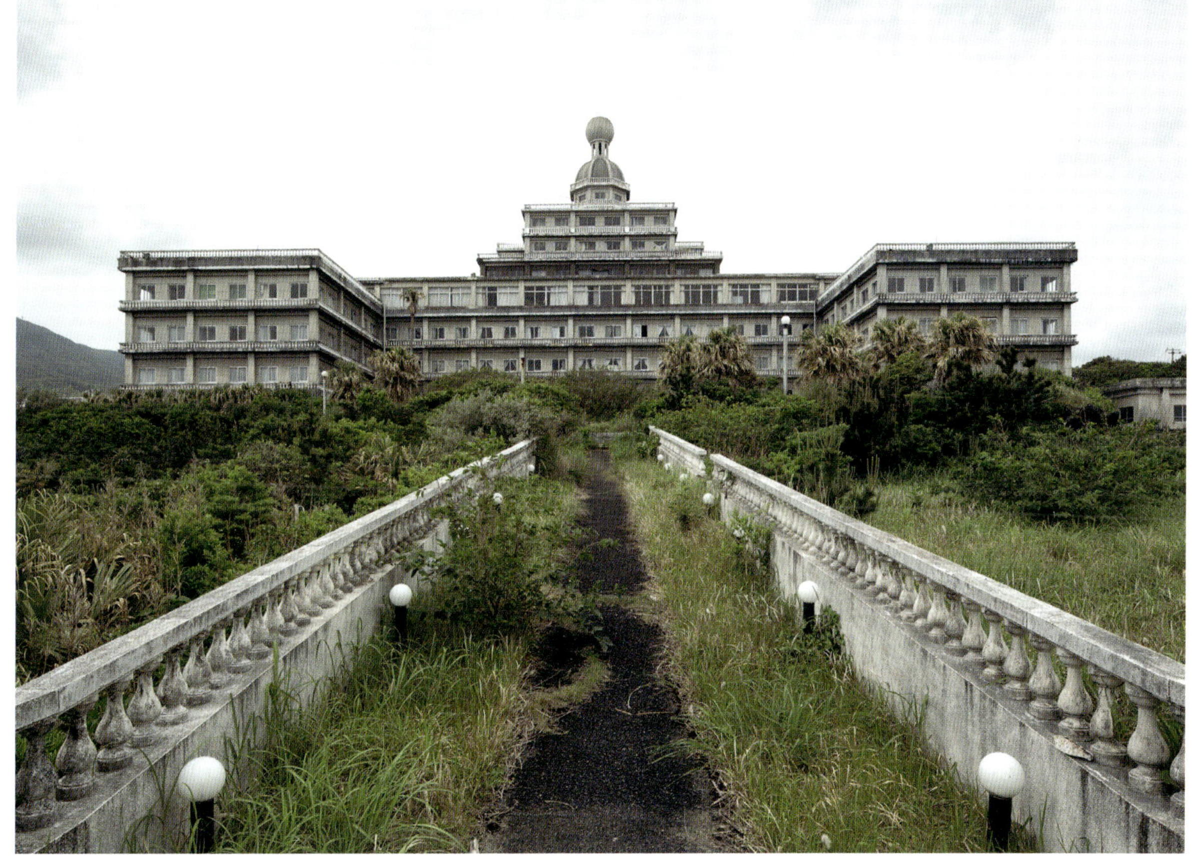

Black Sand Beach Hotel, Japan, 2014

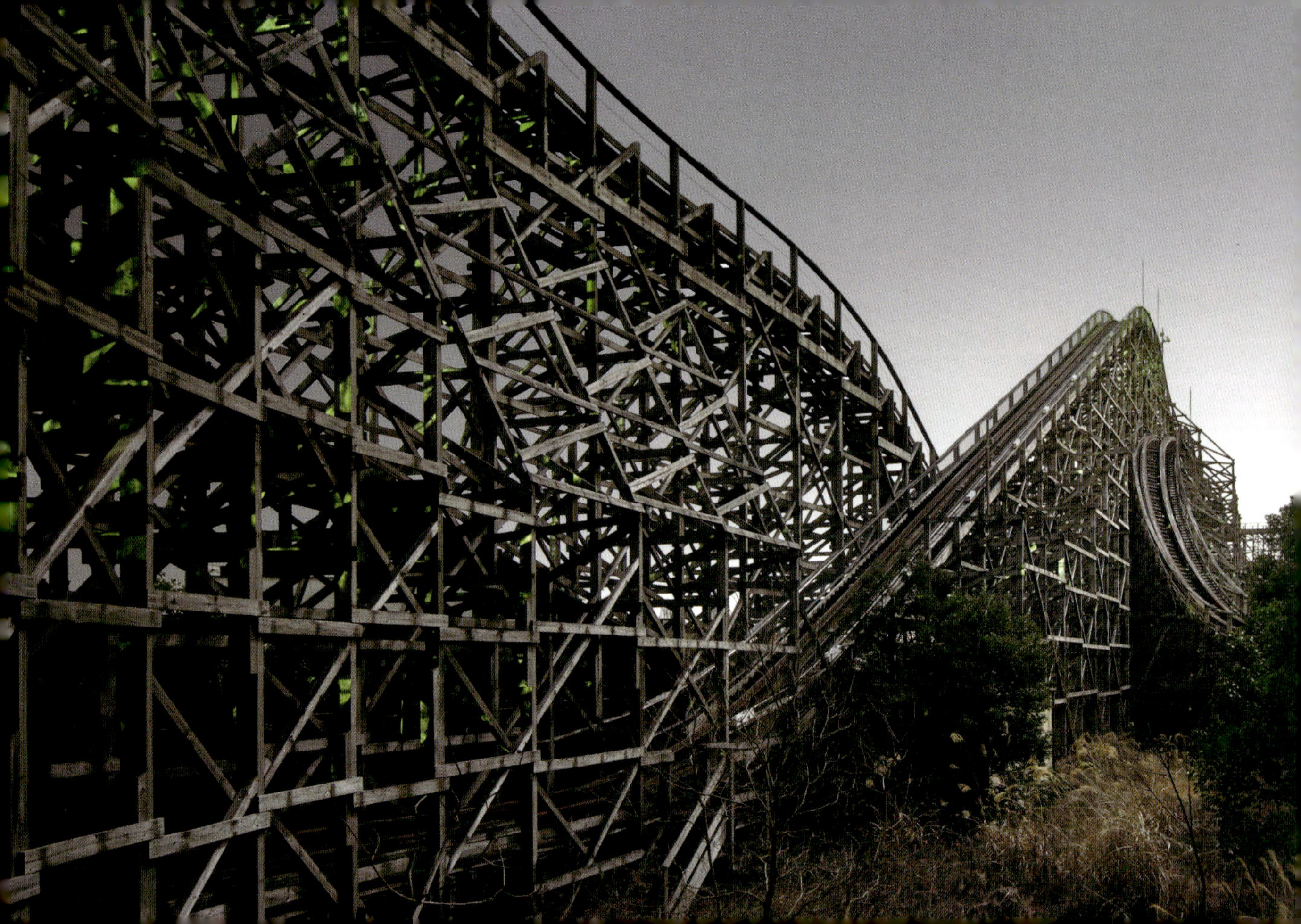

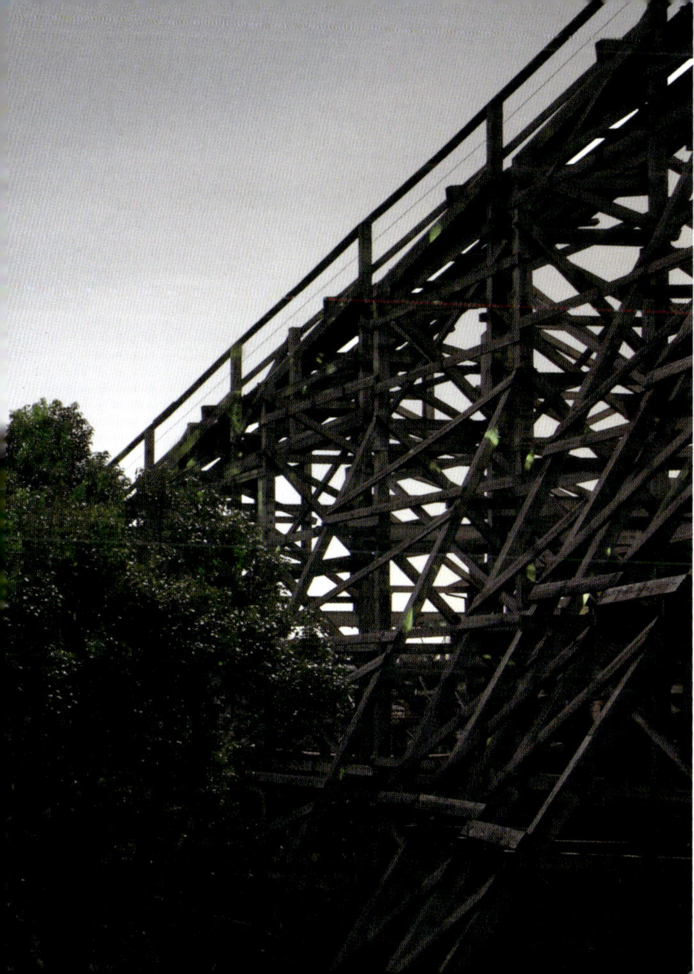

◃ **NARA DREAMLAND**

JAPAN, 2012

A nocturnal exploration is always special. Darkness sharpens the senses, arouses our animal instincts: seeing without light, walking without noise, climbing like a Ninja, blending invisibly into the environment (yet terrified by a life-size dummy of a cowboy in the bushes).

The park was pitch-black. A quarter moon was visible and the sky was slightly lit by the city lights in the background. At the highest point of the roller coaster, balancing between vertigo and ecstasy, I saw the guard's car. ◆

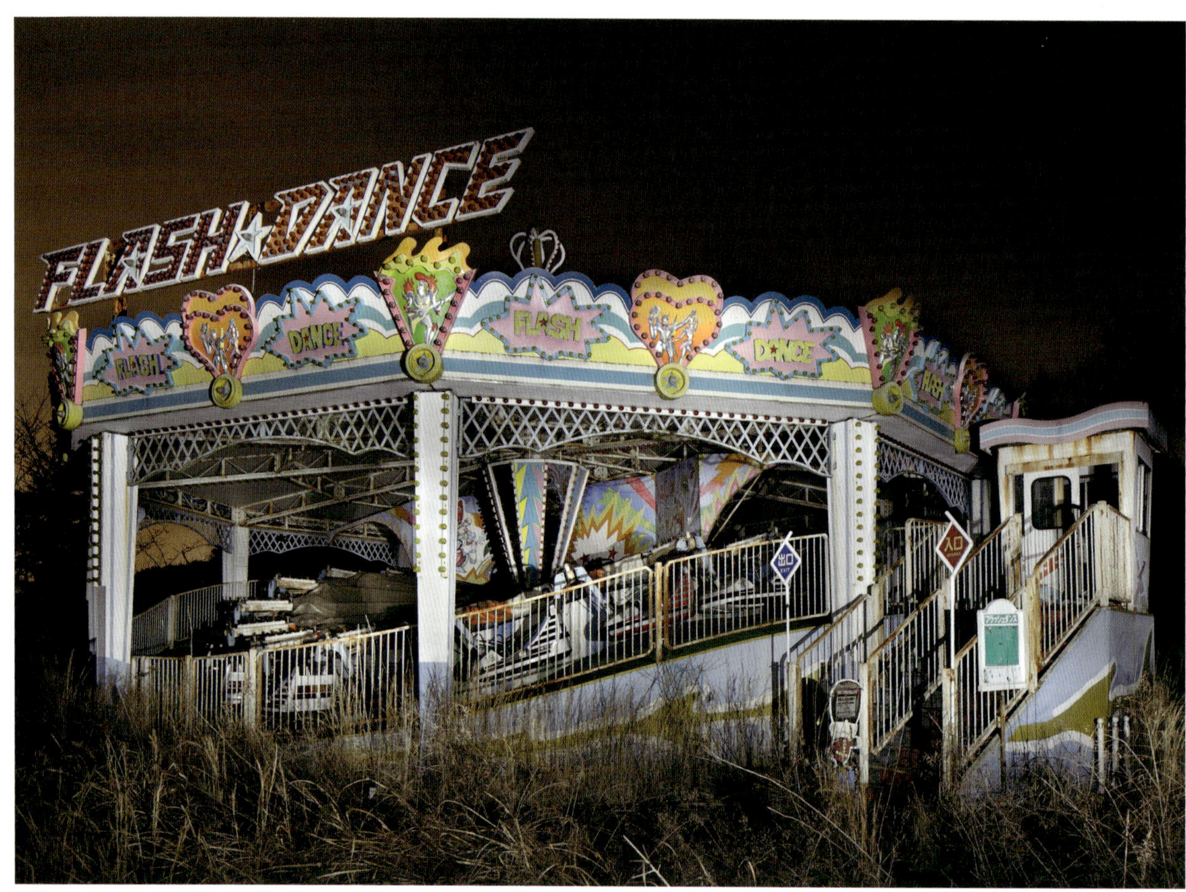

△ Nara Dreamland, Japan, 2012

▽ Nara Dreamland, Japan, 2012

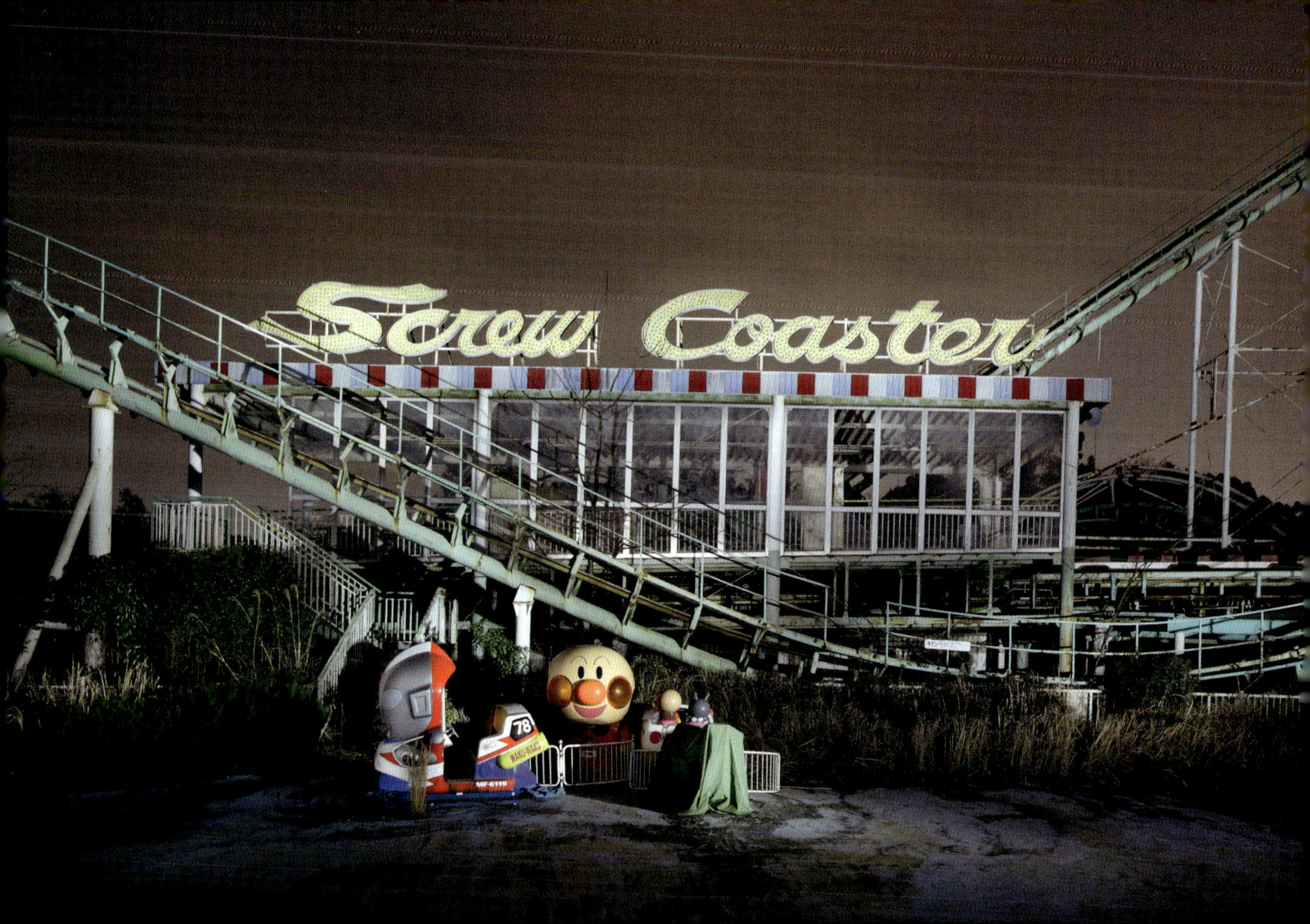
Screw Coaster
78
WAKU-WAKU
MF-6119

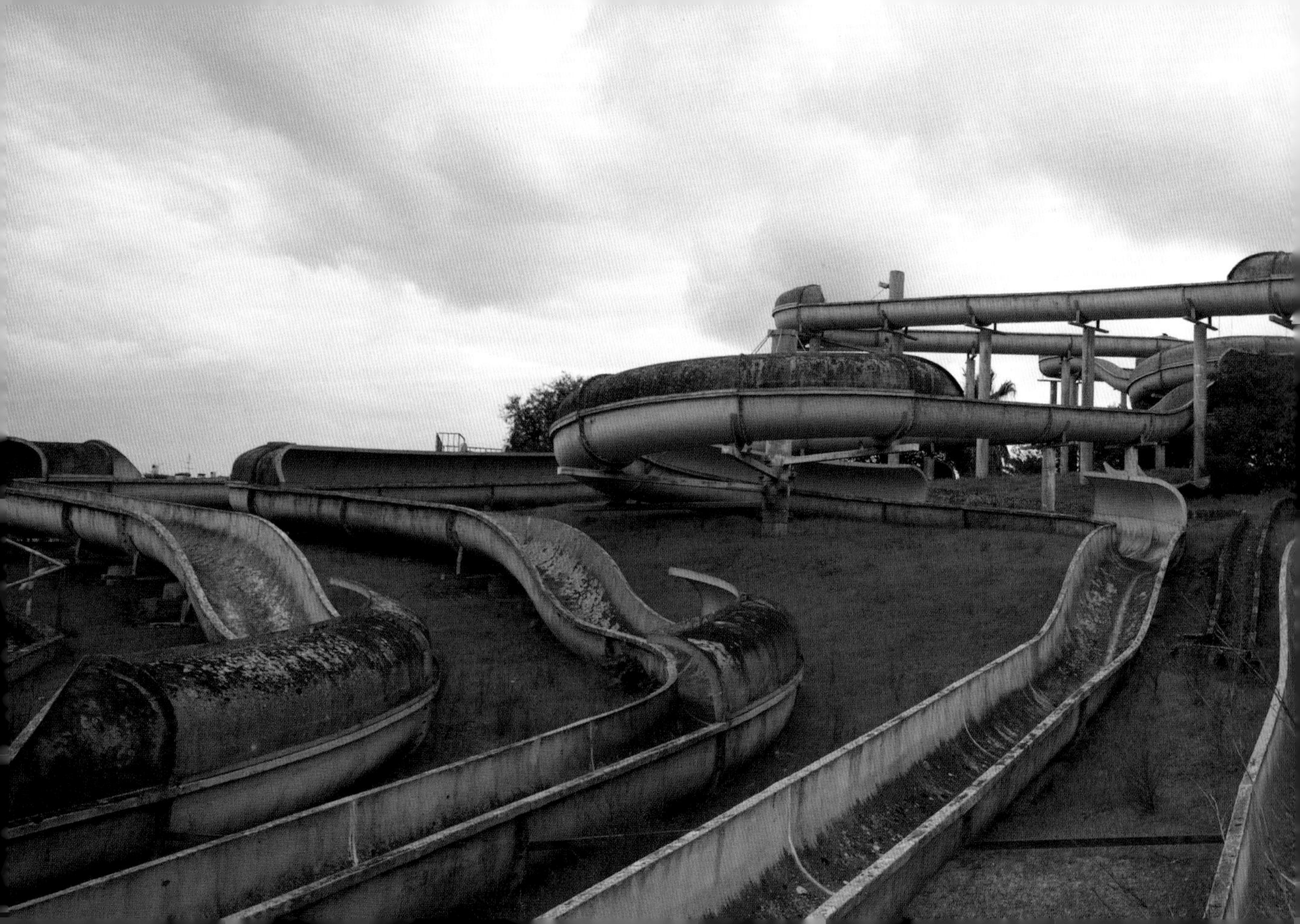

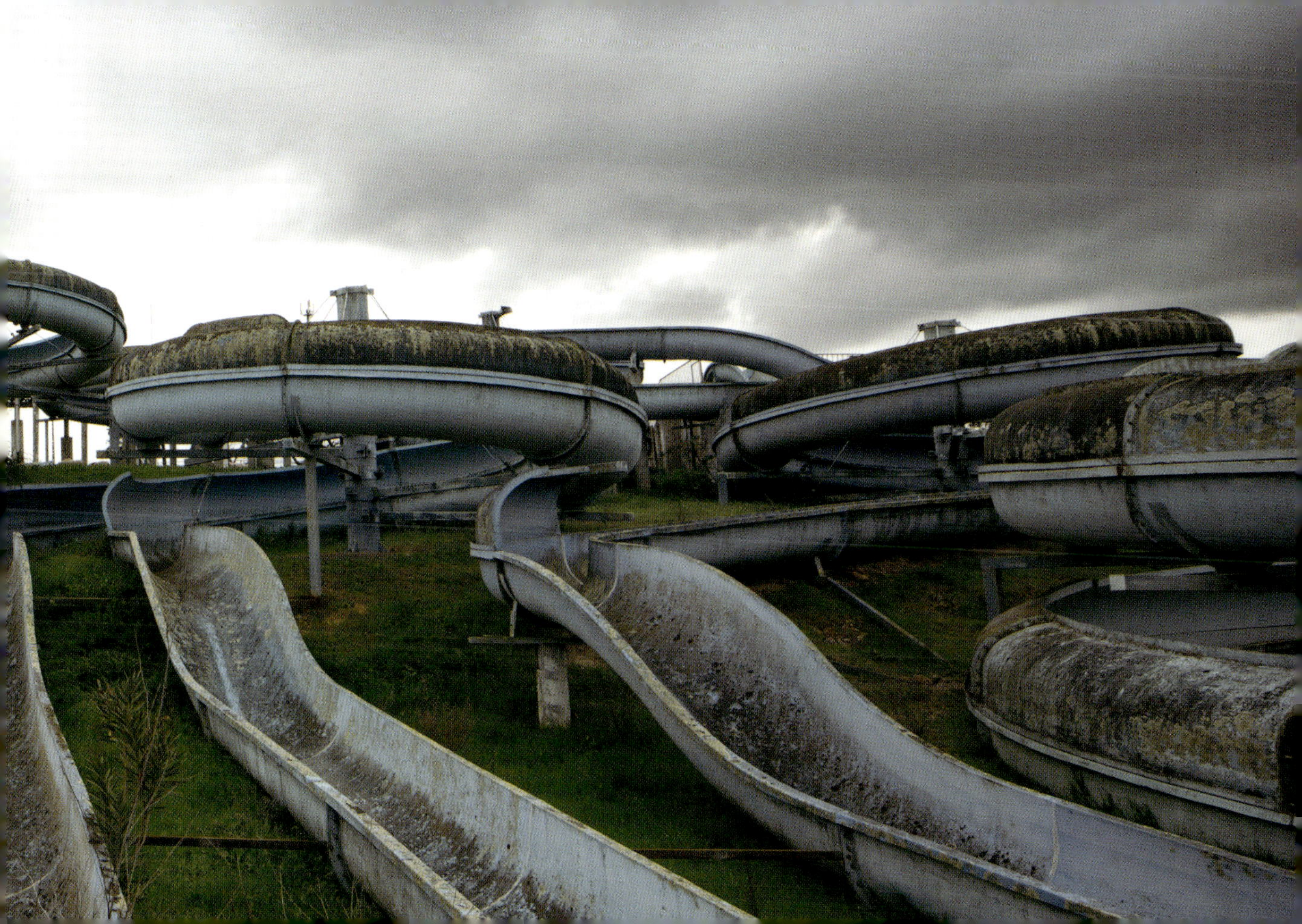

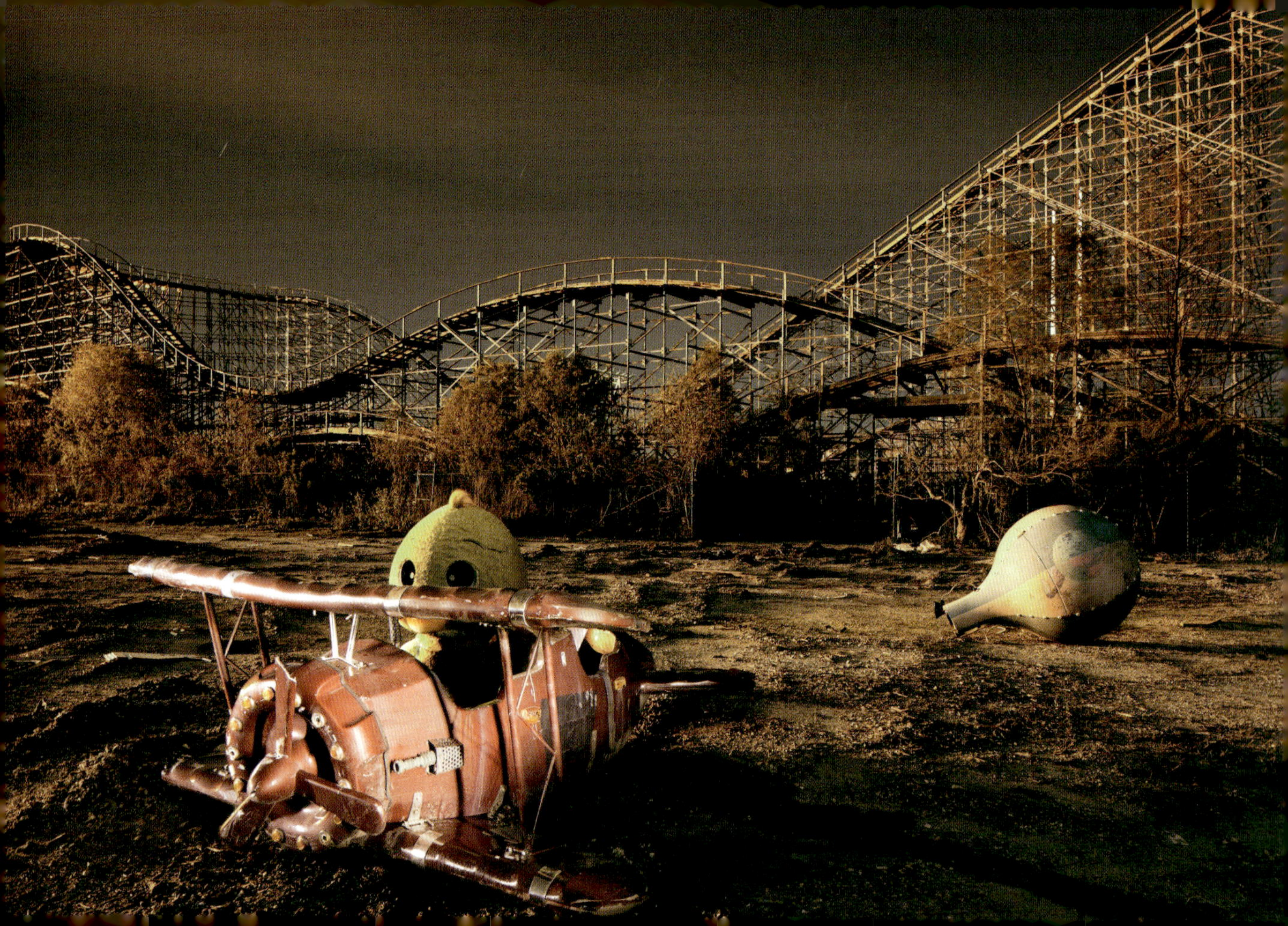

◃ SIX FLAGS NEW ORLEANS

USA, 2013

Six Flags New Orleans has been closed since hurricane Katrina struck in August 2005, flooding and destroying the theme park.

The park is guarded and the police regularly patrol it to keep out curious visitors. The plan was to explore the potential access points during the day and to return in the evening for the real visit.

Most of the park is encircled by swamps. Using rubble from an abandoned villa, we built a bridge up to the fence, where we found a hole. Further on we still had to cross a stretch of a swamp until we arrived at the large parking lot.

During the day, everything looked easy-going, but when we came back at night, the entire place was suddenly transformed. The street lamps created eerie shadows over the swamps as if alligators were lying about everywhere. The rubble that we used for crossing the swamp had sunk so deep in the mud that we barely made it to the other side, let alone returning over it in order to exit the park.

On the way, we were surprised by a pack of coyotes that had dug their burrow behind the bumper cars. Their whining, snoring and gnashing teeth gave us the chills. The image of these beasts running around cowardly with their tails between their legs, made each one of our imaginary primal hairs curl.

It was only once we stood safely near the roller coasters, that we could finally breathe freely again. The tension and the magic of the night blended with the endless buzzing of mosquitoes. And then time stood still. ◆

ADAM'S THEATER ▷

NEW JERSEY, USA, 2009

In this area with its homeless people and vagrants, everything is carefully sealed off. I had a chat with the parking lot security guard. I won his trust and he showed us the easiest place to climb over the barbed wire. He warned us that the fire escape was rusty and on the point of collapse.

It was impossible to do this discreetly, and we made a terrible racket as we climbed over the rusty, sharp wire. The rubbish belt behind the fence mirrored the dark side of this city, with its broken bottles of cheap liquor, its cans and needles.

The iron of the fire escape crumbled beneath our feet. I went in front as I weighed the least. The doors on the first and second floors were closed. On the third floor, two steps broke off and clattered to the ground. I clung to the railing and asked myself what *on earth* was I doing in that place.

The last door at the top was jammed but not locked. When I put pressure on it, it opened a little way, but at the same time I felt the fire escape give way beneath my feet...

I slowly pushed open the door. Cool, damp air wafted out to greet me. As my eyes adjusted to the darkness, I could make out the contours of the gigantic theater. ◆

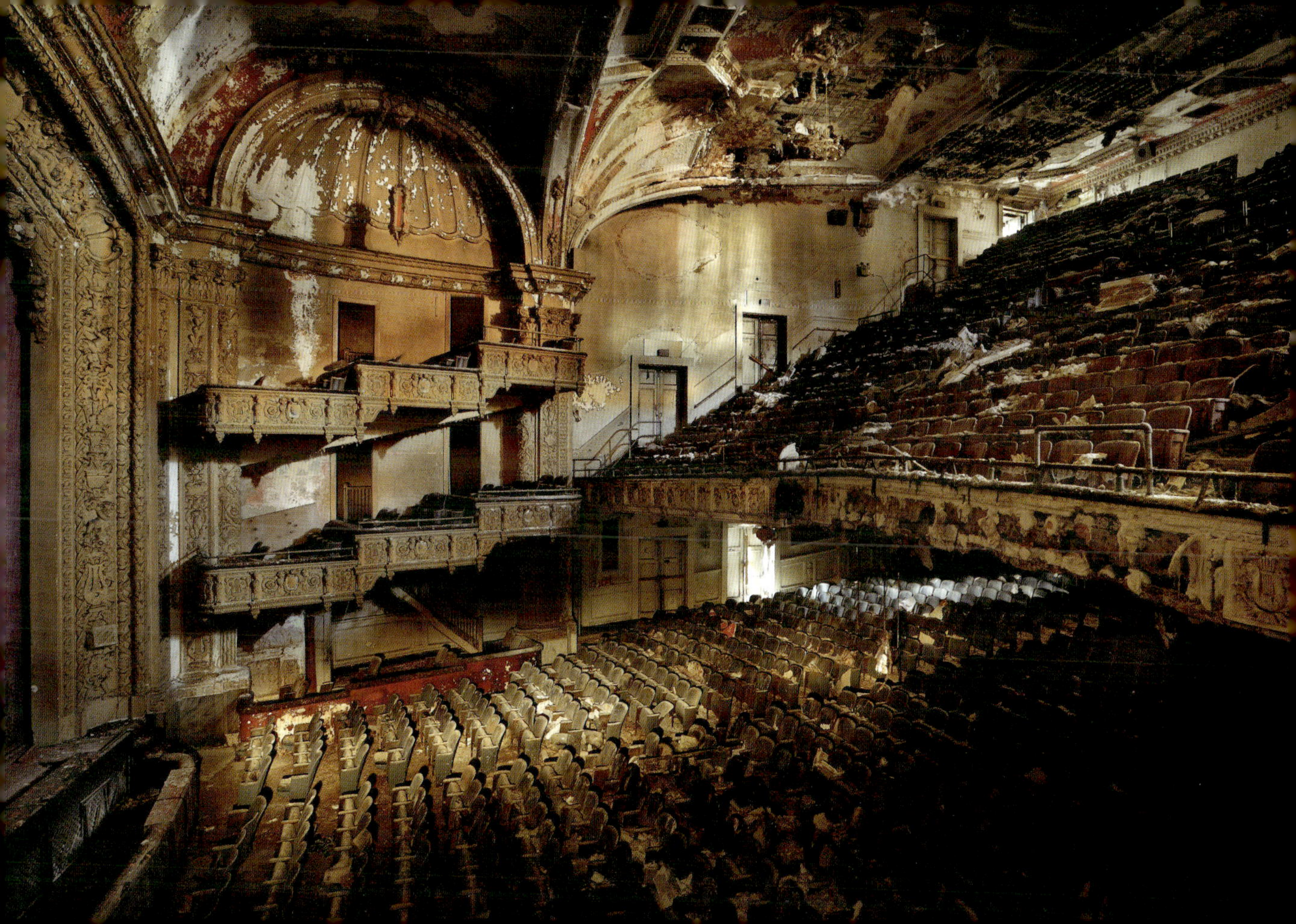

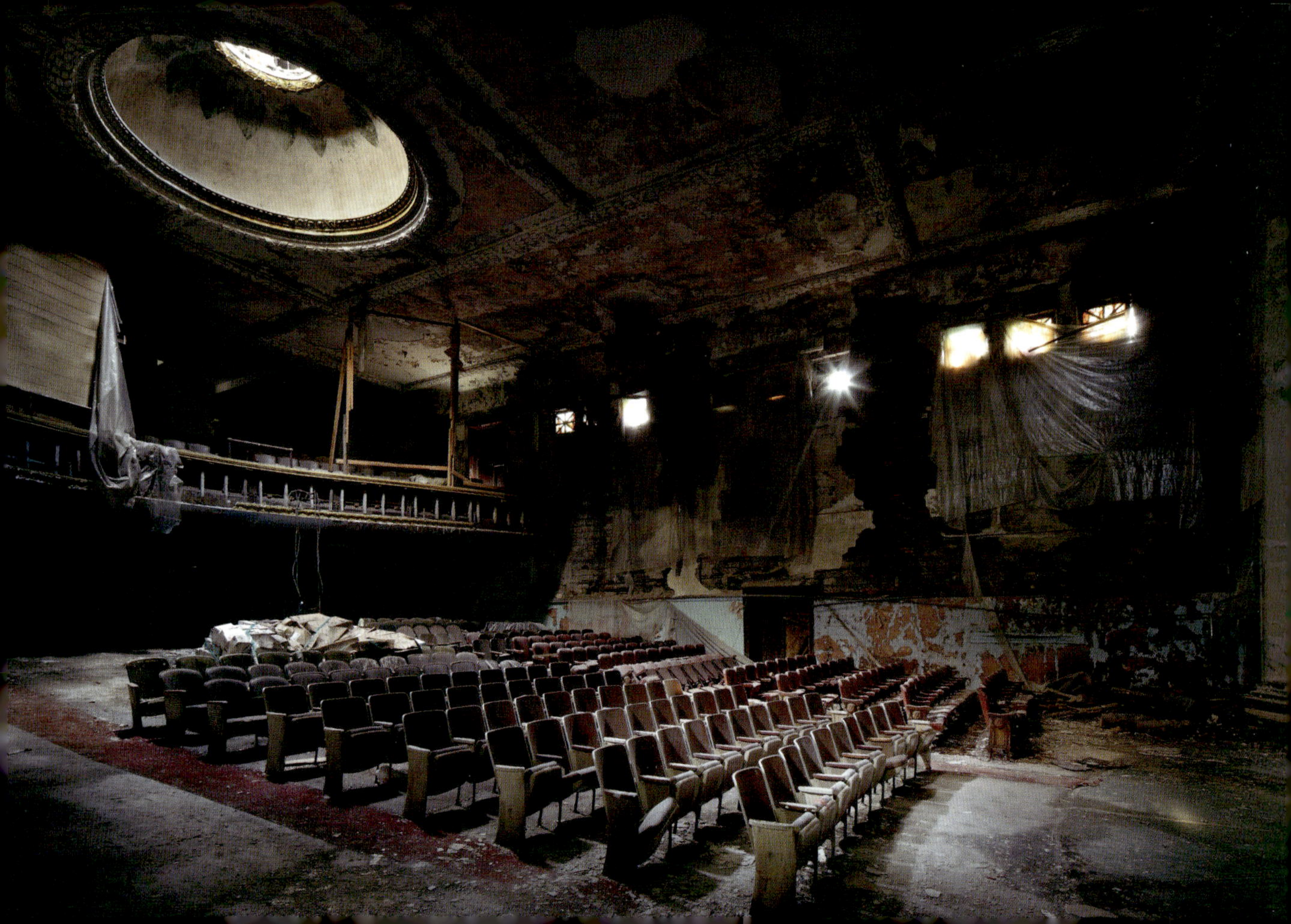

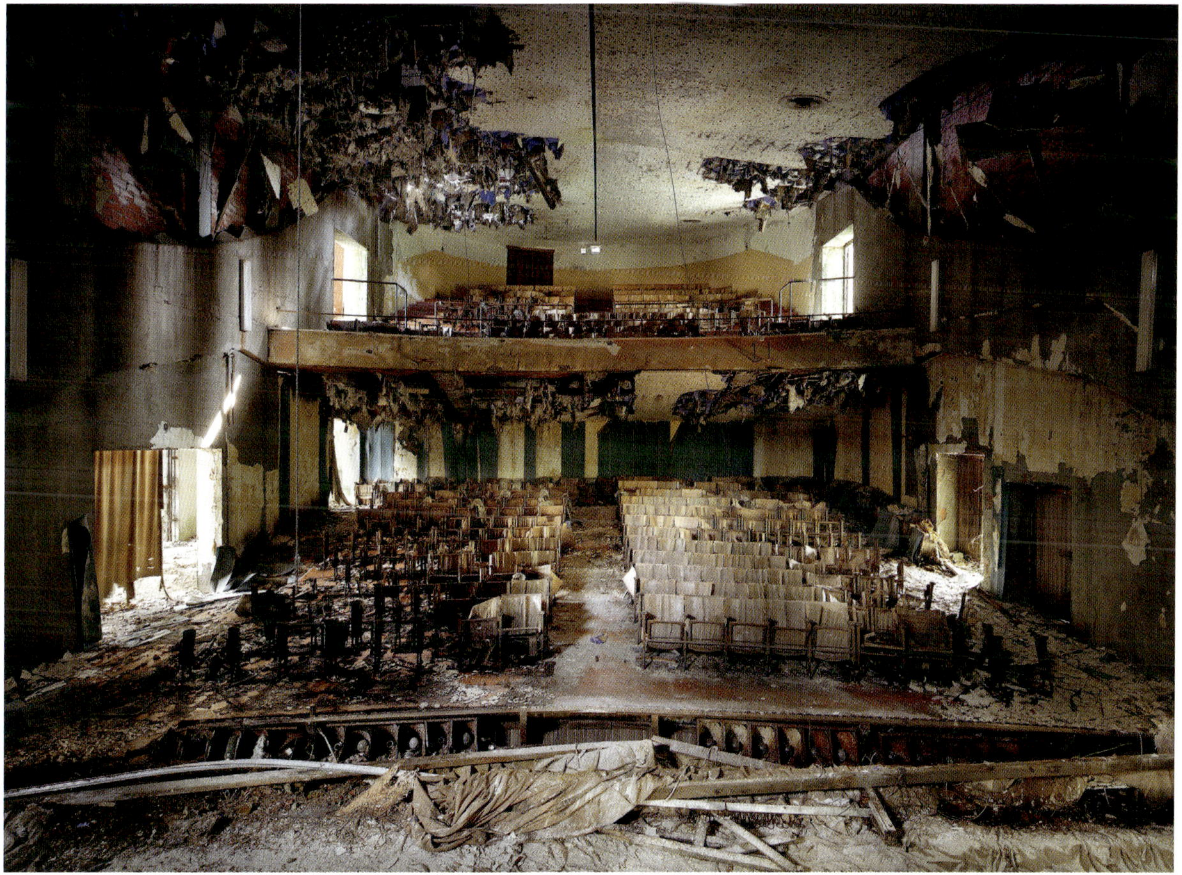

▵ Sattler Theater, Buffalo, USA, 2011 ▿ Vercelli Mosquito Theatre, Italy, 2011

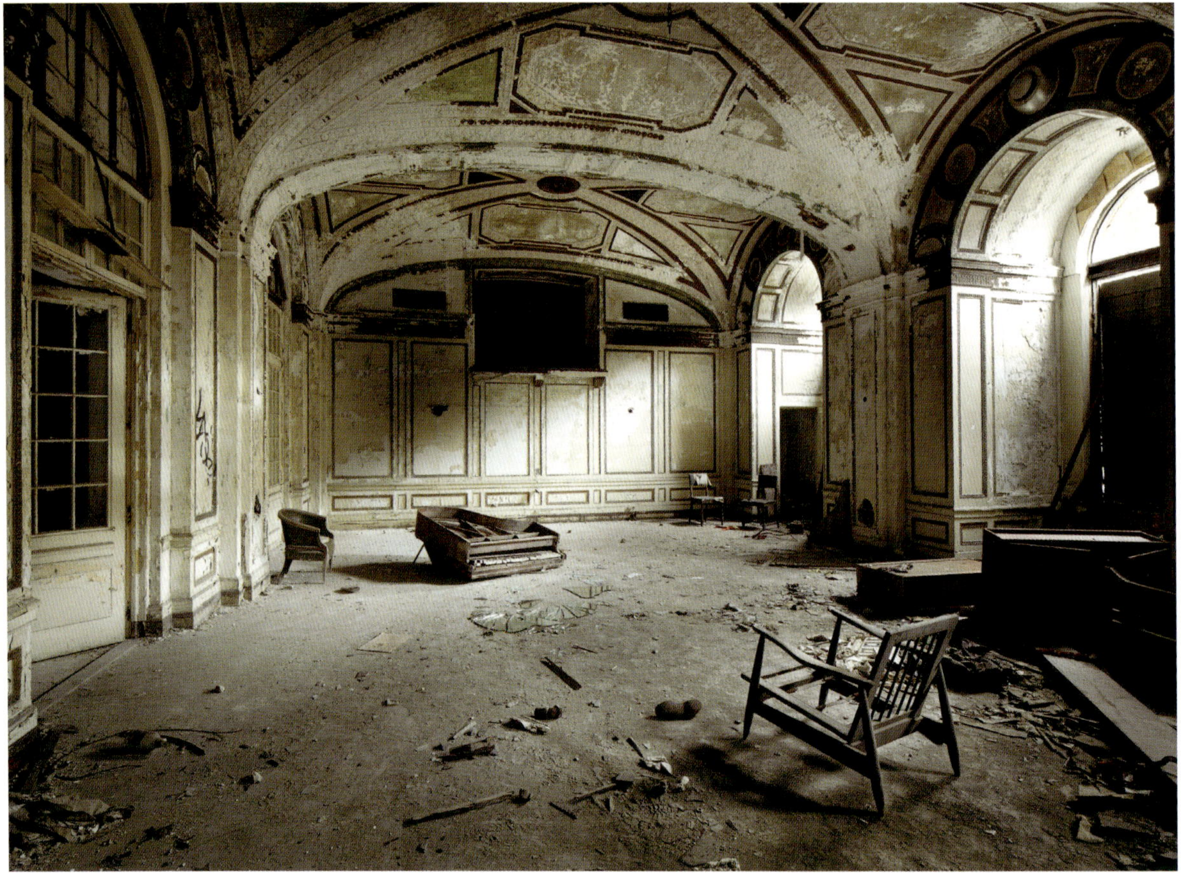

Lee Plaza Hotel lobby, Detroit, 2010

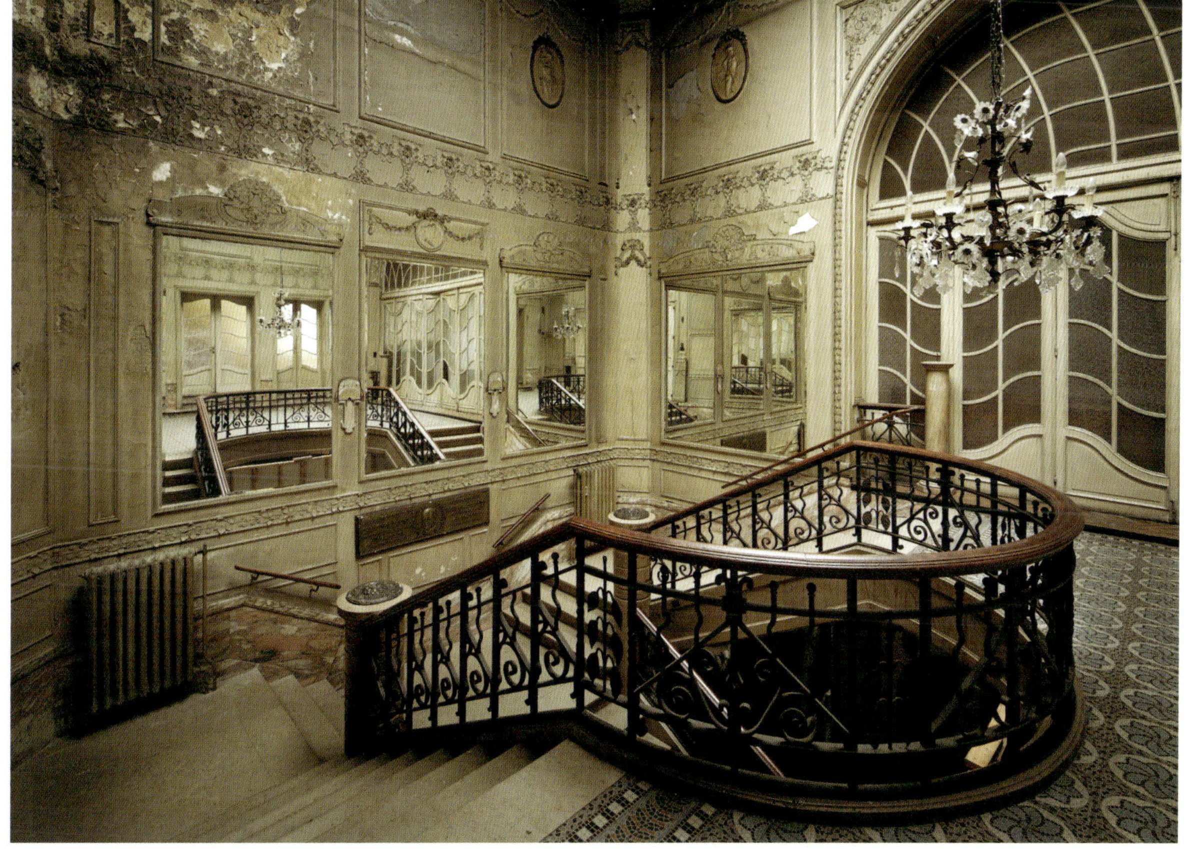

Aegidium, Belgium, 2012

HUNTER'S CASTLE ▷

BELGIUM, 2008

This is a charming, dilapidated, 17th century country estate located amidst orchards and meadows.

In 1763 Mozart spent the night at the castle while touring, and aviation pioneer, Louis Blériot, found a bed here after an emergency landing in the park.

The last lord of this castle lived here until the end of his life, occupying only the scullery and a bedroom. The rest of the house was no longer heated, the roof leaked and the walls were covered with moss. There was no money for repairs and the lord's two nephews, the only remaining members of his family, couldn't afford to pay for the upkeep of the castle. An alarm system and a neighbor kept a watch on things. A farmer picked the fruits and used the stables for his equipment.

The silence inside doesn't really spoil the fun. In the living room, several animal heads mounted on the walls stare at each other while they muse over their glorious past. Every year, the layer of dust on their fur grows a little thicker. ◆

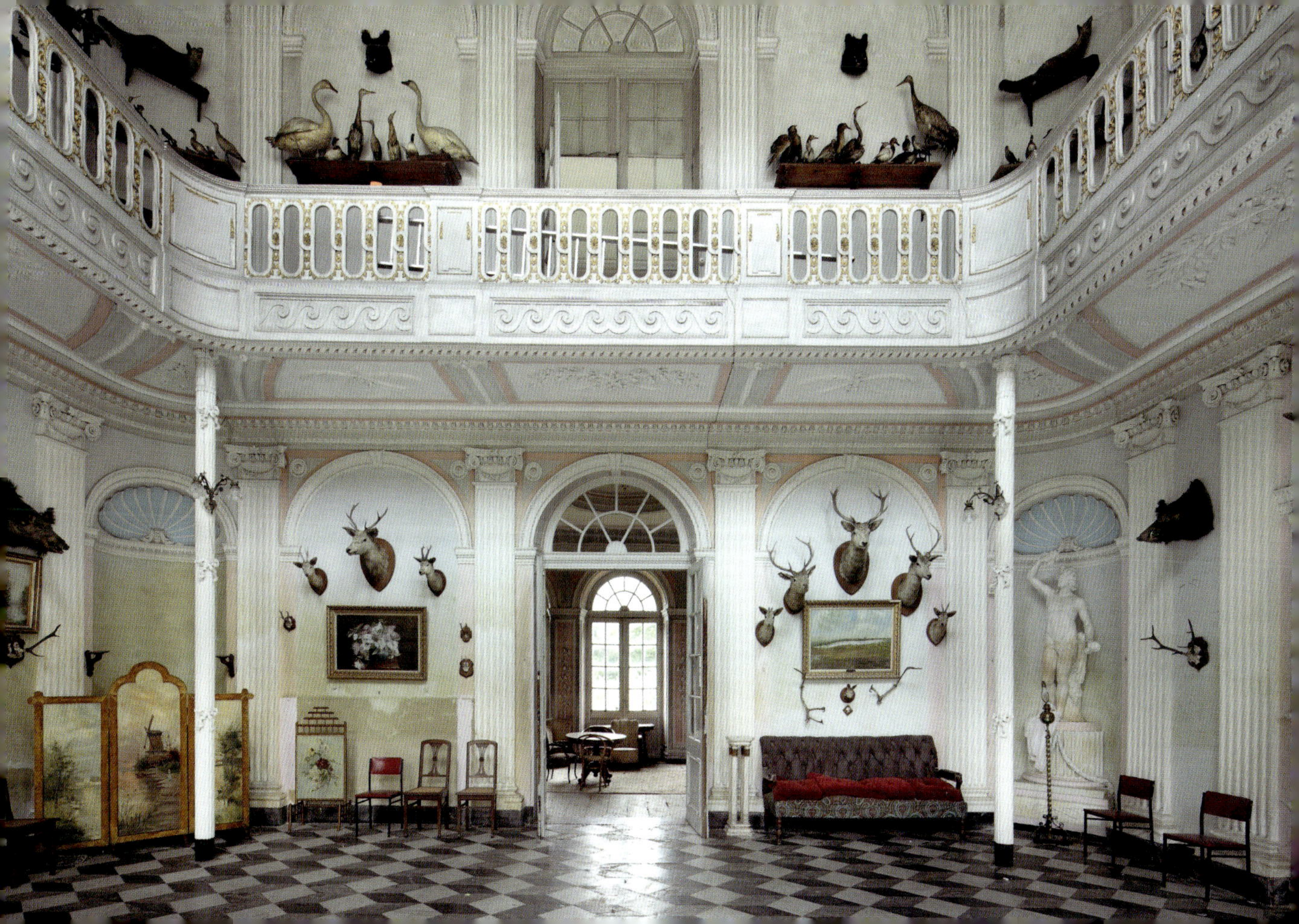

CHÂTEAU NOISY ▹

BELGIUM, 2007

Hidden deep in the woods, guarded by foresters and hunters, stands an old castle. Abandoned since the last of the railway children left in the 1980s.

The long climb to the castle on the hill was not without risk: showers of birdshot, aimed at unsuspecting pheasants, whistled past my ears. What was I to do? Put on a fluorescent jacket in an attempt not to become an innocent victim? Better to move stealthily, wait and chase away the pheasants around me!

Then suddenly I stood face to face with a fairy-tale castle, ravishing yet vulnerable. From a distance I wondered for a while whether the place was really abandoned, but the signs left no doubt: a broken window, a burnt roof, the front door boarded up, the driveway full of puddles and the park totally neglected. ◆

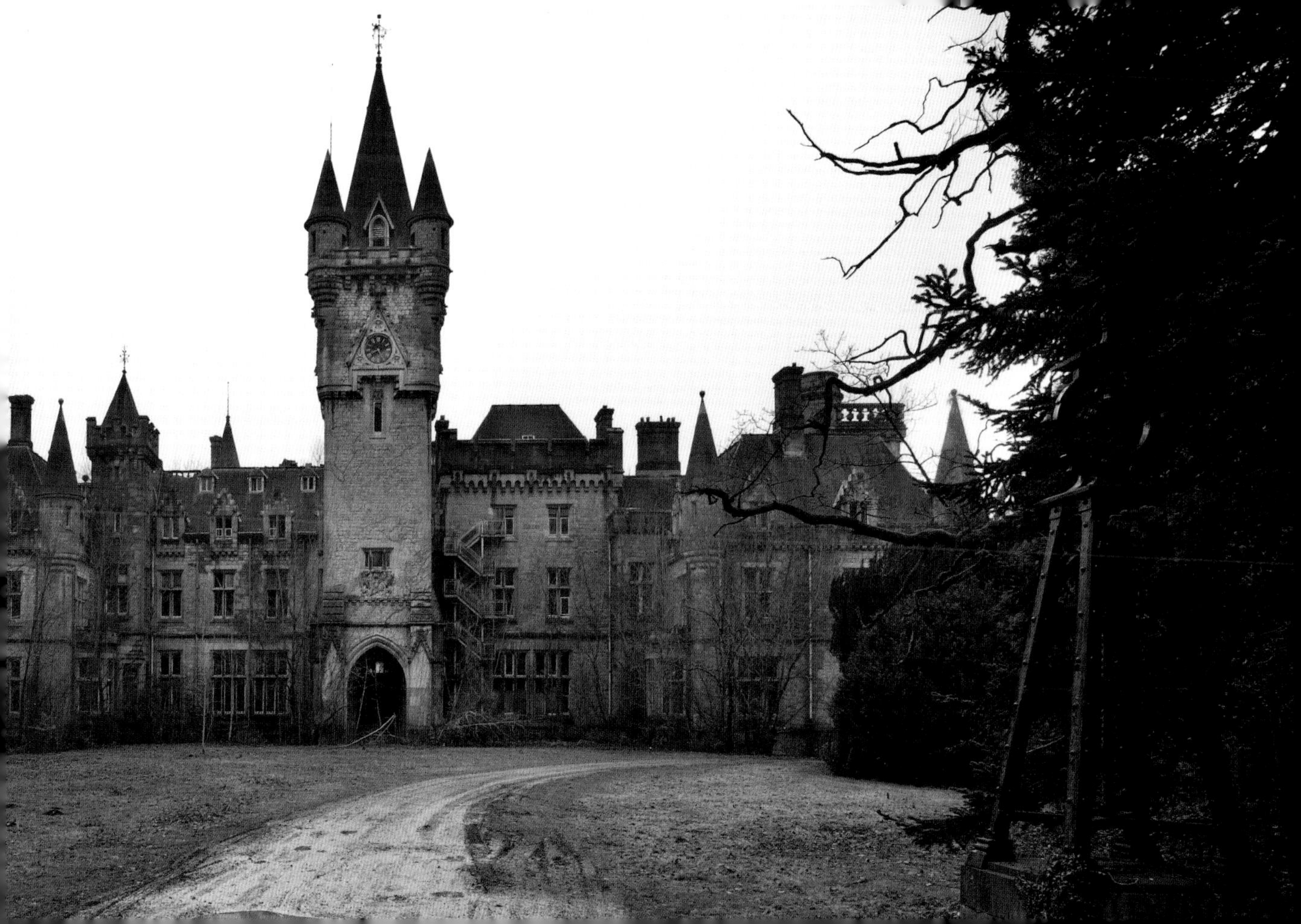

PLASTER STAIRWAY ▹

VILLA DECADIMENTO, ITALY, 2011

Down winding streets too tight even for the smallest Fiat, we were looking for Villa Decadimento. Trampled weeds, an iron gate, a hole in the high wall... and there stands the majestic villa in the middle of an arboretum with the best view ever of the Lago Maggiore. The garden is still maintained, the grass around the villa neatly clipped. Long ago thieves forced the door open, now climbing plants block the passage. Downstairs it is dark and damp. Over the years the decor has adapted itself perfectly to the 1970s Zanussi refrigerator, standing motionless like a chameleon in an upside-down world.

The large central staircase is a real beauty. The stairs are covered with a white layer of powdered plaster. Light penetrates through a landing window and a hole in the wall. It is dark and light simultaneously, as in a fairy tale.

Later that day, traveling by car, we found another villa that looked deserted. Just to make sure I knocked on the door, waited a minute, knocked again, but got no answer. I walked cautiously around the house. Coming back to the front door from the other side, a woman now stood there shouting out angrily at me. Behind her was a man with a shotgun! All I could do was look innocent like a silly tourist and ask if I could take photos of the villa, to which she responded: 'Get the hell off my property.' ◆

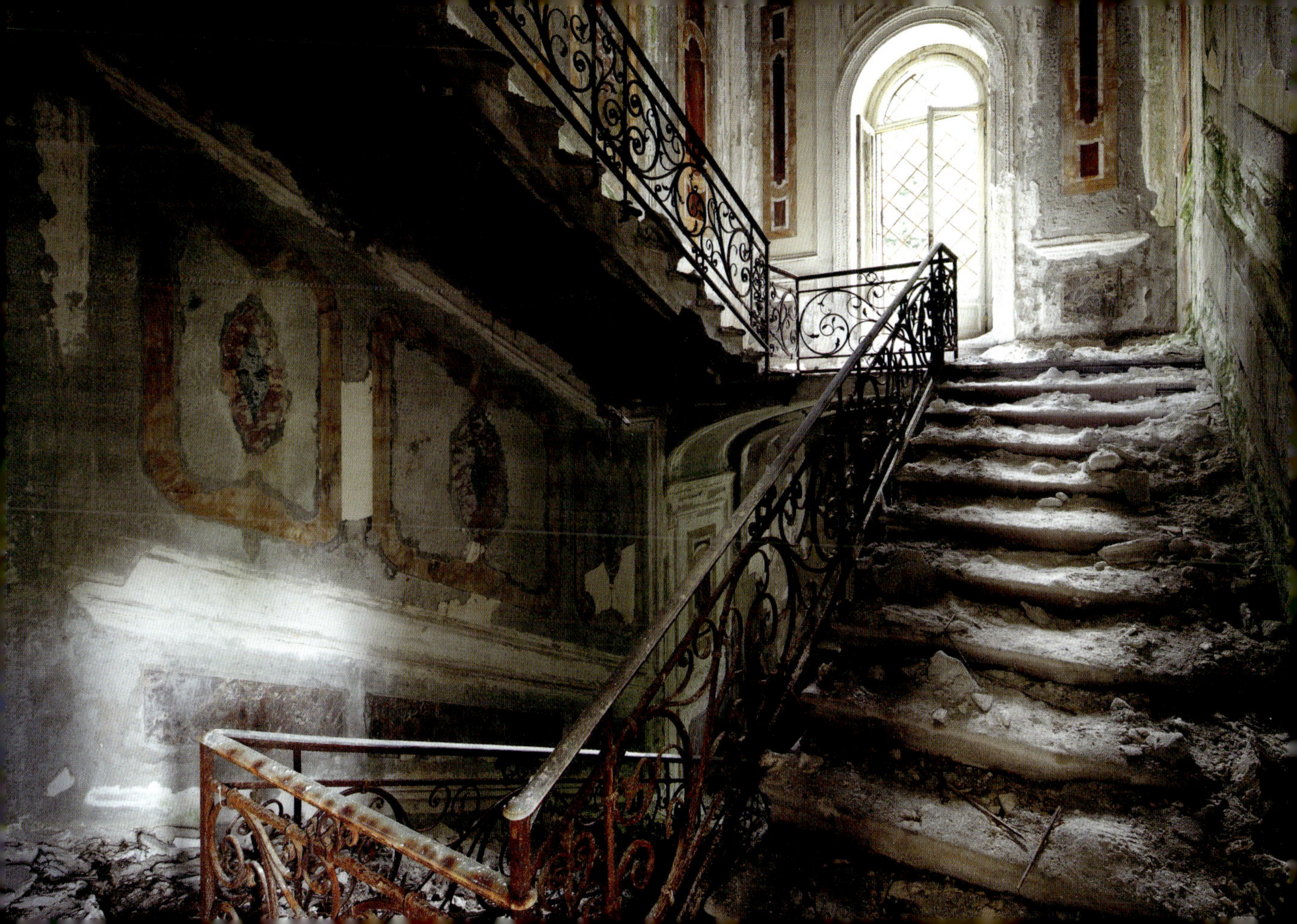

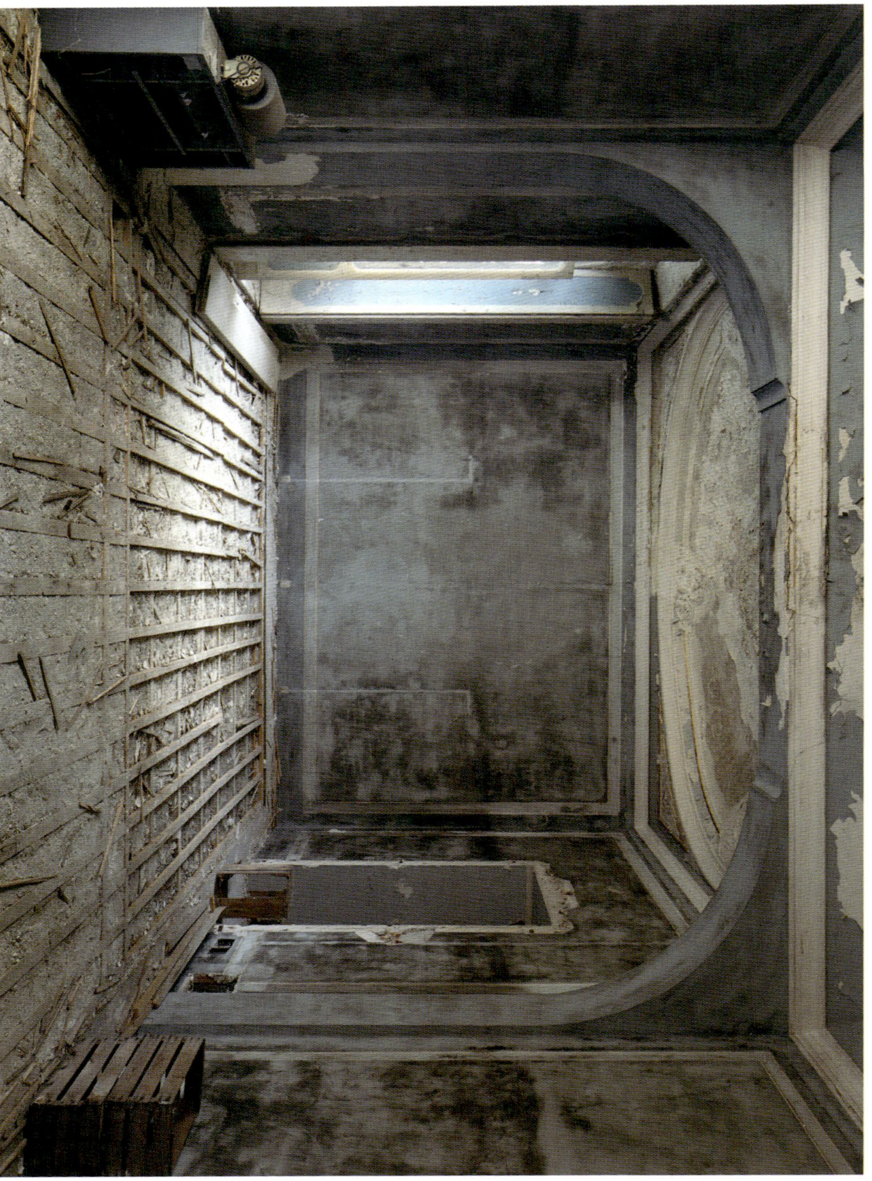

 The Blue Room, Italy, 2016

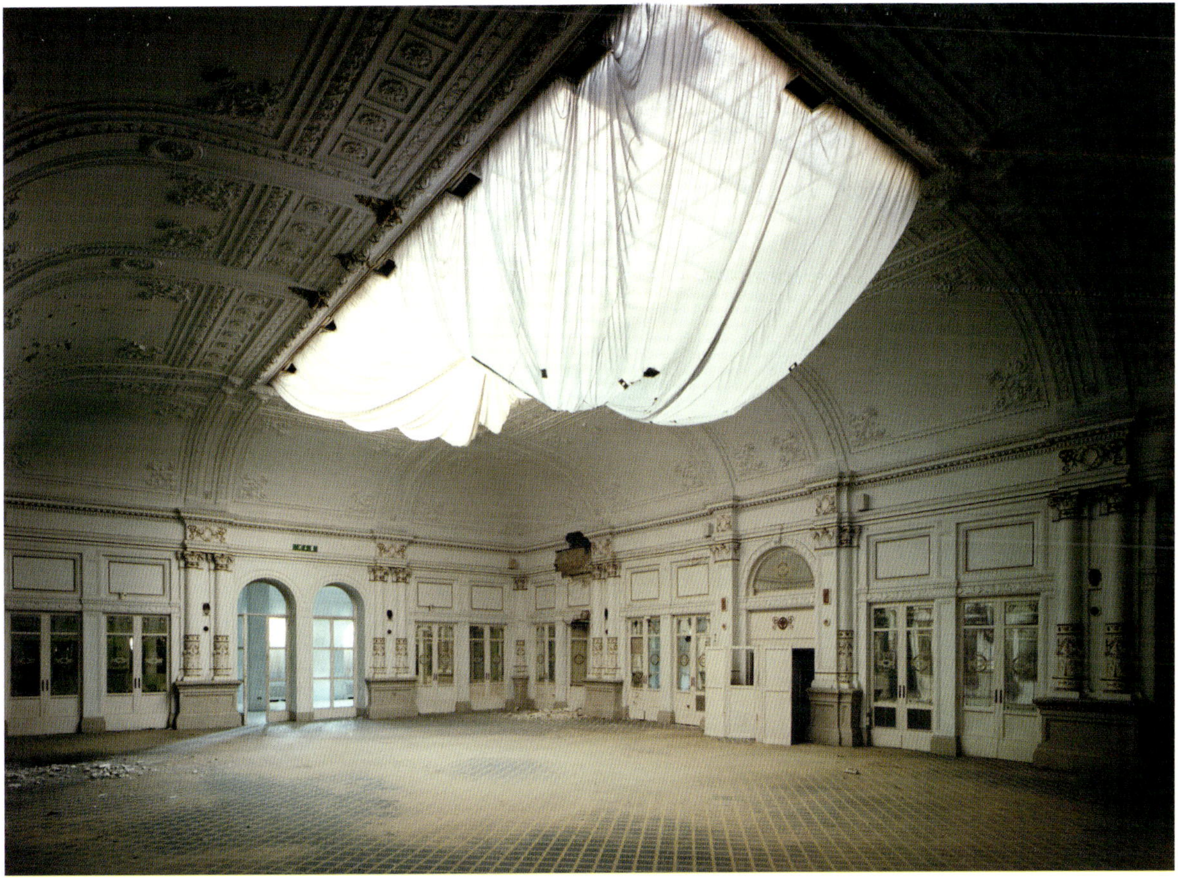

Grand Hotel Ballroom, Italy, 2016

Villa Maledetto, Italy, 2016

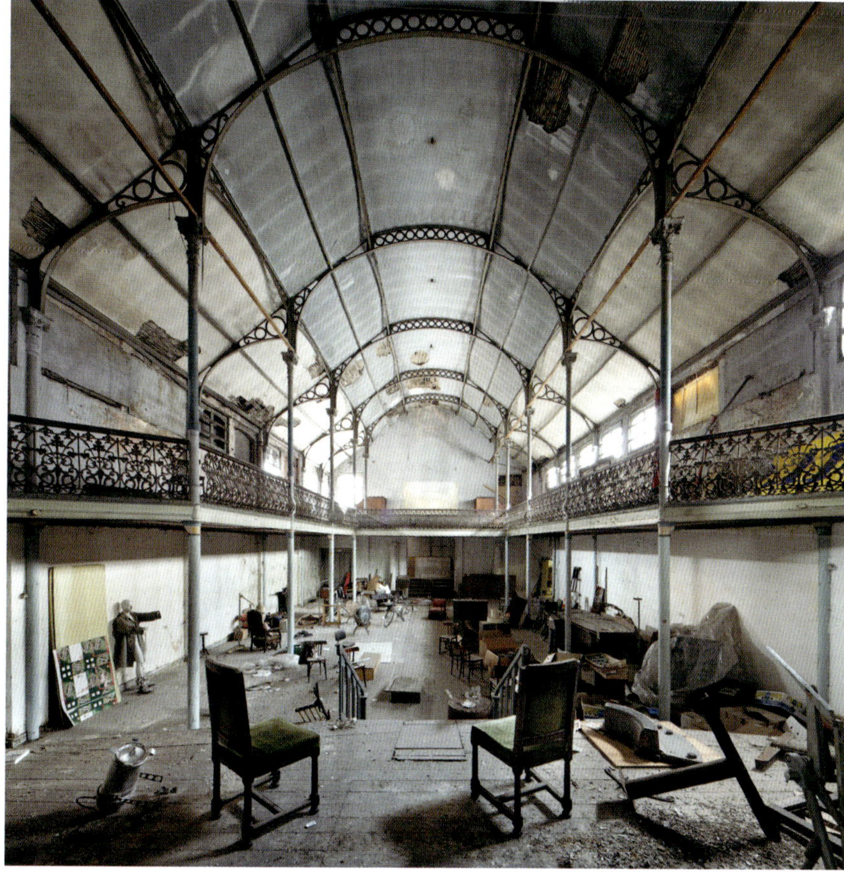

Theater 1900, Belgium, 2010

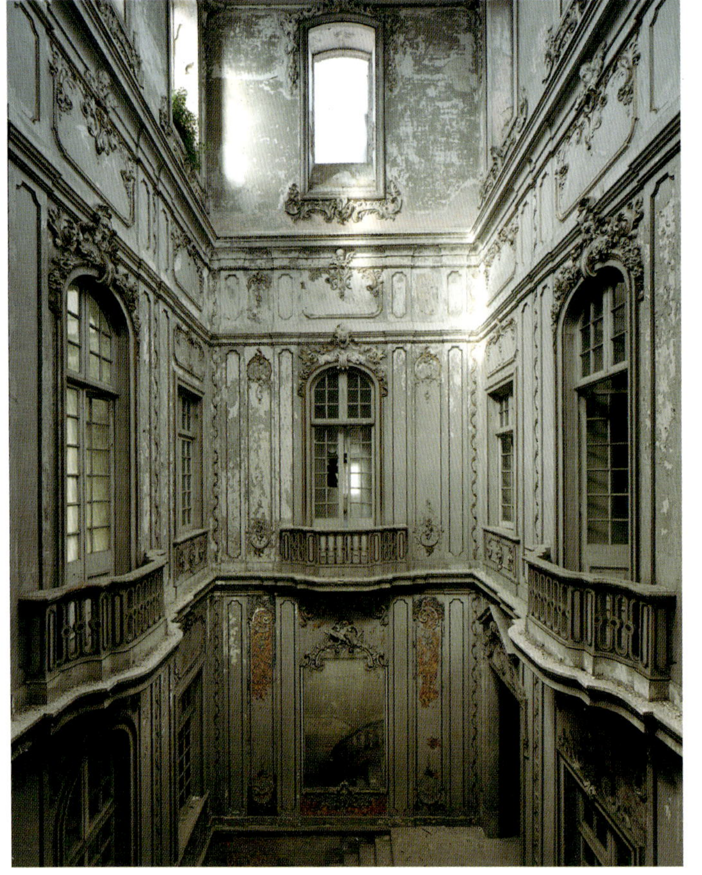

Montezuma, Portugal, 2017

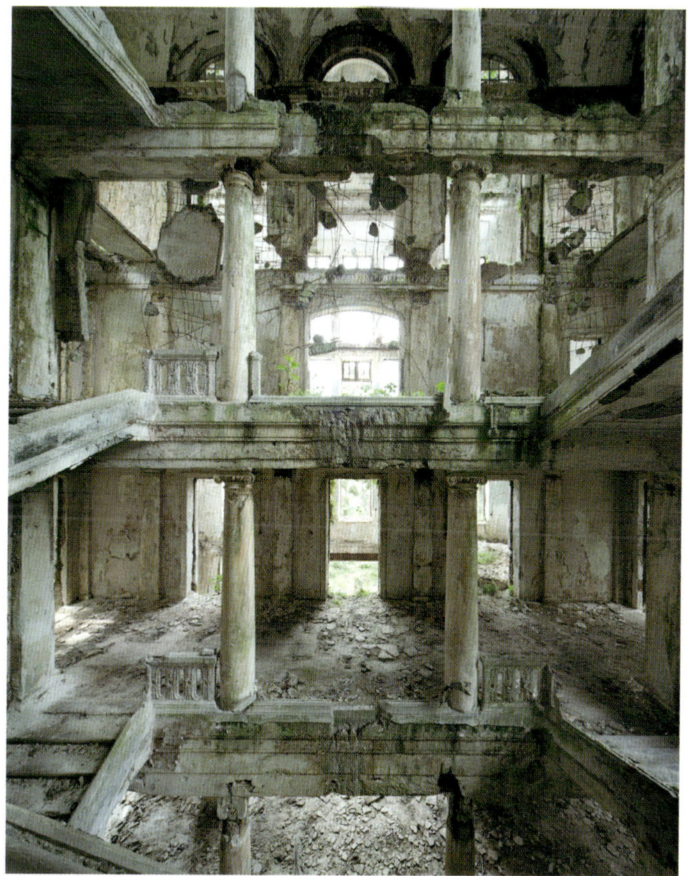

Prince Smetski Sanatorium, Abkhazia, 2018

THE BURNT LIBRARY ▷

ITALY, 2011

CORRIDOR OF ZEN ▷

ITALY, 2013

In a small town in the Po Valley this hospital stands like an impregnable fortress.

Some of the newer buildings on the estate are easily accessible, but not very interesting. The shepherd, whose sheep graze the grass short on the lawns, was keeping an eye on things. While avoiding him, I stumbled upon a confused old man collecting dead twigs in the park. We shook hands and babbled mutually unintelligible Italian. I asked him if he knew a way inside. But he didn't seem to grasp why I wanted to enter a building which for years he probably wanted to escape...

The solution ultimately appeared in the form of a rotten ladder hidden in the tall grass.

The covered passageway radiated such improbable peace and harmony that a daily walk must have had more effect than the medicine of the day. I call it 'The Corridor of Zen'.

The old building is incredibly big. The fire was on the first floor. The story that goes around is that the archive contained mainly material about the mafia. An identical cupboard in an office next door was spared. Its doors stand haphazardly open as if a mischievous wind is blowing through the room. ◆

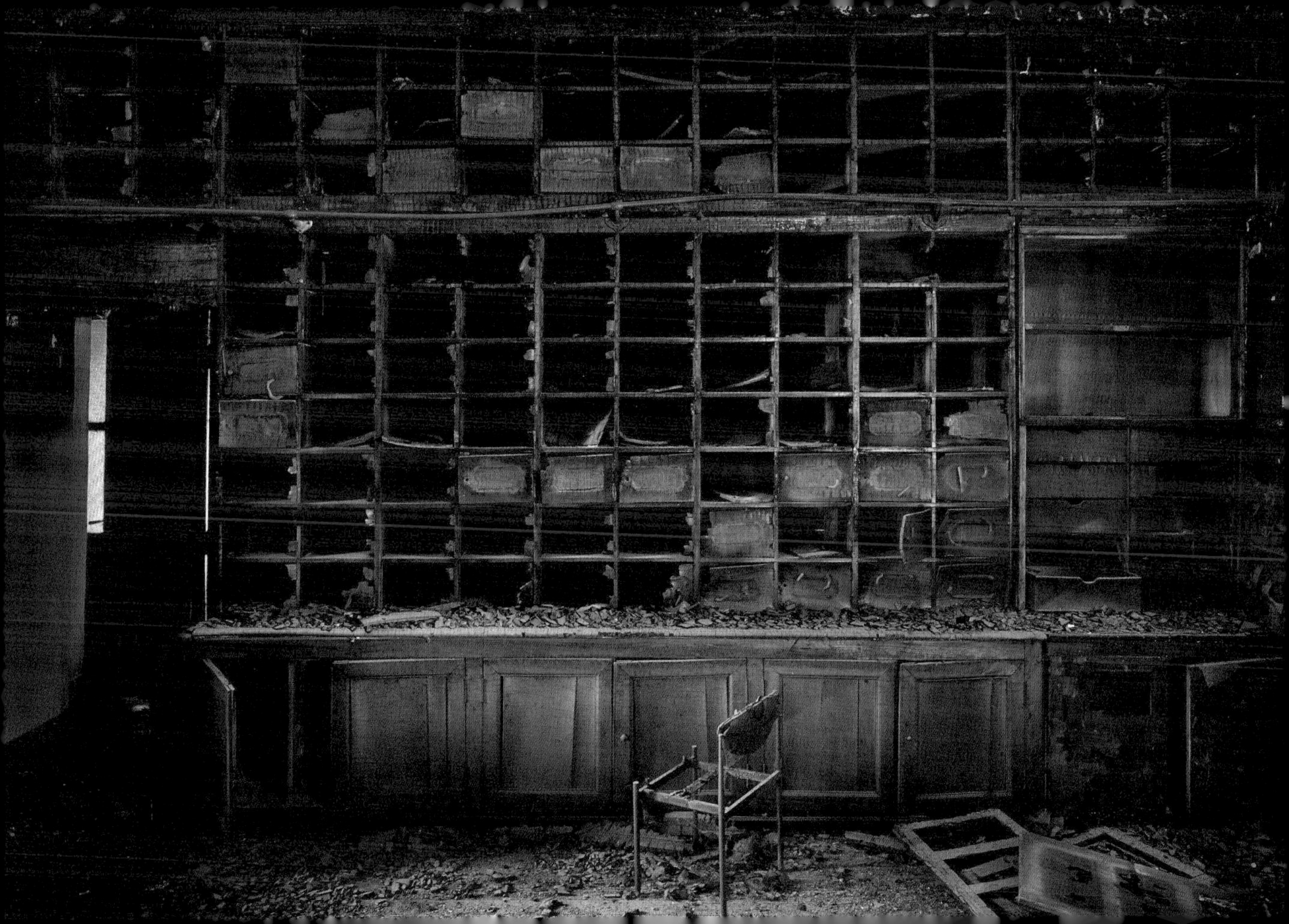

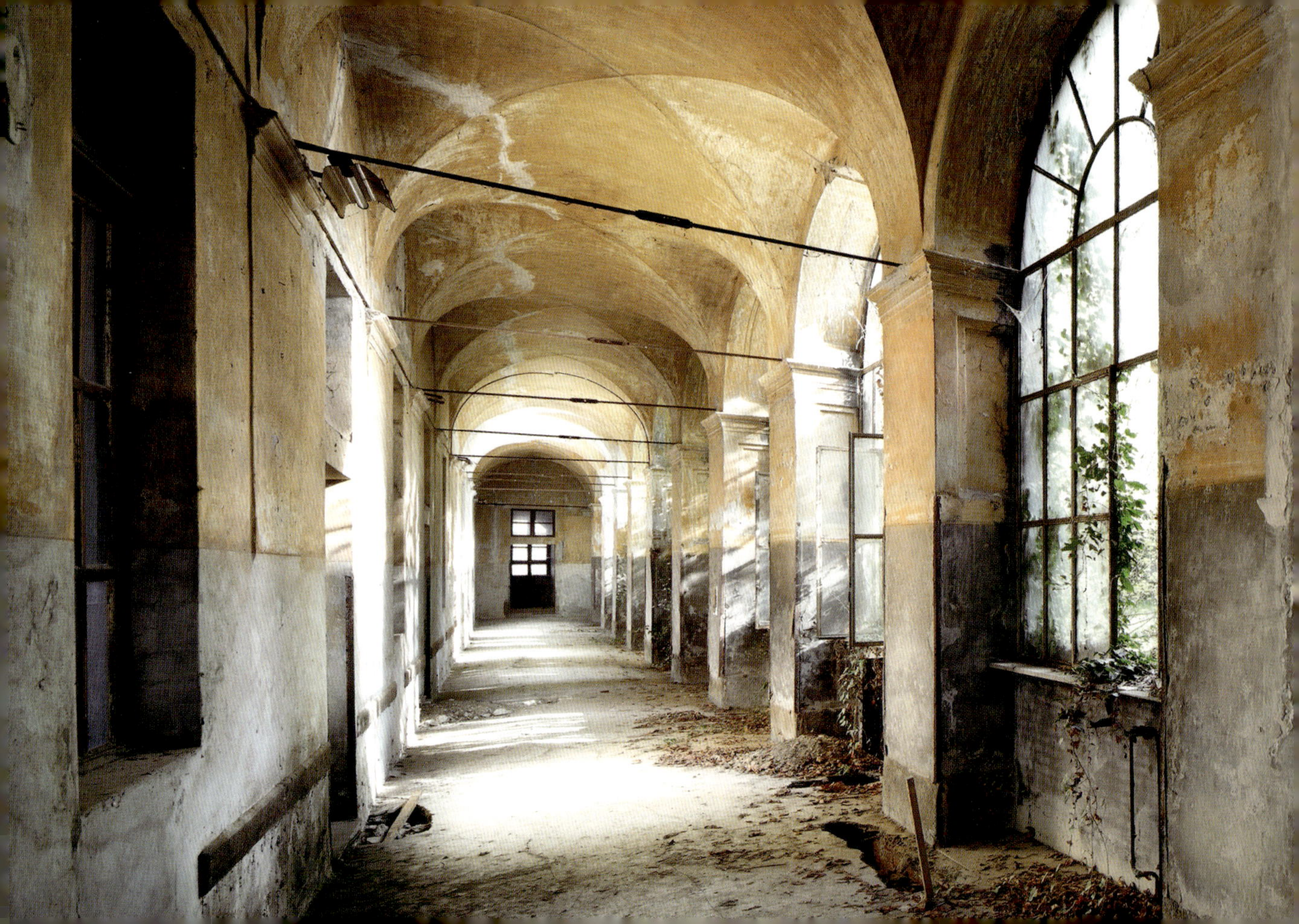

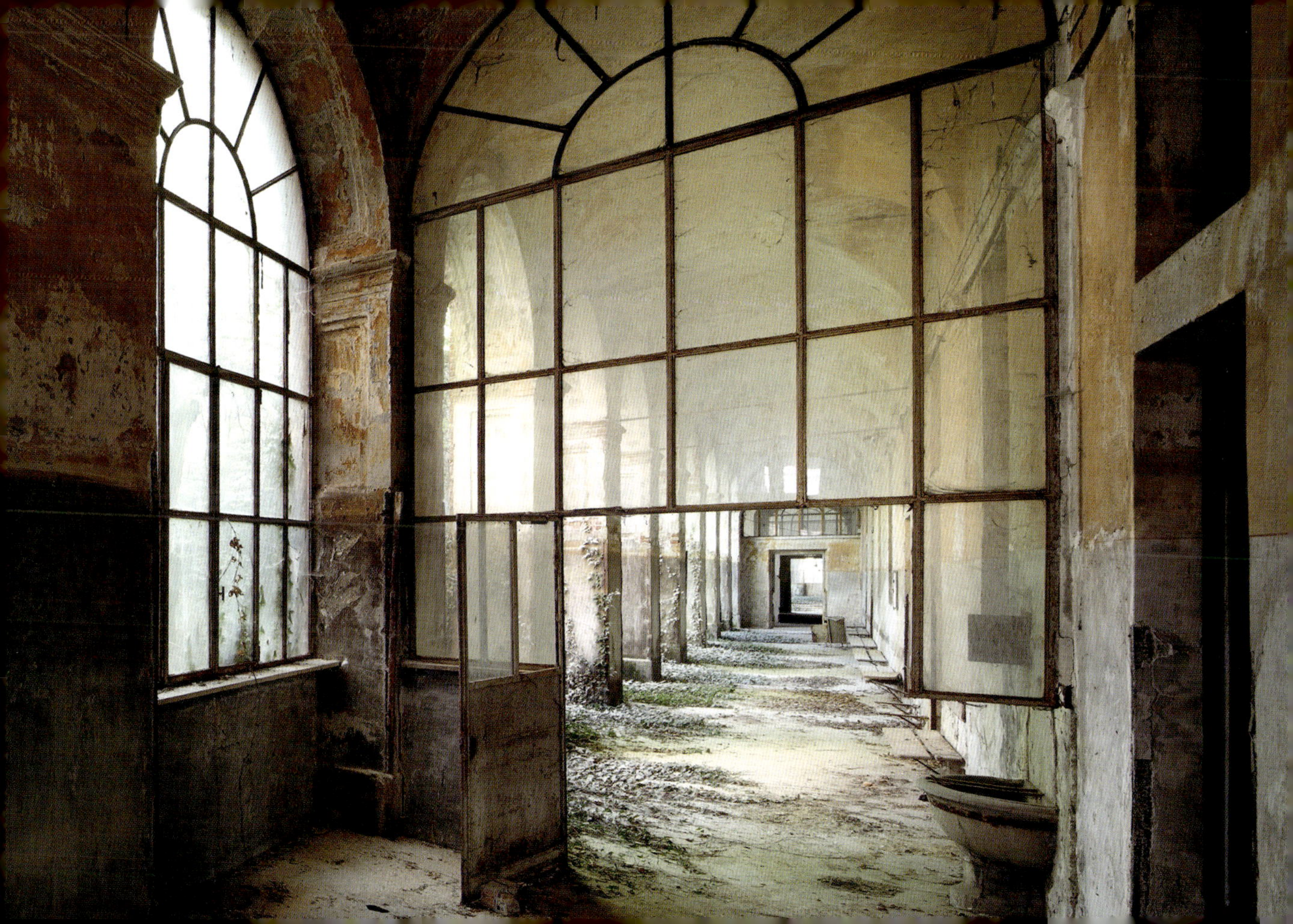

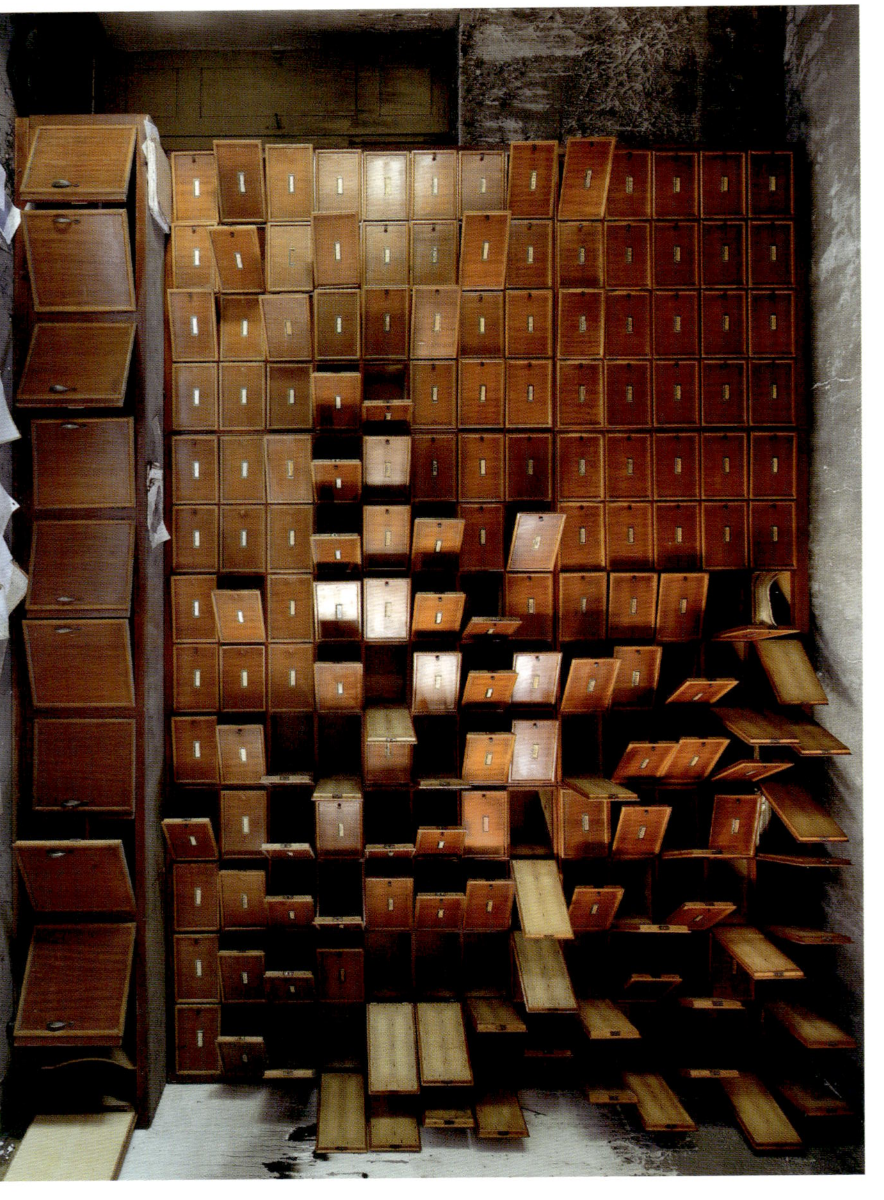

 The Unburnt Library, Italy, 2013

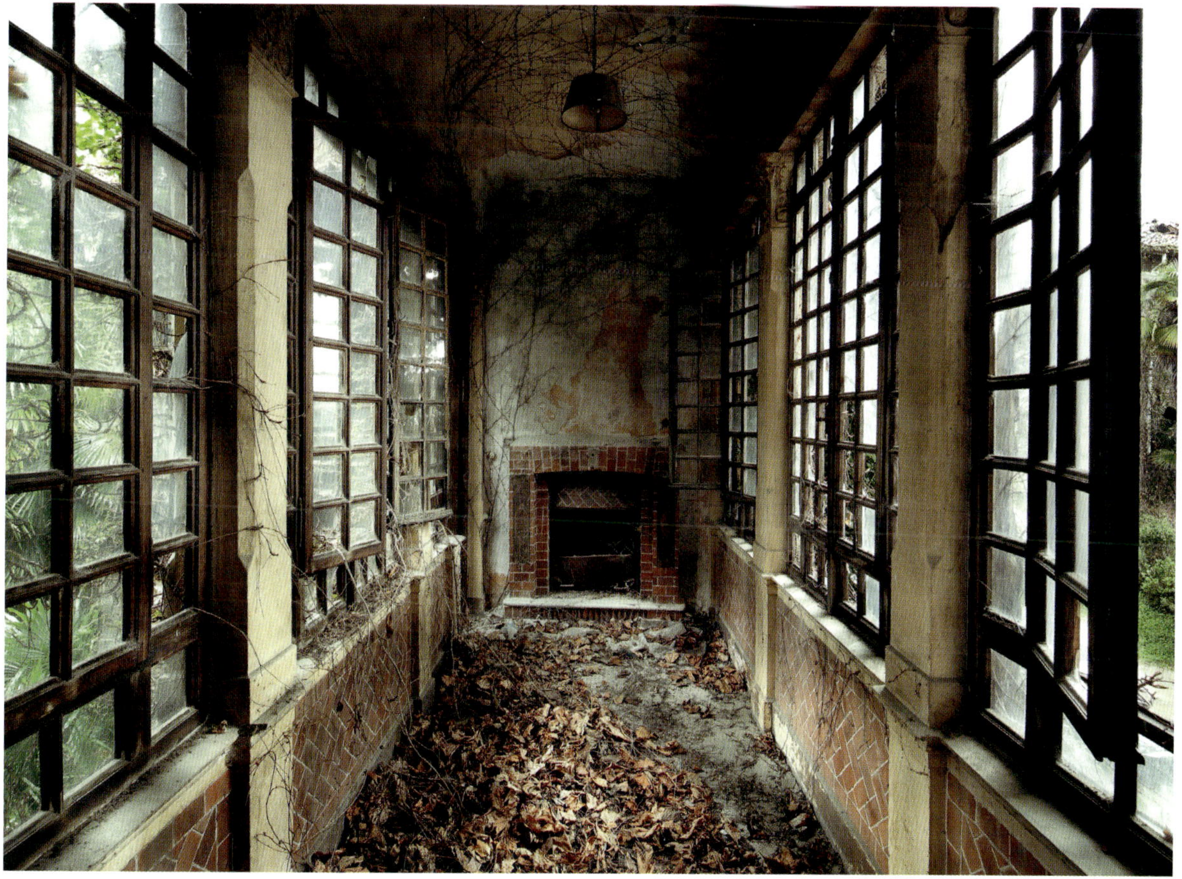

Castello Duchessa di Genova, Italy, 2013

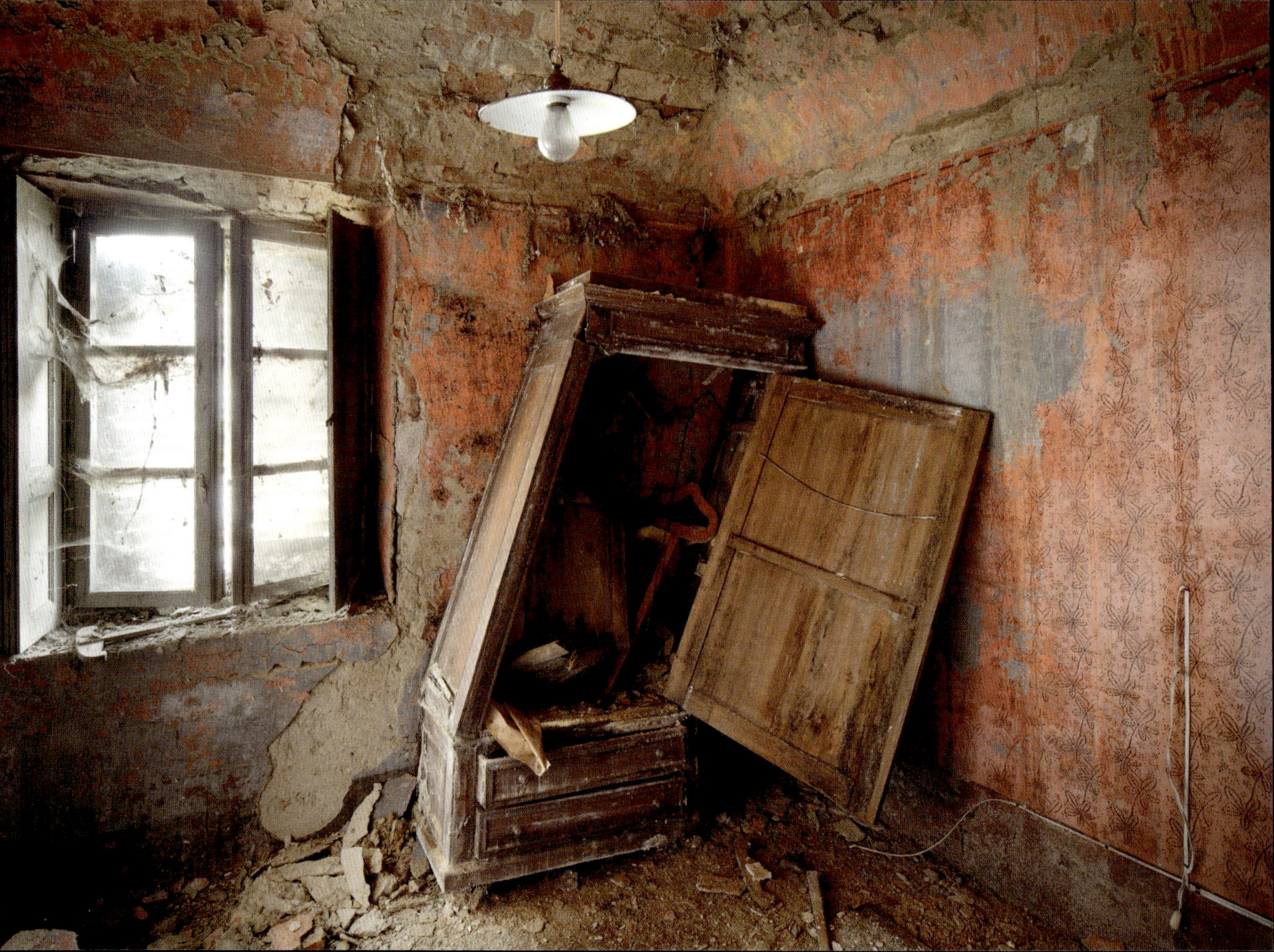

△ Castello Albano, Italy, 2011 ▽ Castello Albano - Paris Match, Italy, 2011

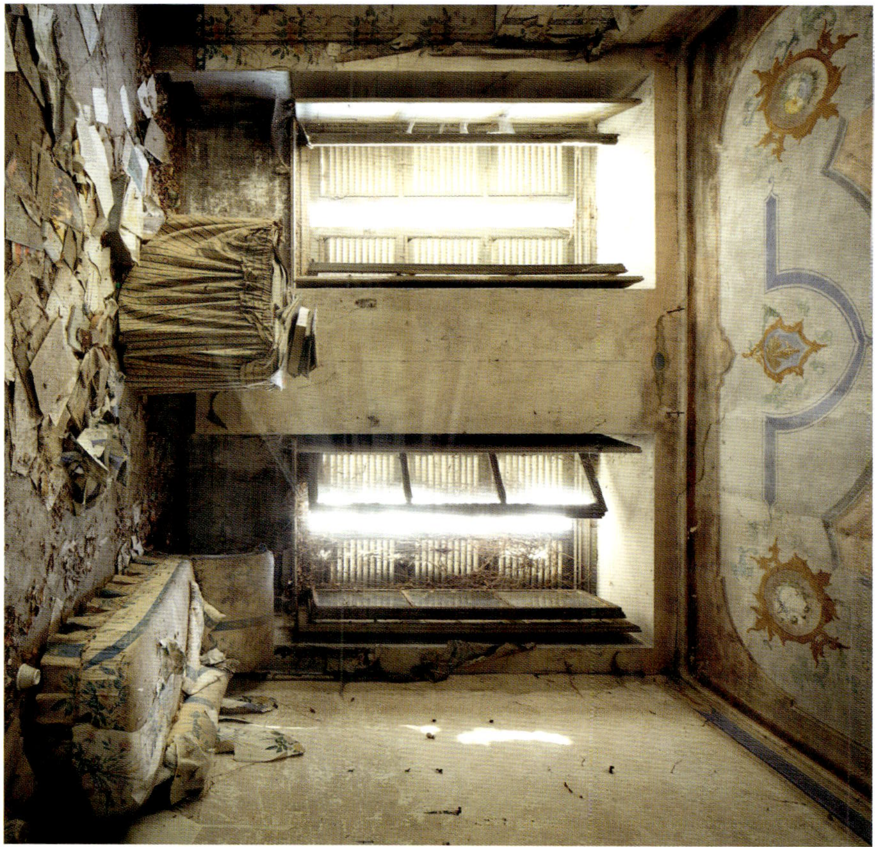

VILLA FORTUNA ▹

ITALY, 2016

A cappuccino for breakfast. Pasta and a glass of Chianti for dinner. Beauties talk into their mobiles as they zigzag trendy Vespas single-handedly through the traffic jam. I pay the motorway toll and leave the drab industrial suburbs. Driving through breathtaking scenery, I take an exit to the middle of nowhere and come upon a picturesque village in search of a long wall with a wrought iron gate. Peering eyes watch me from behind curtains. Through a jungle of brambles, I arrive at the little castle. With every step I take, the floor gives way a little and the neighbour's dog barks at me for minutes on end. ◆

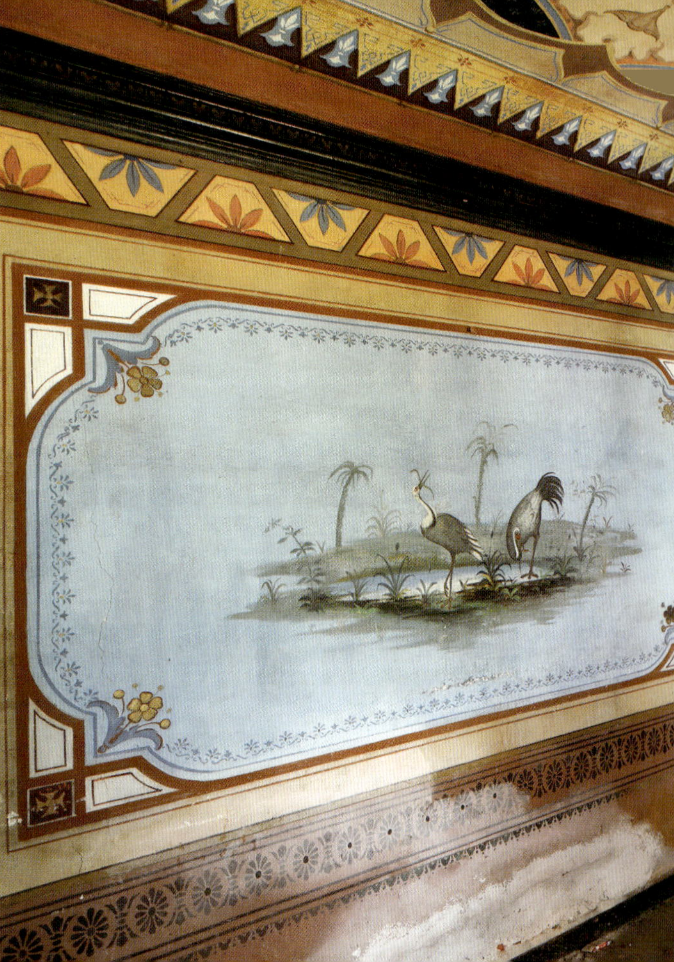

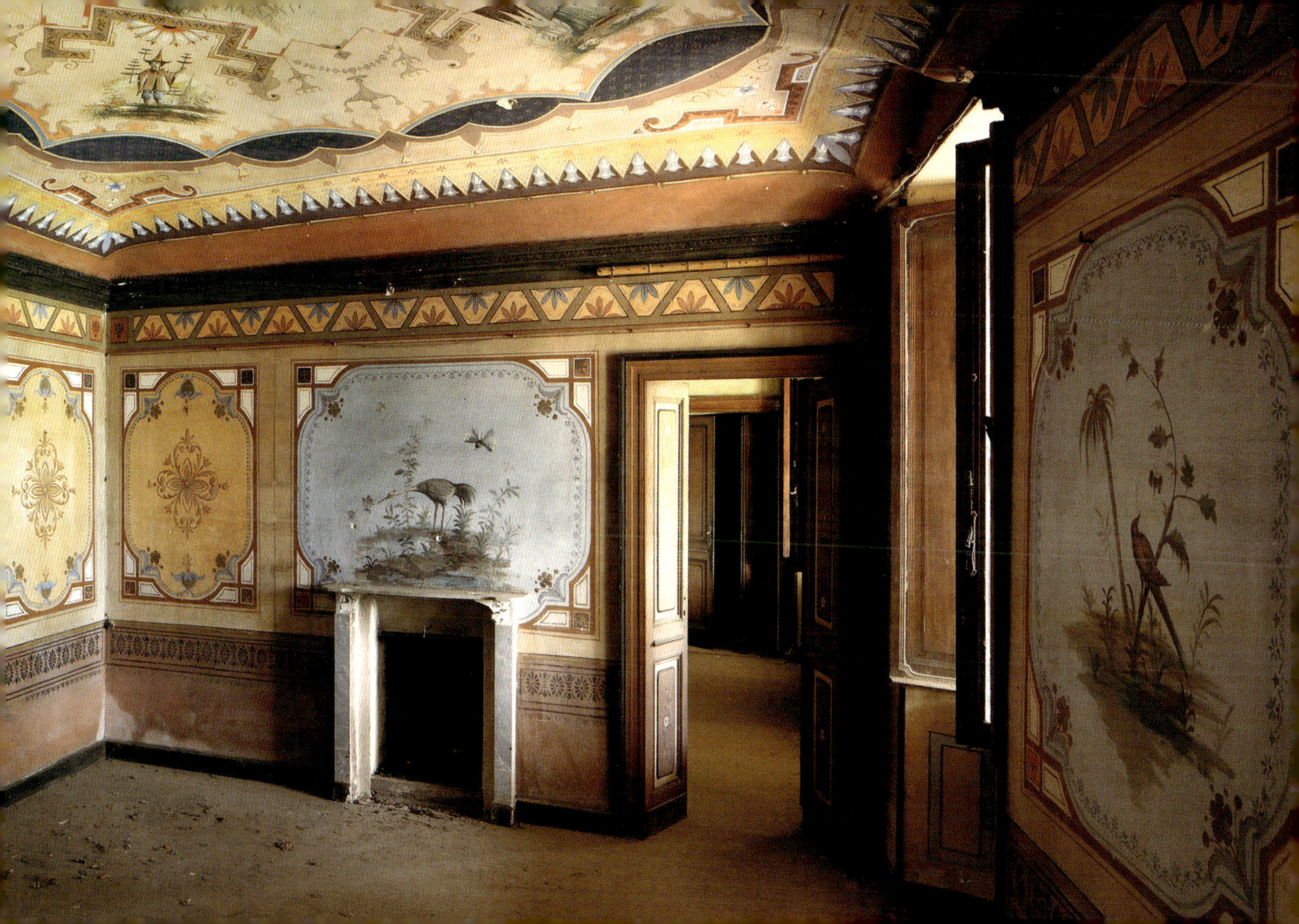

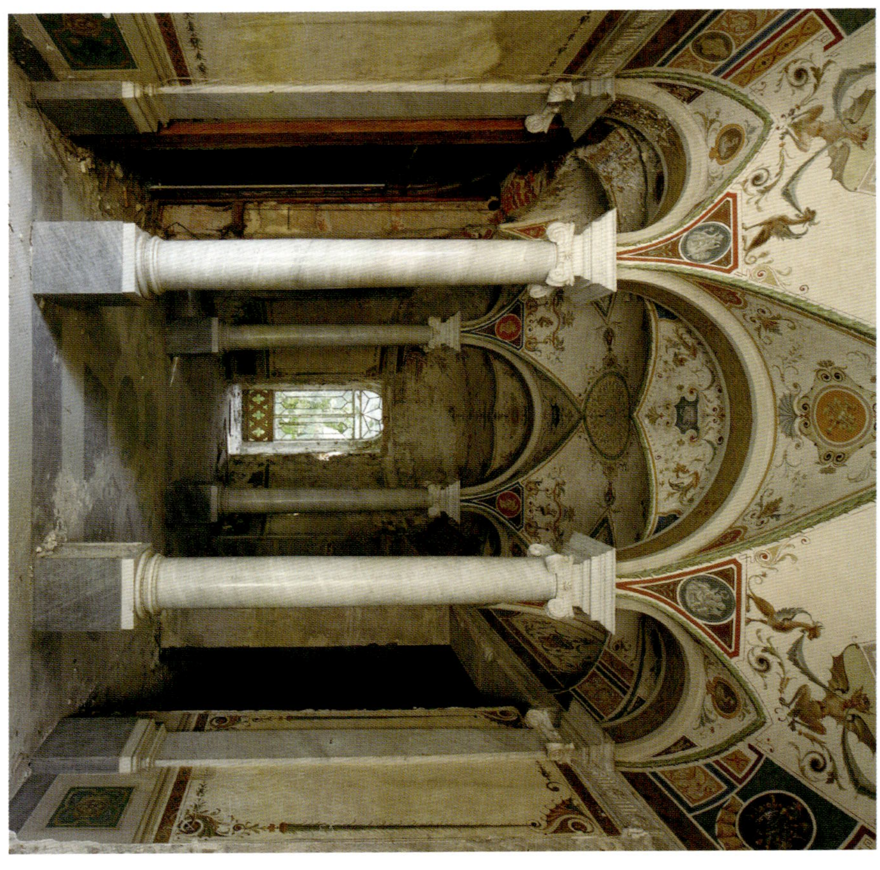

 La Villa del diavolo, Italy, 2016

Betoane, Romania, 2015

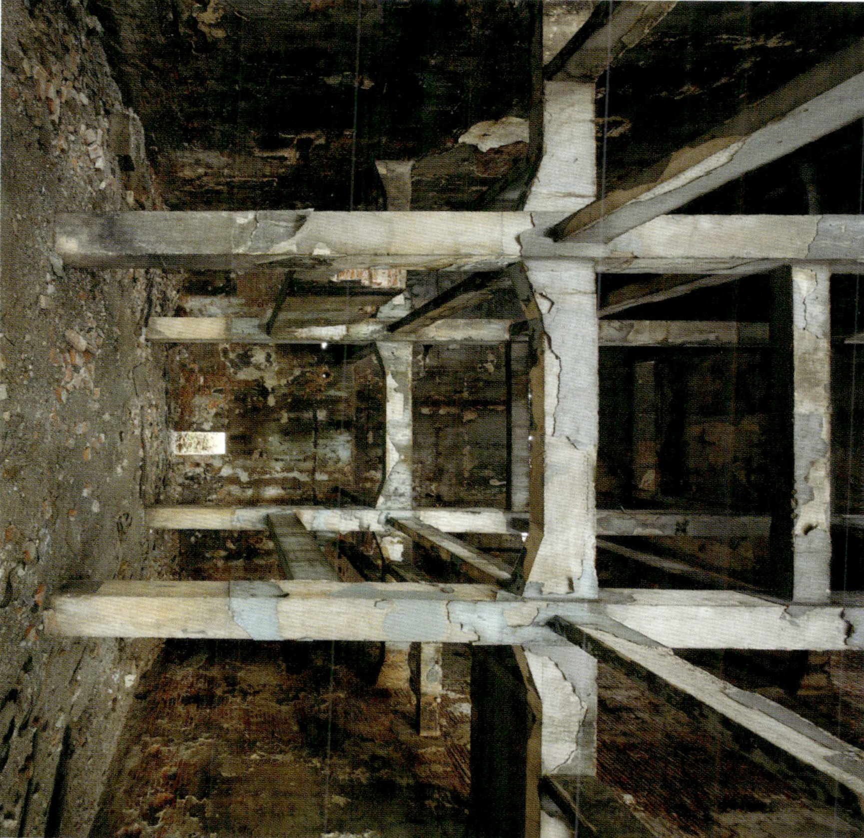

RAYS OF SUN ▷

ZELISZOW, POLAND, 2012

Just outside the village there is a football field, a bus stop, a few houses, fields and a church. More reminiscent of a theater than a church, all in wood, with warm colors and graceful arches. The sun's beams are a sign that an empty church is never forsaken by God. Here once sounded the words of Martin Luther's German bible and the enchanting music of Bach's St. Matthew Passion.

I spent the entire day at this magical place. When it got dark, an owl, perched on the ridge of a roof, called out to me to stay just a little longer... ◆

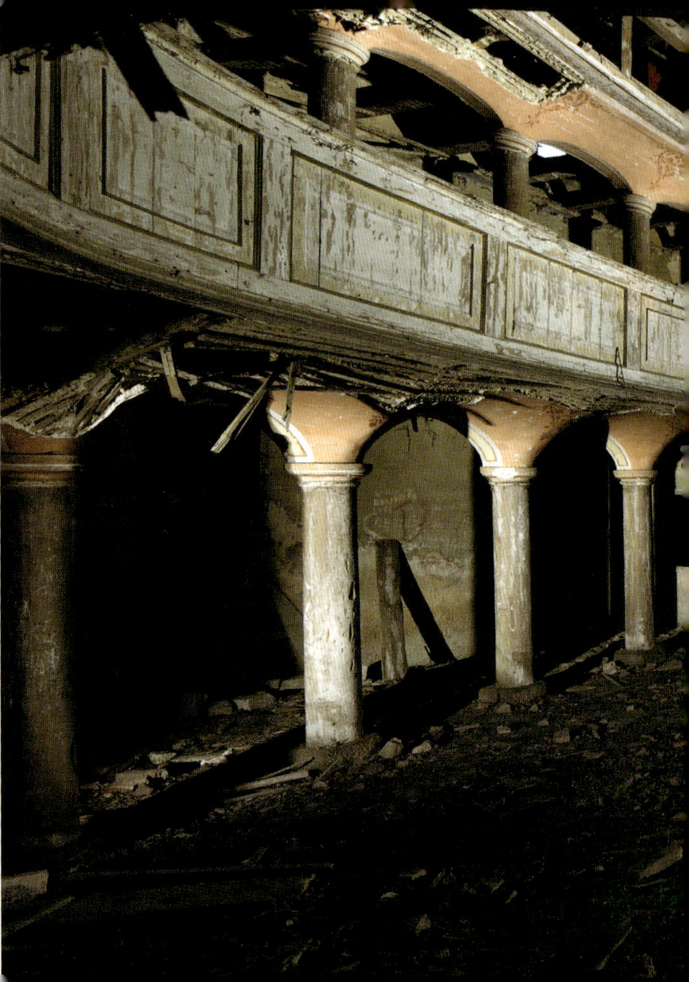

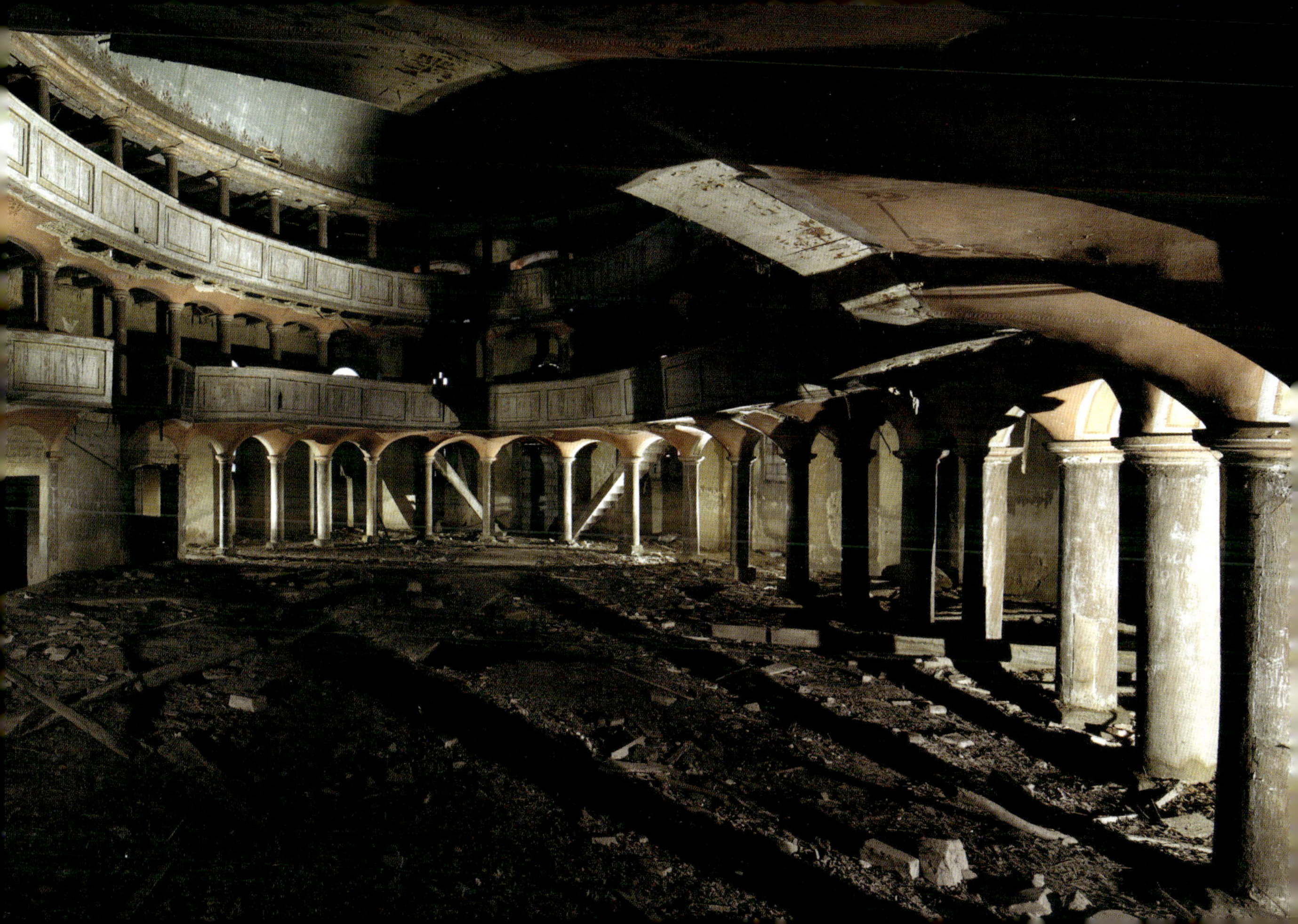

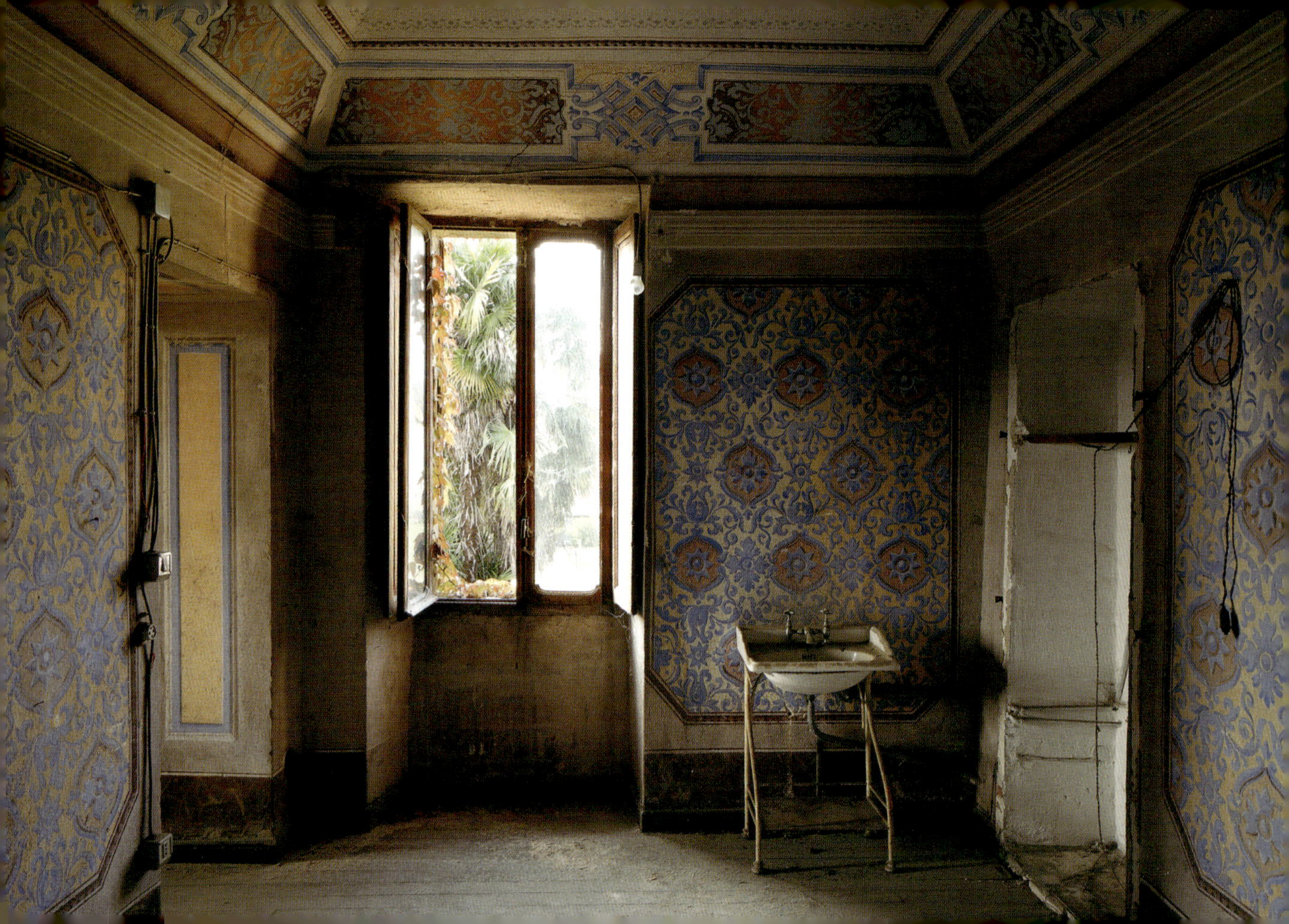

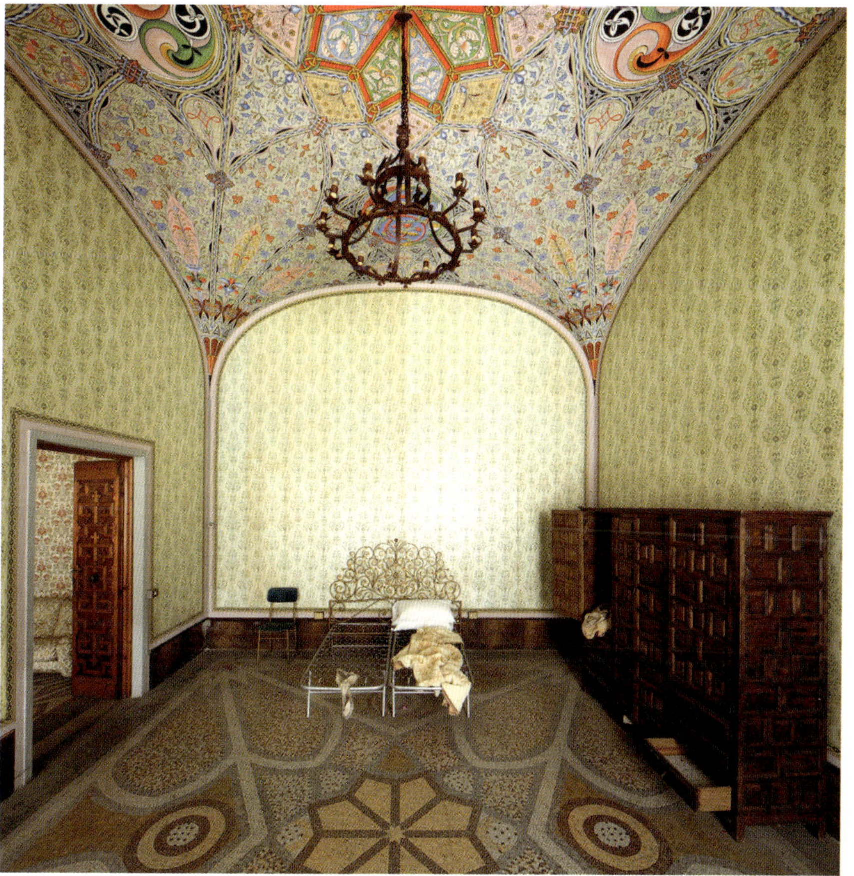

△ Villa Ronis, Italy, 2016 ▽ Castello di Sammezzano, Italy, 2013

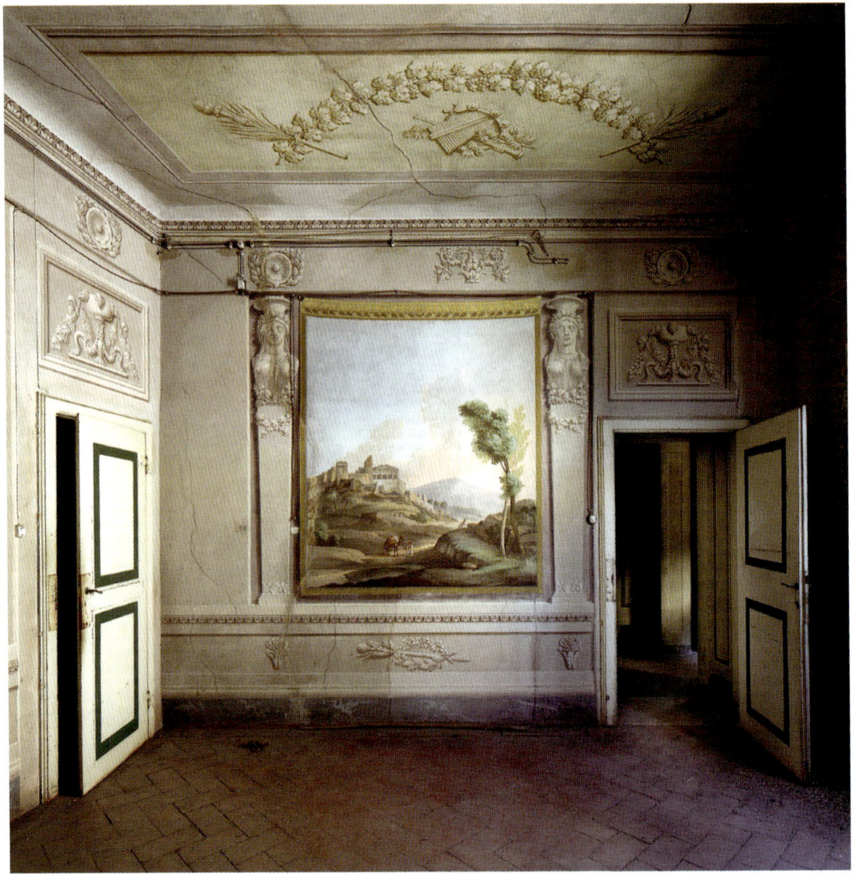

△ Villa Bastia, Italy, 2011

▽ Villa Quiete, Italy, 2013

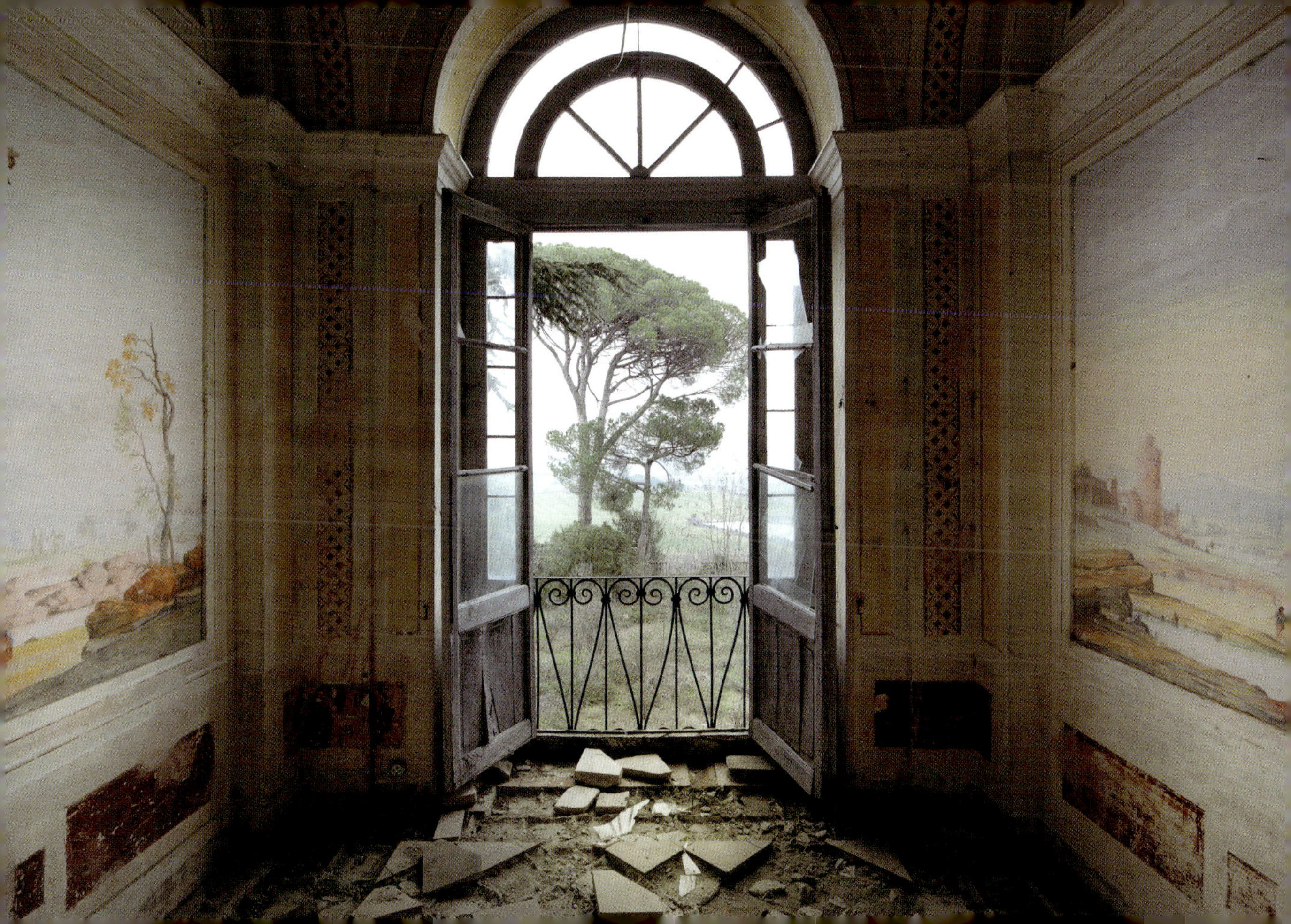

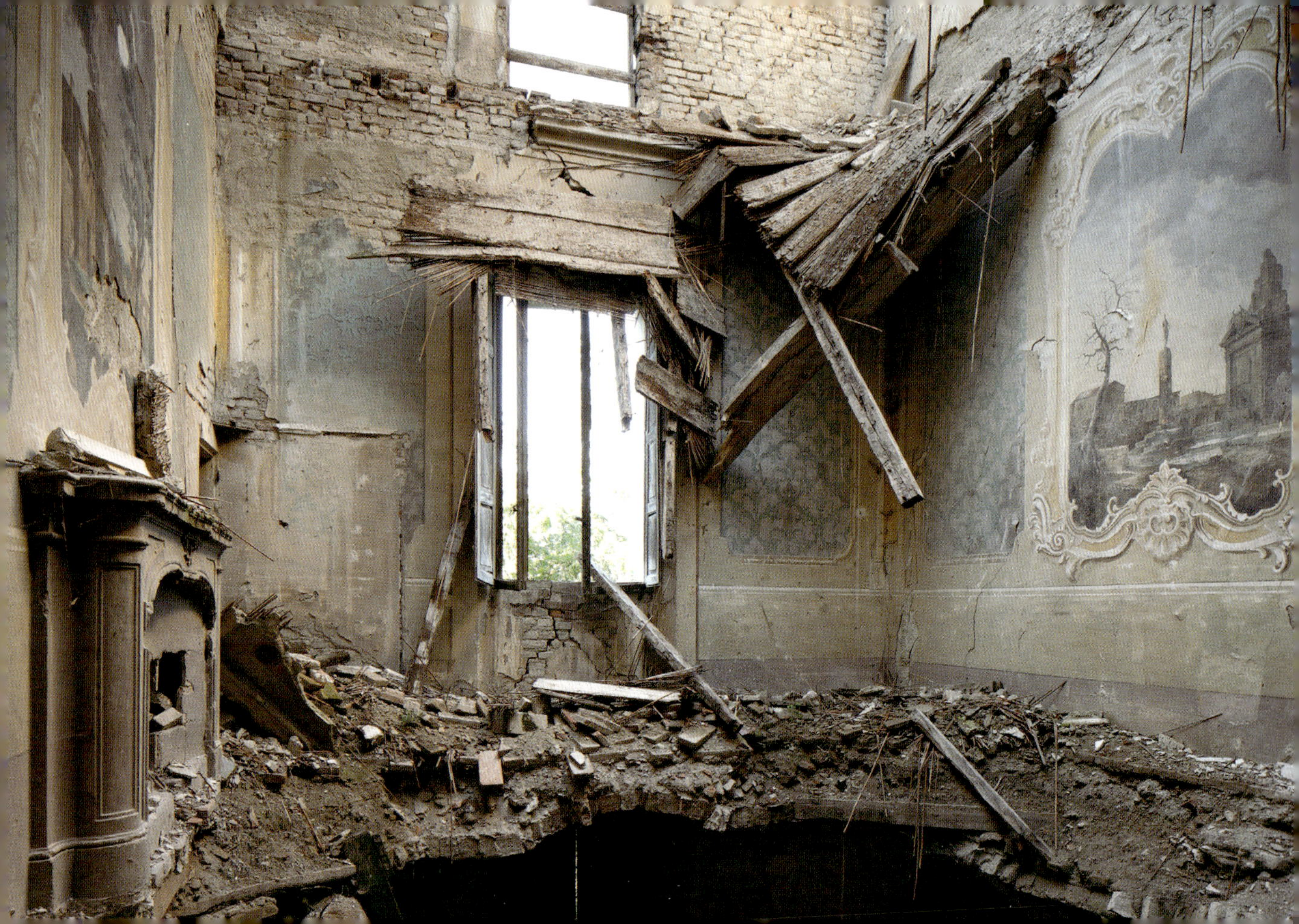

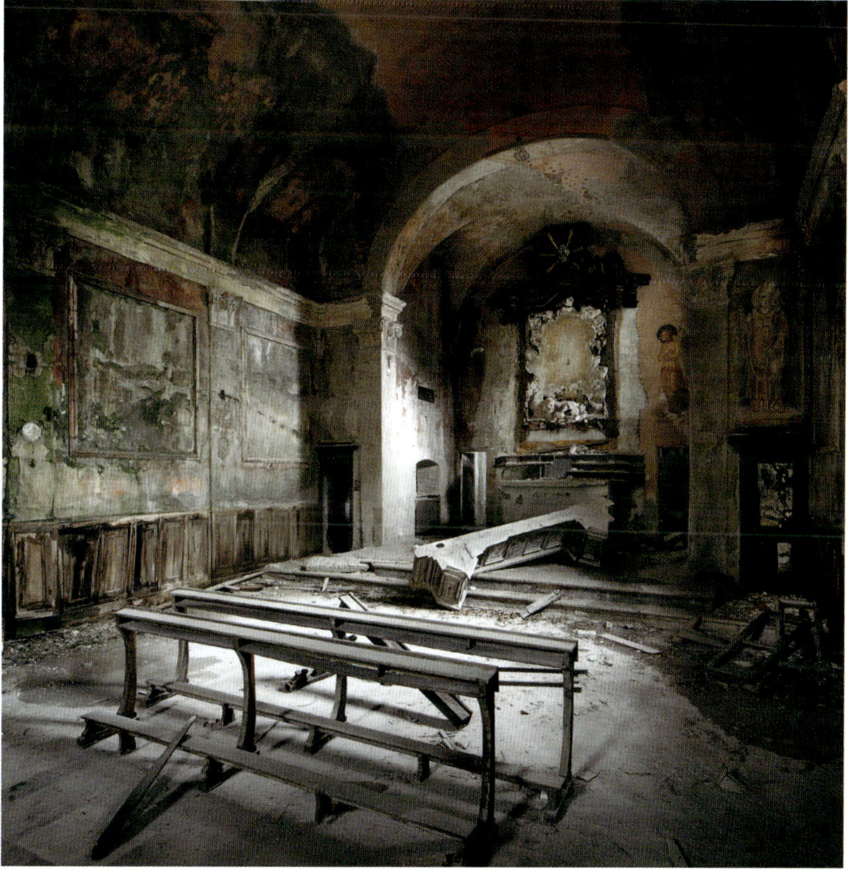

▵ Villa Crollata, Italy, 2016 ▿ Sant'Ambrogio, Italy, 2013

COLONIA MONTANA ▹

ITALY, 2013

The sky was clear, there was still a bit of snow on the ground, the mountain air was at its purest.

Not too much traffic at the border crossing. It's really not more than a village street. The guardsmen were hanging around the electric heater in their shed. The windows were fogged over so I doubt that they could see me creeping into the gigantic building that stands literally on the border. This is where children from the working class were sent on vacation to get away from the smog in the Po Valley.

Inside it was as still as a mouse. Just like it probably was the day before the vacation. ◆

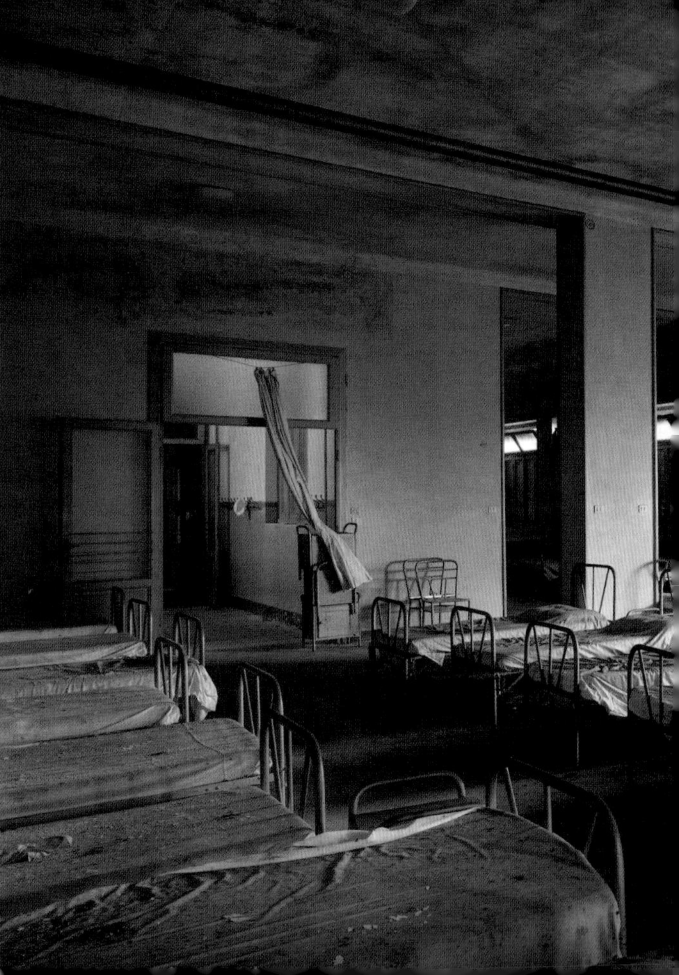

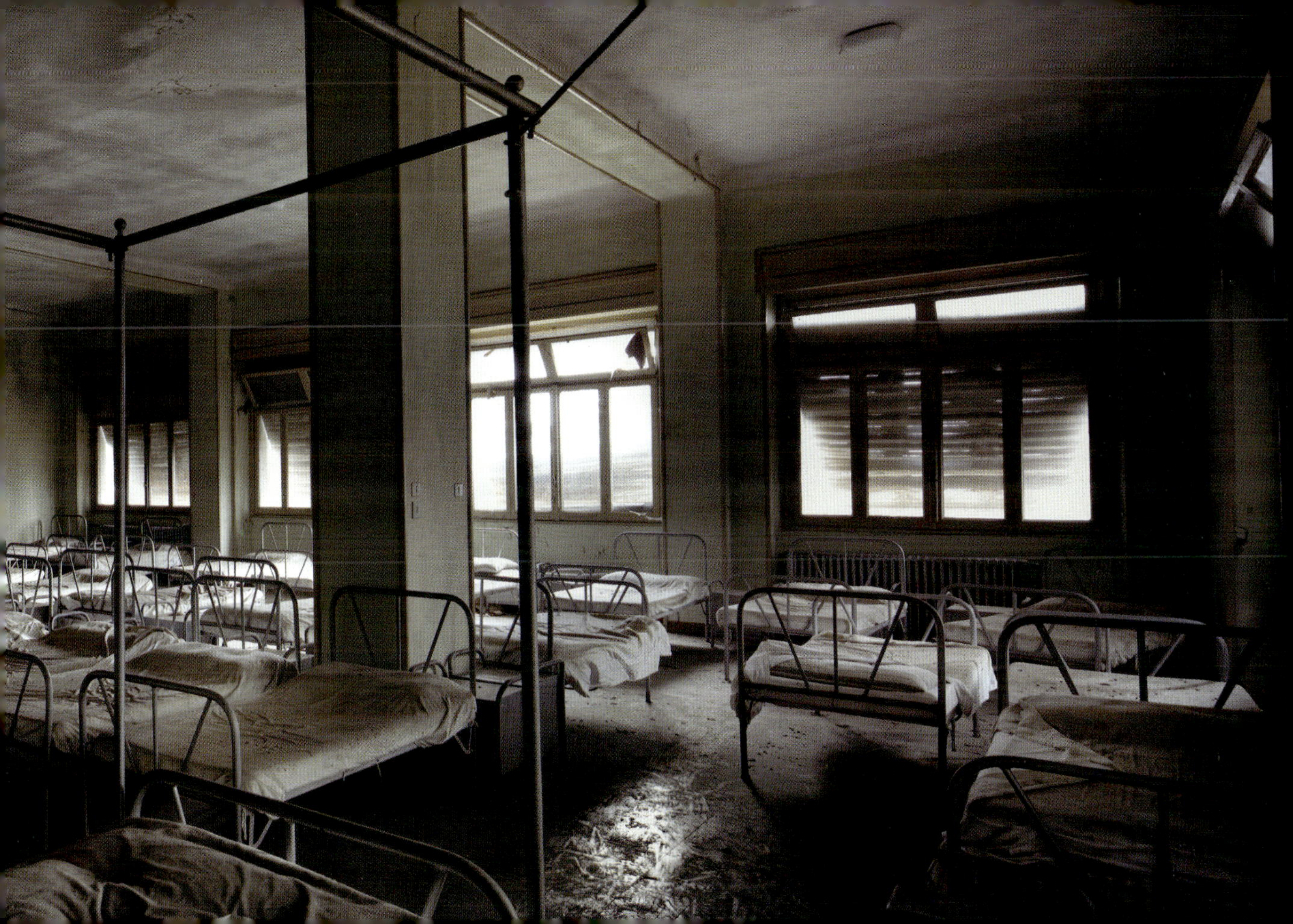

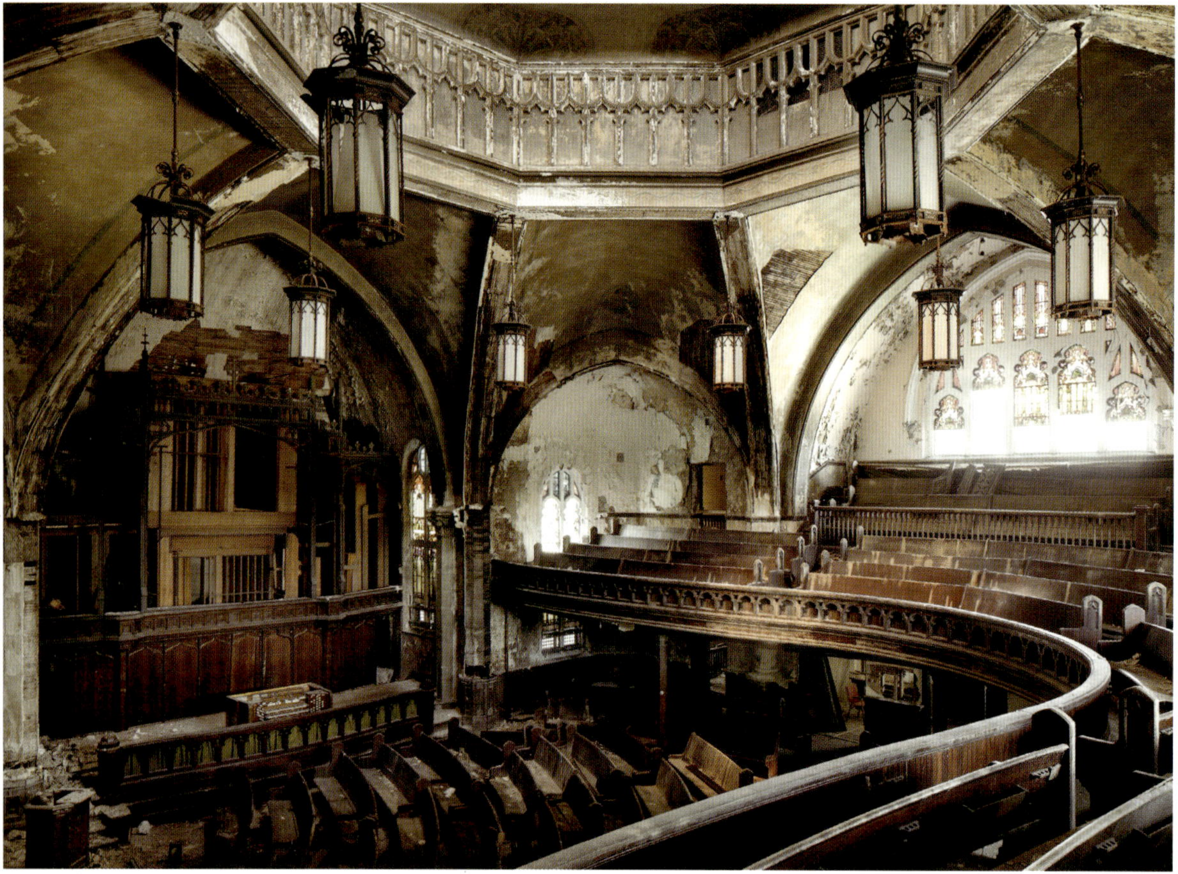

St.-Curvy, Detroit, USA, 2012

95 St.-Curvy, Detroit, USA, 2012

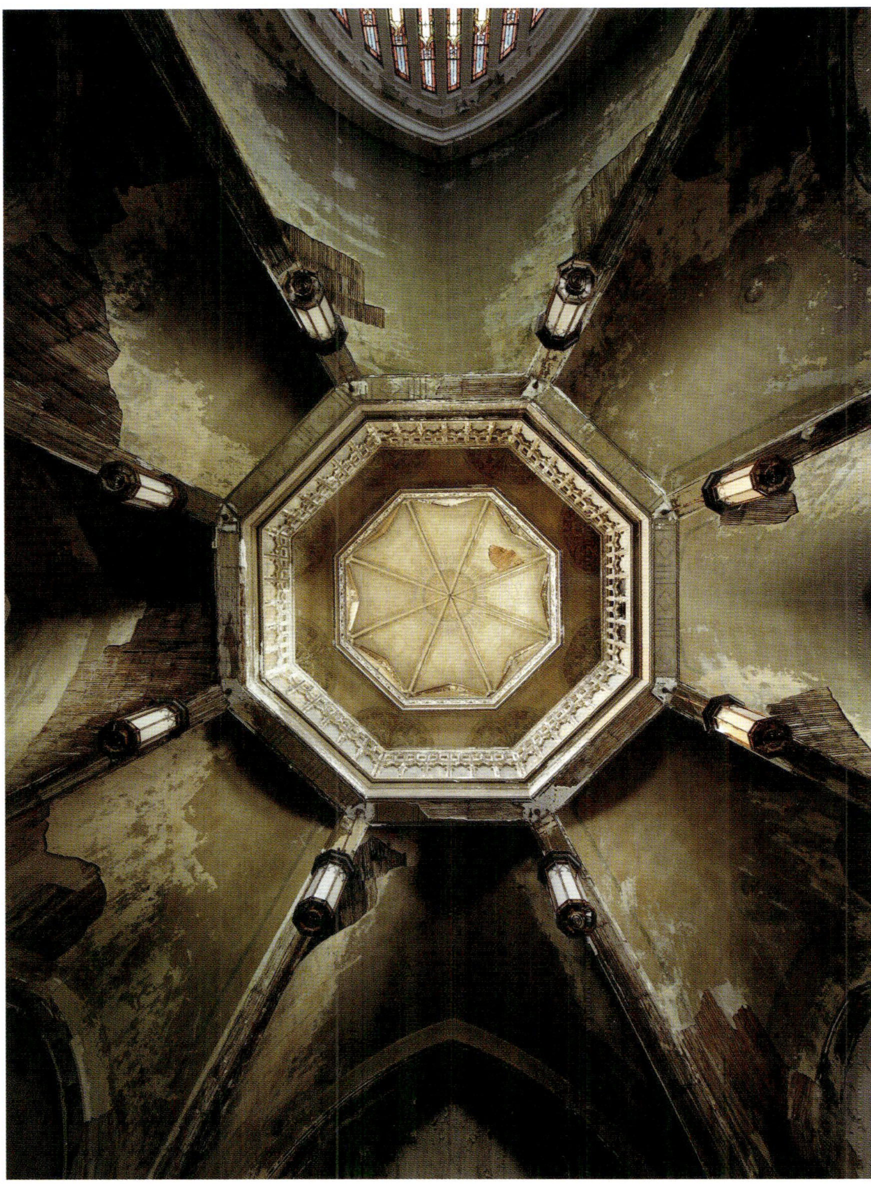

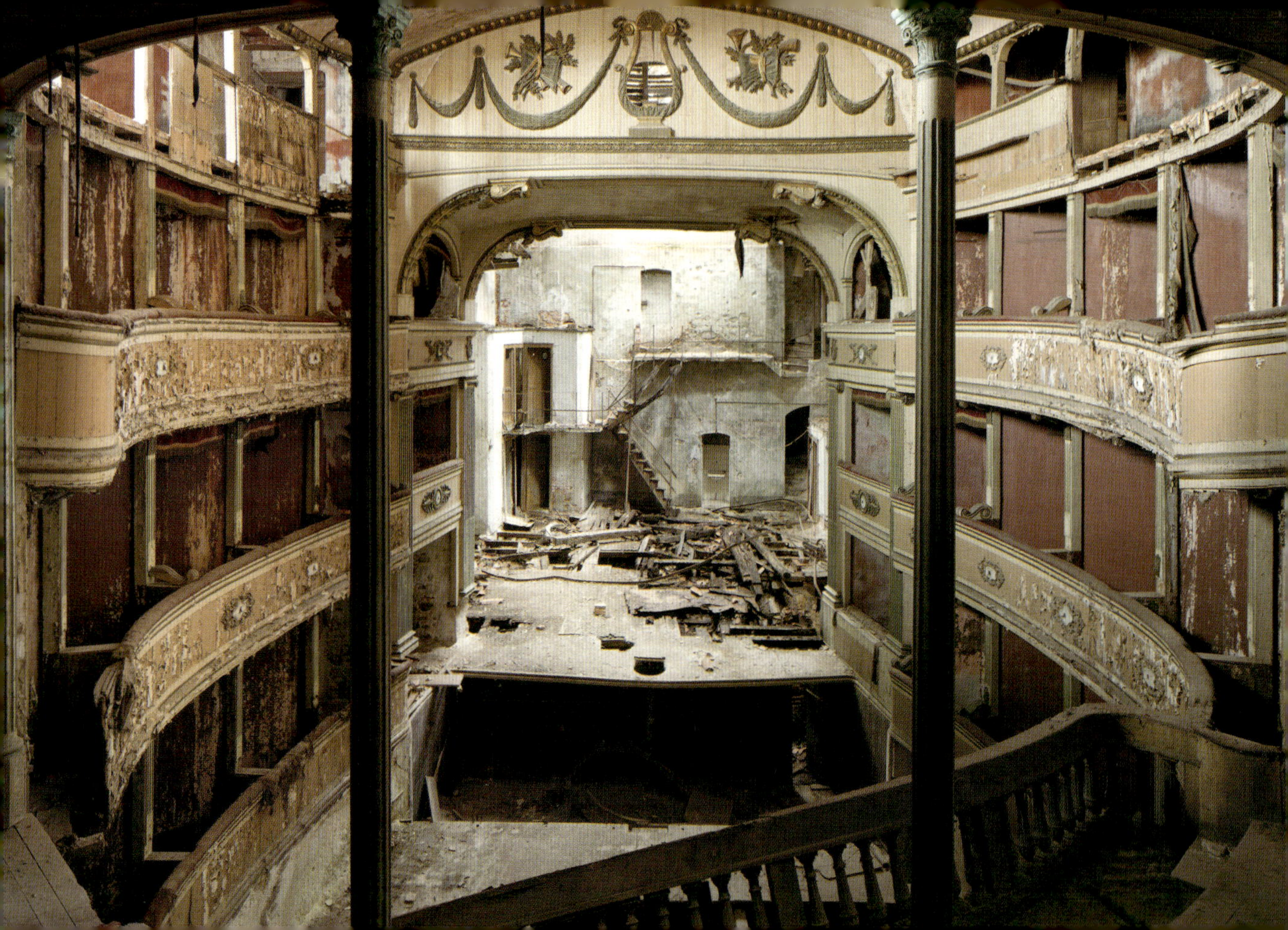

△ Mountain Village Theater, Italy, 2019 ▽ The Torture Bath, Italy, 2019

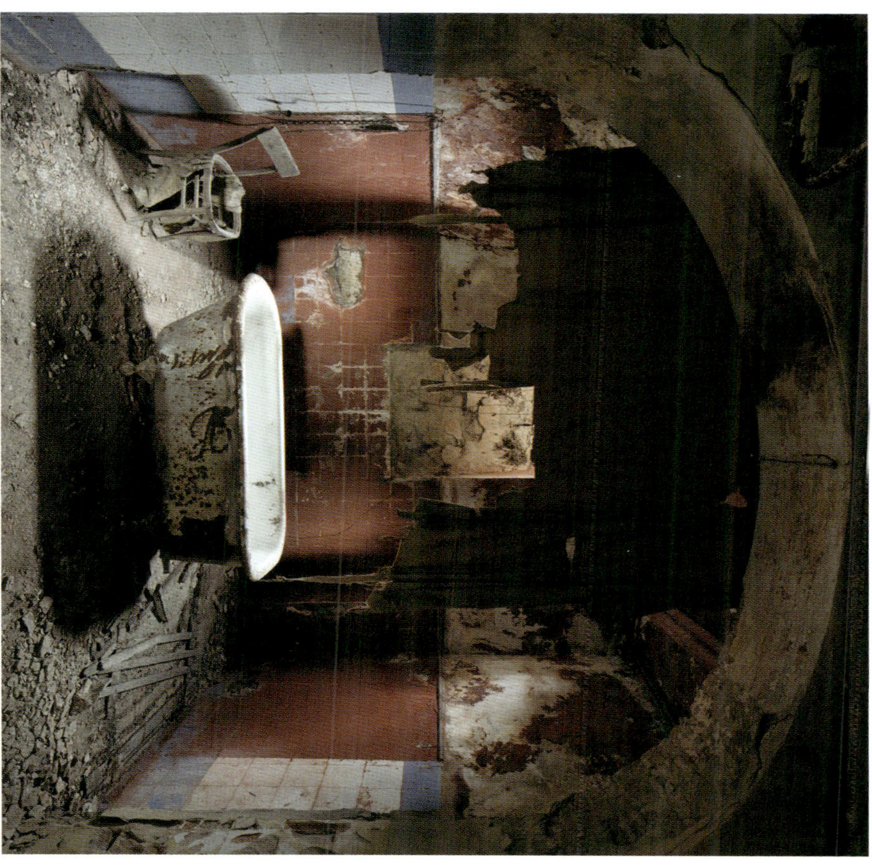

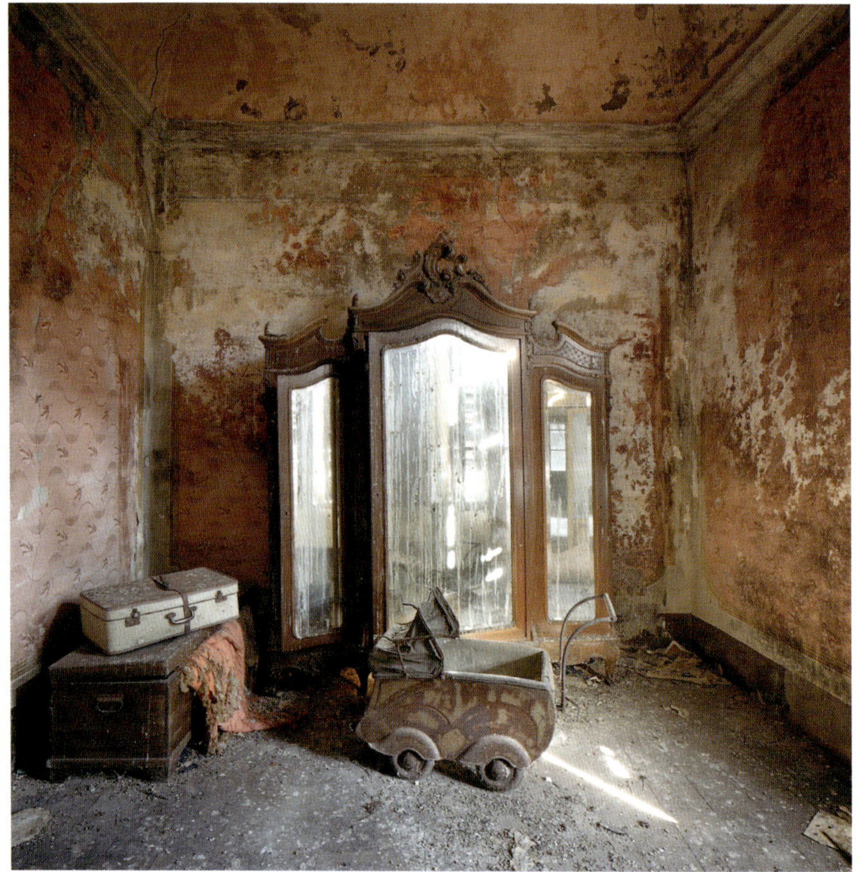

Carrozzina, Italy, 2016

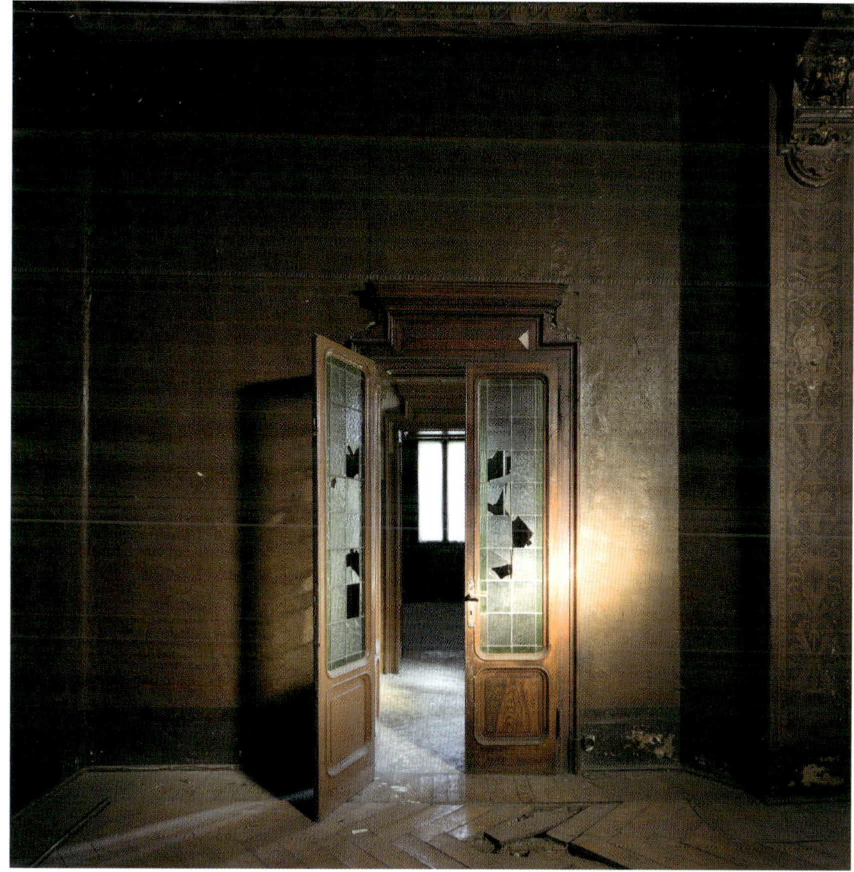

Living Room, Italy, 2016

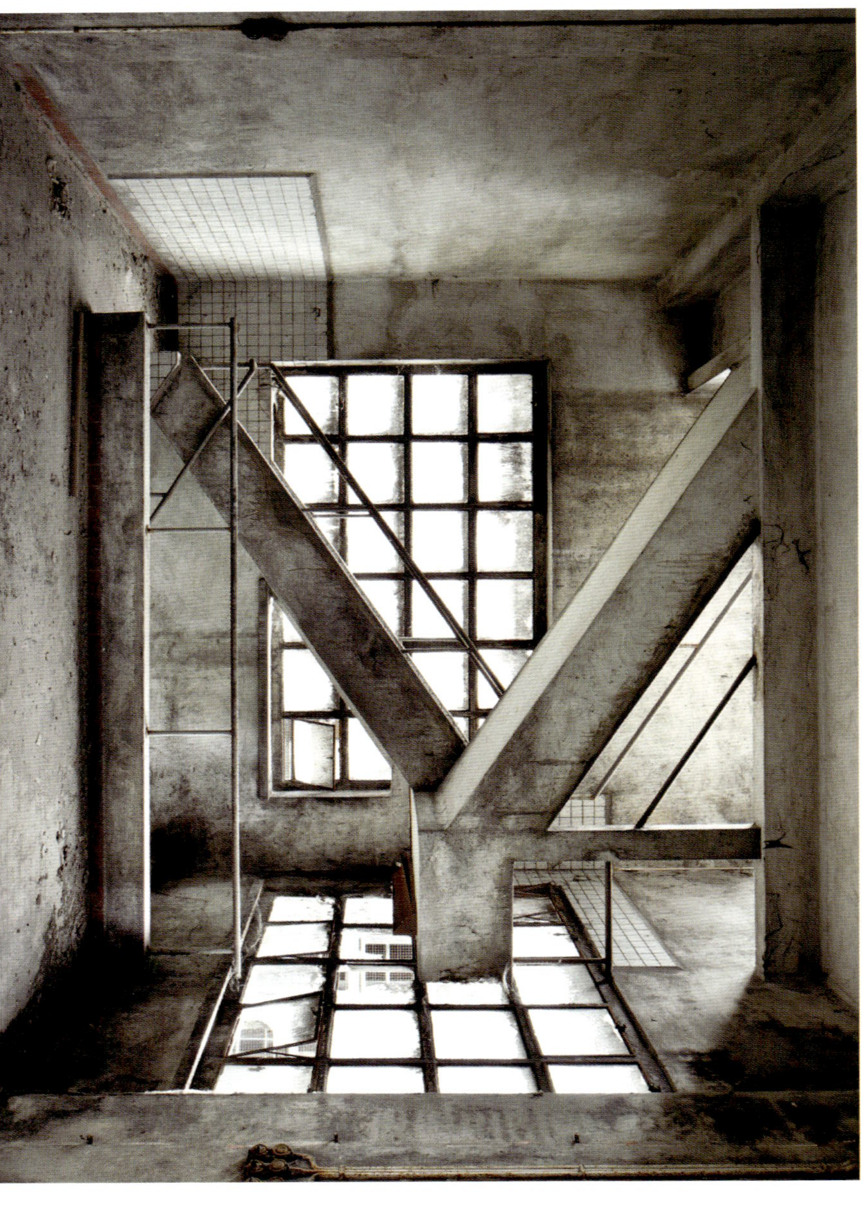

 Factory with Great Round Tower, Italy, 2011

 Farwell Building, Detroit, USA, 2012

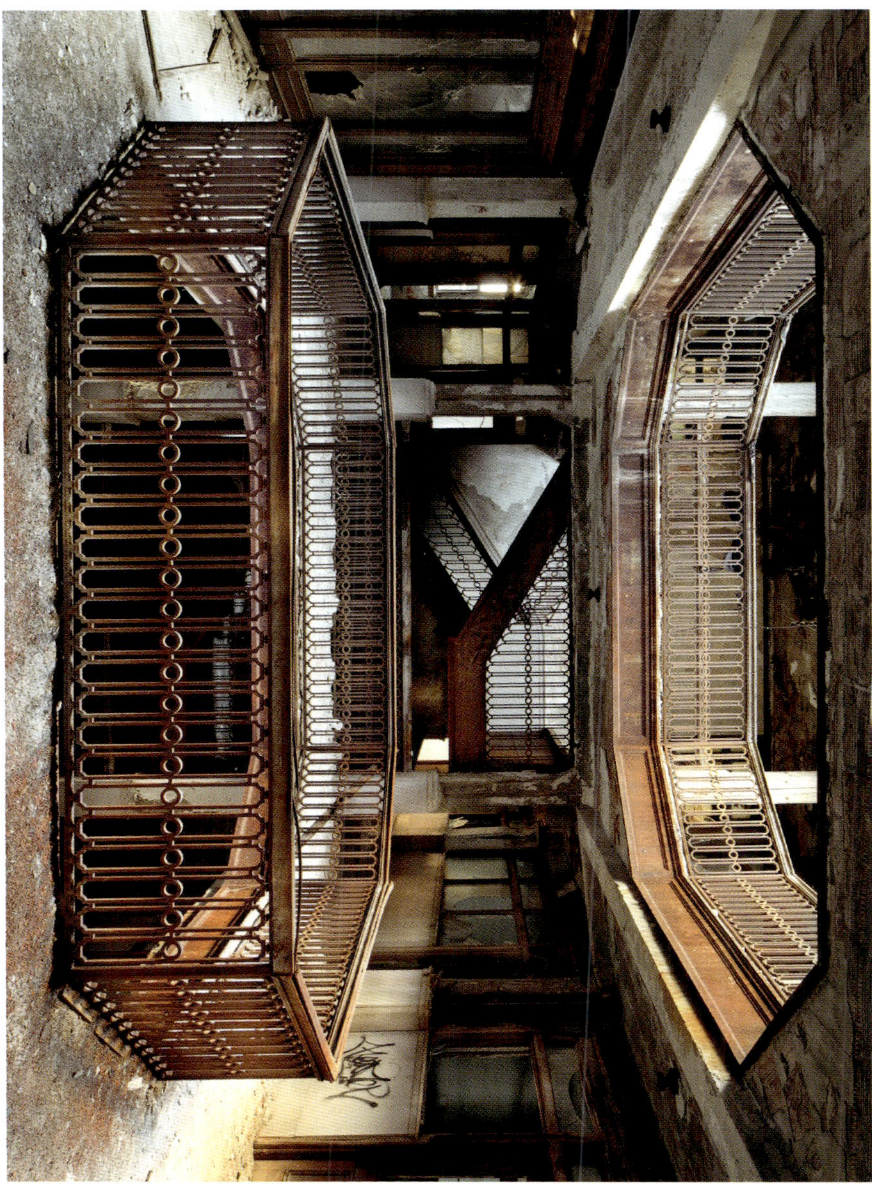

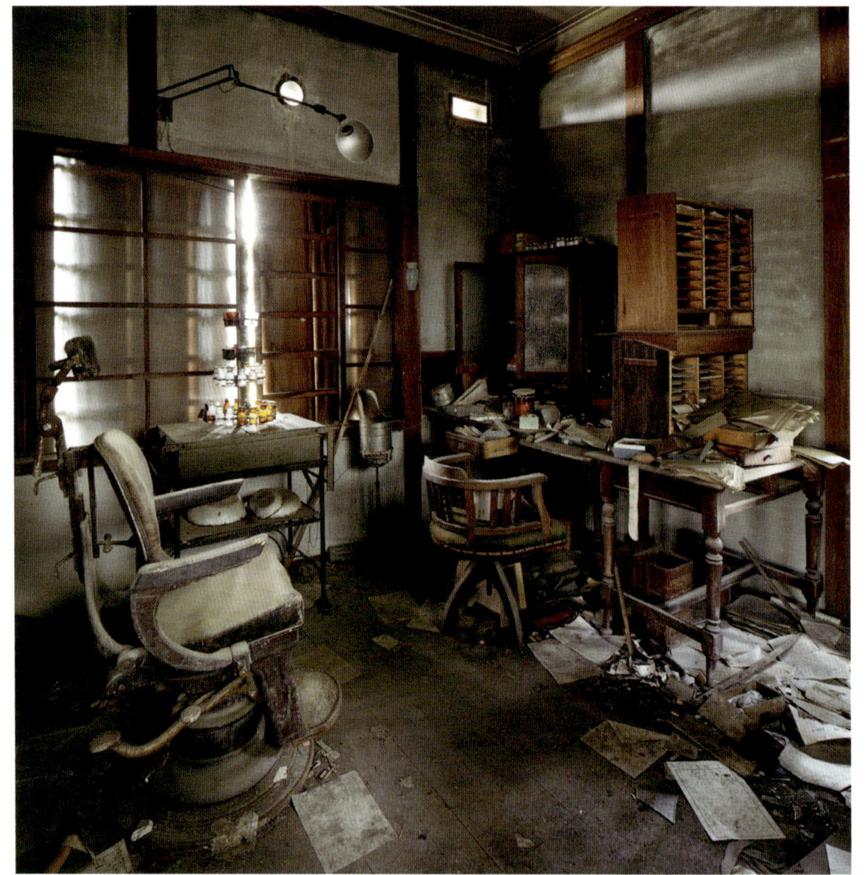

▵ Ghost Clinic, Japan, 2012 ▿ Dentist's Chair - Broderick Tower, Detroit, USA, 2010

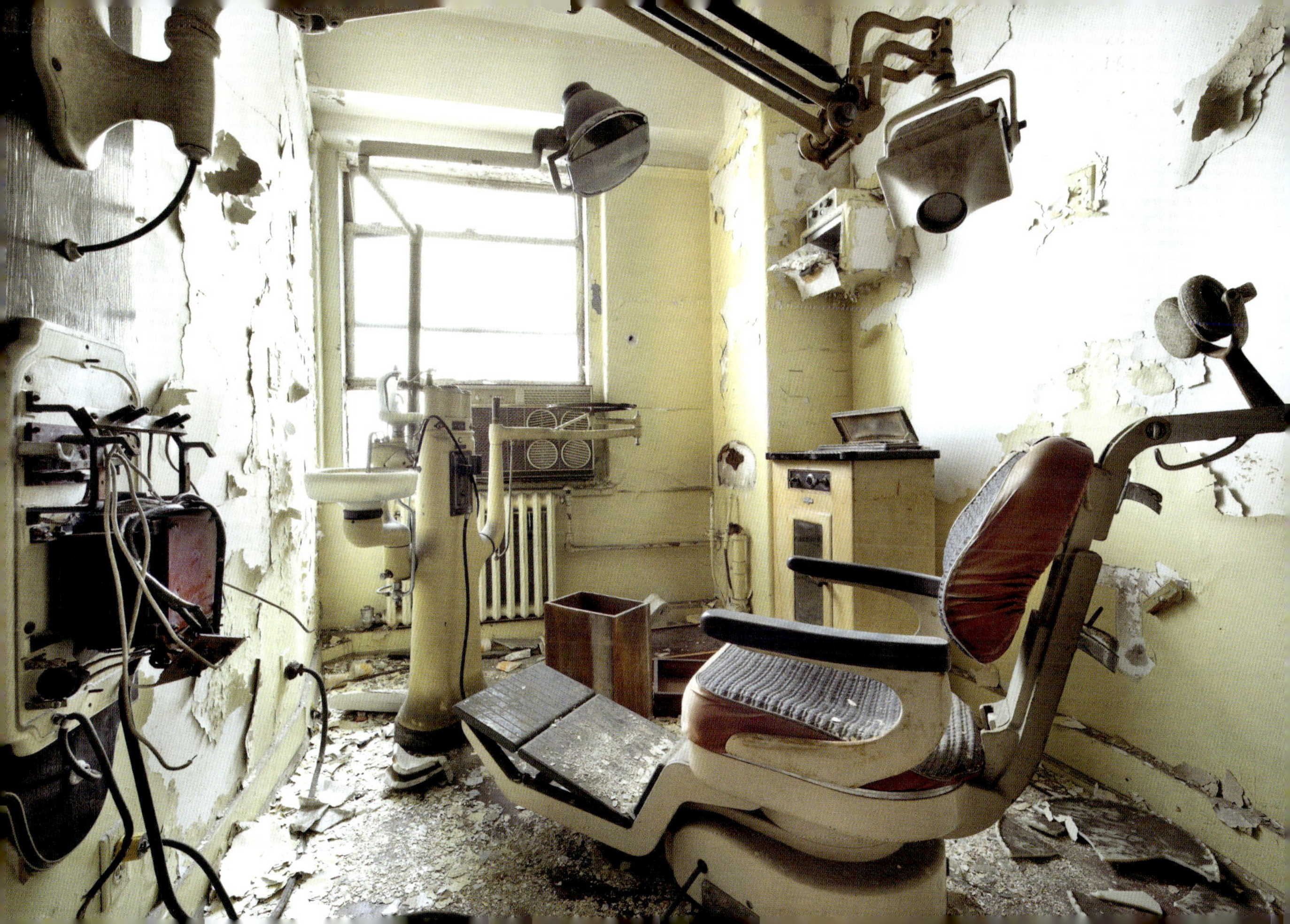

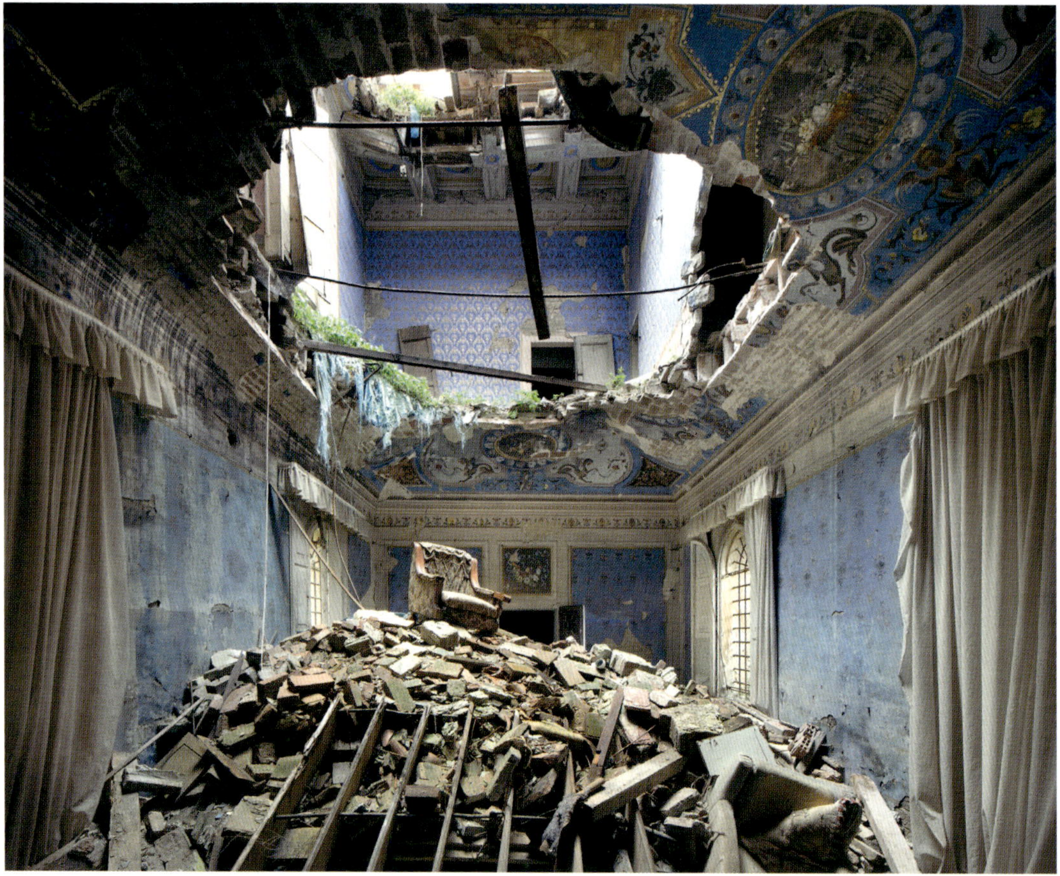

 Teatro Blu, Italy, 2019

Biblioteca, Italy, 2019

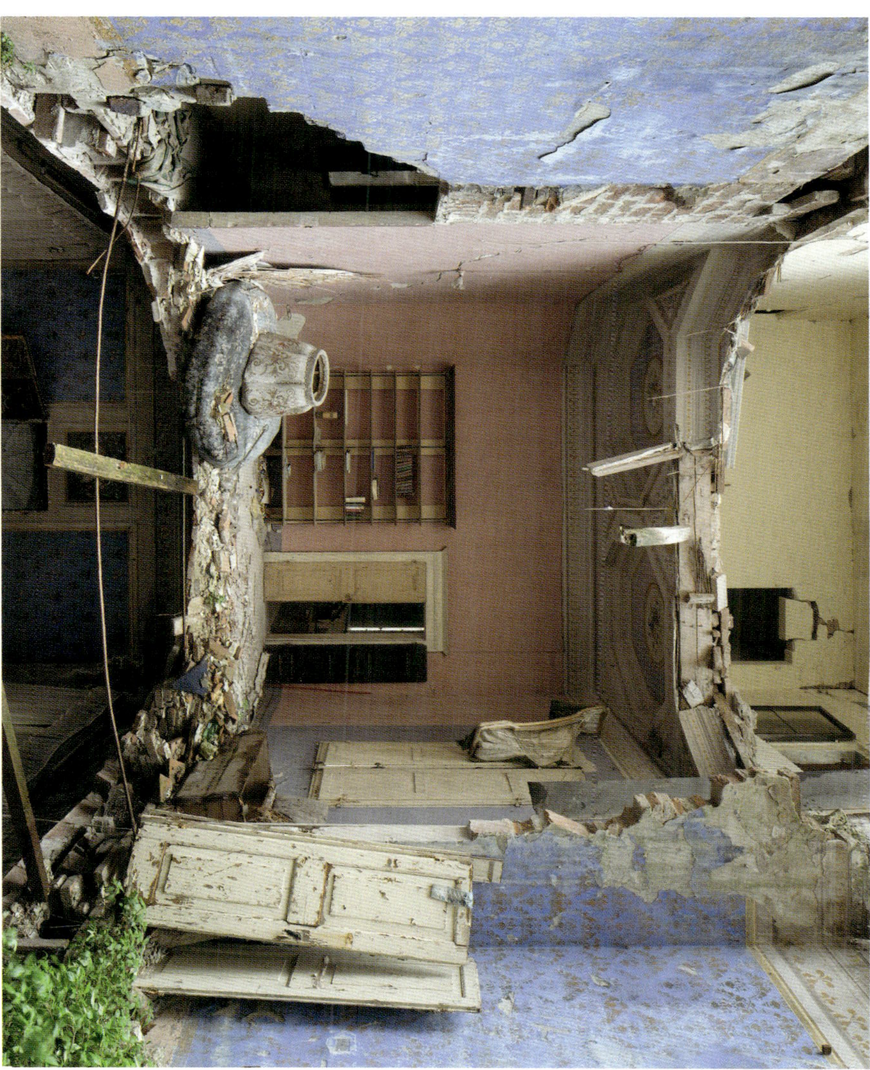

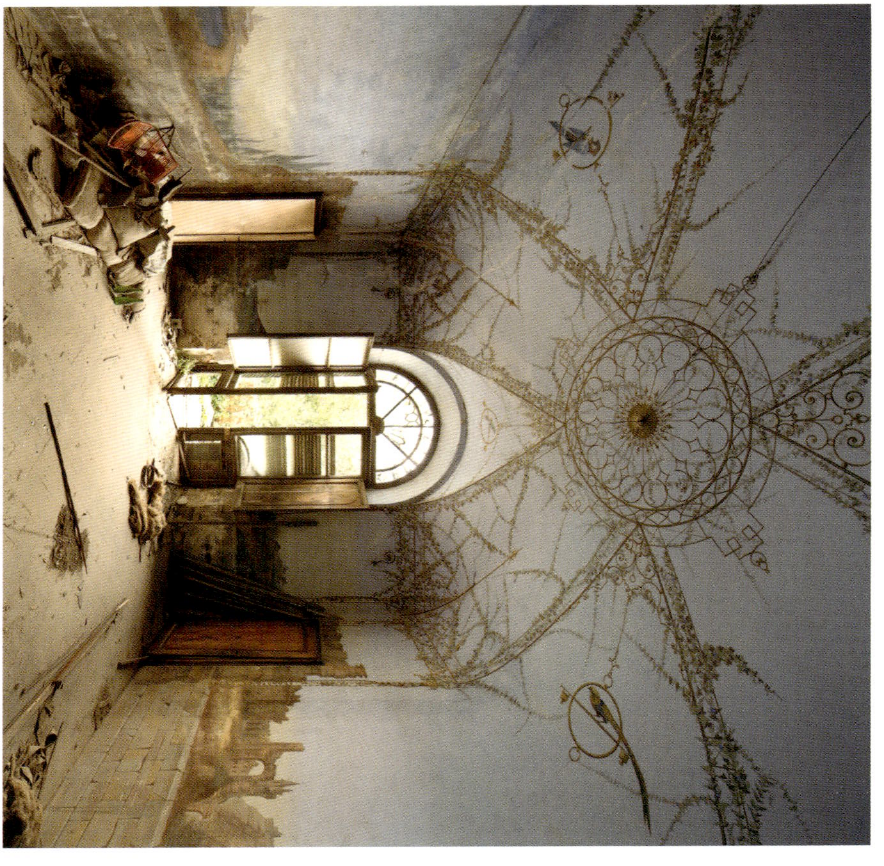

 △ Due Bottiglie, Italy, 2019 ▽ Lago, Italy, 2019

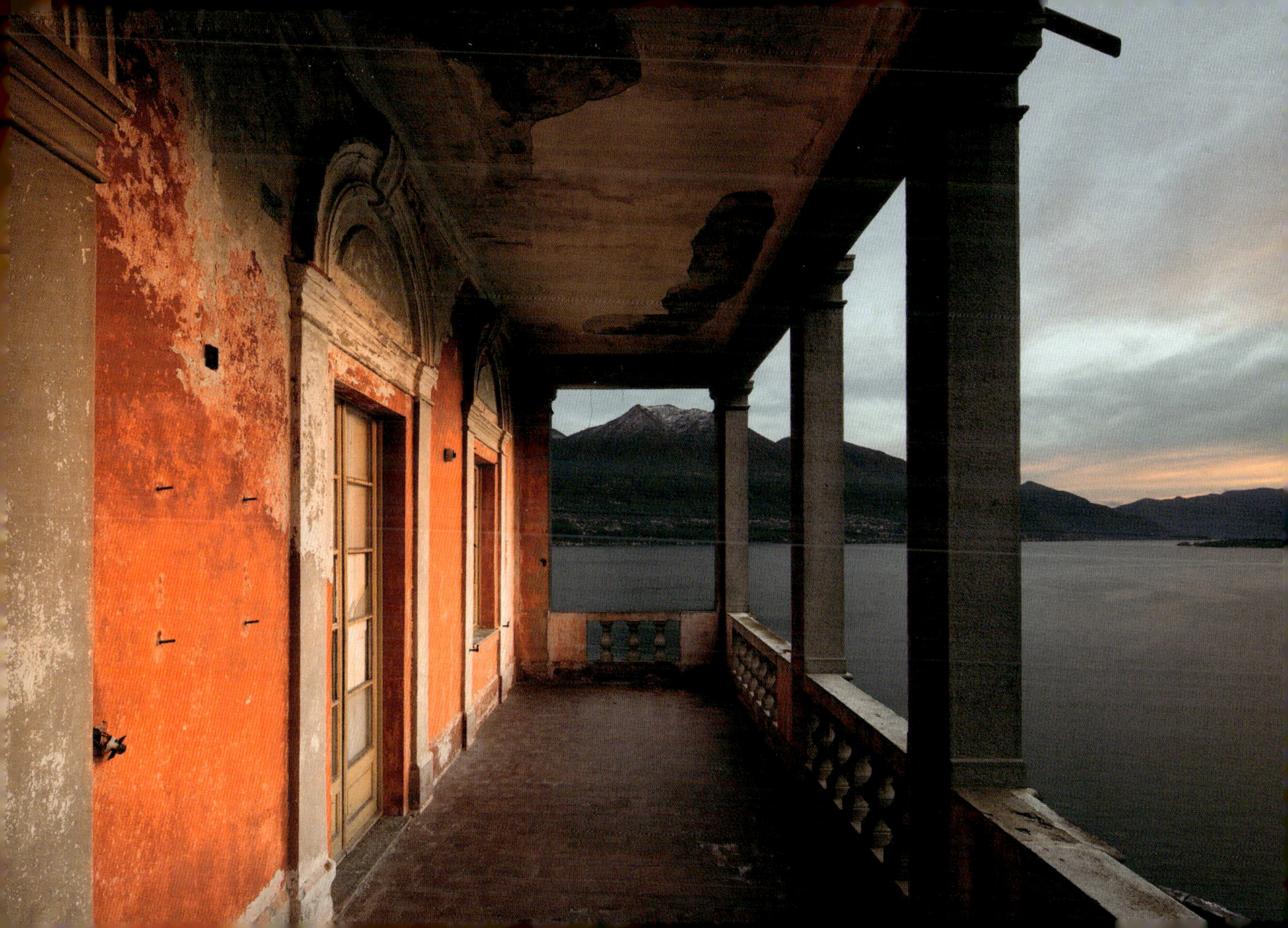

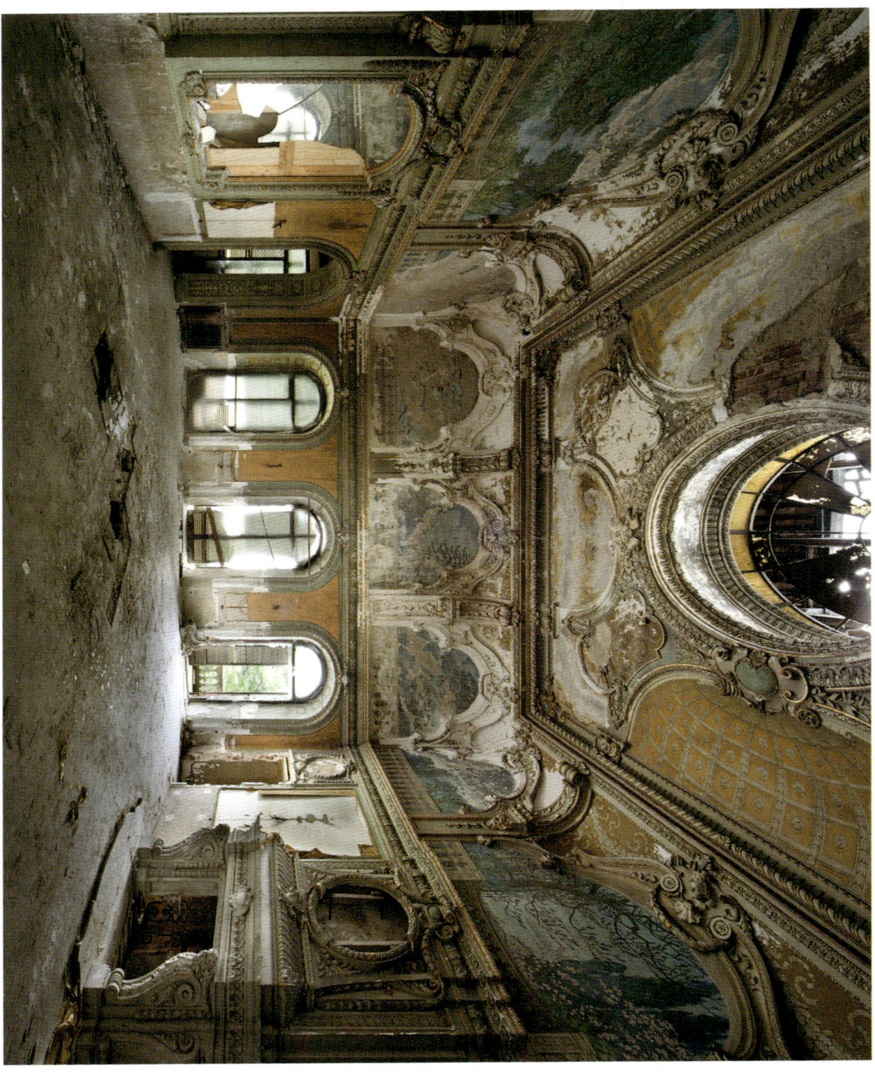

 Gesso, Italy, 2019

Antichambre, Italy, 2019

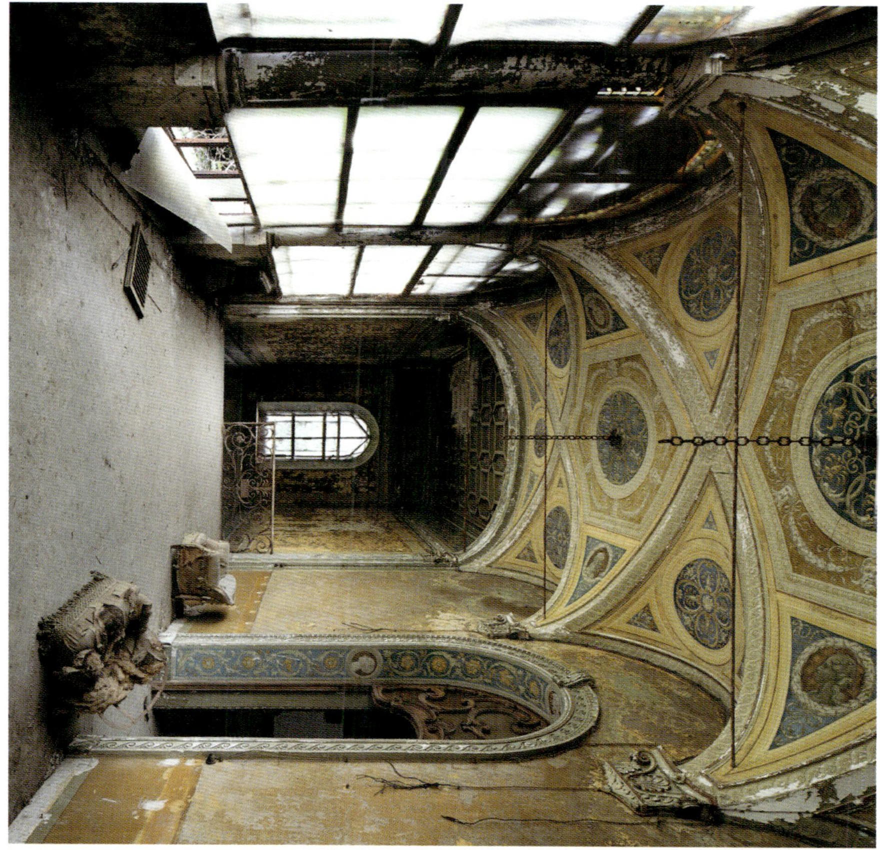

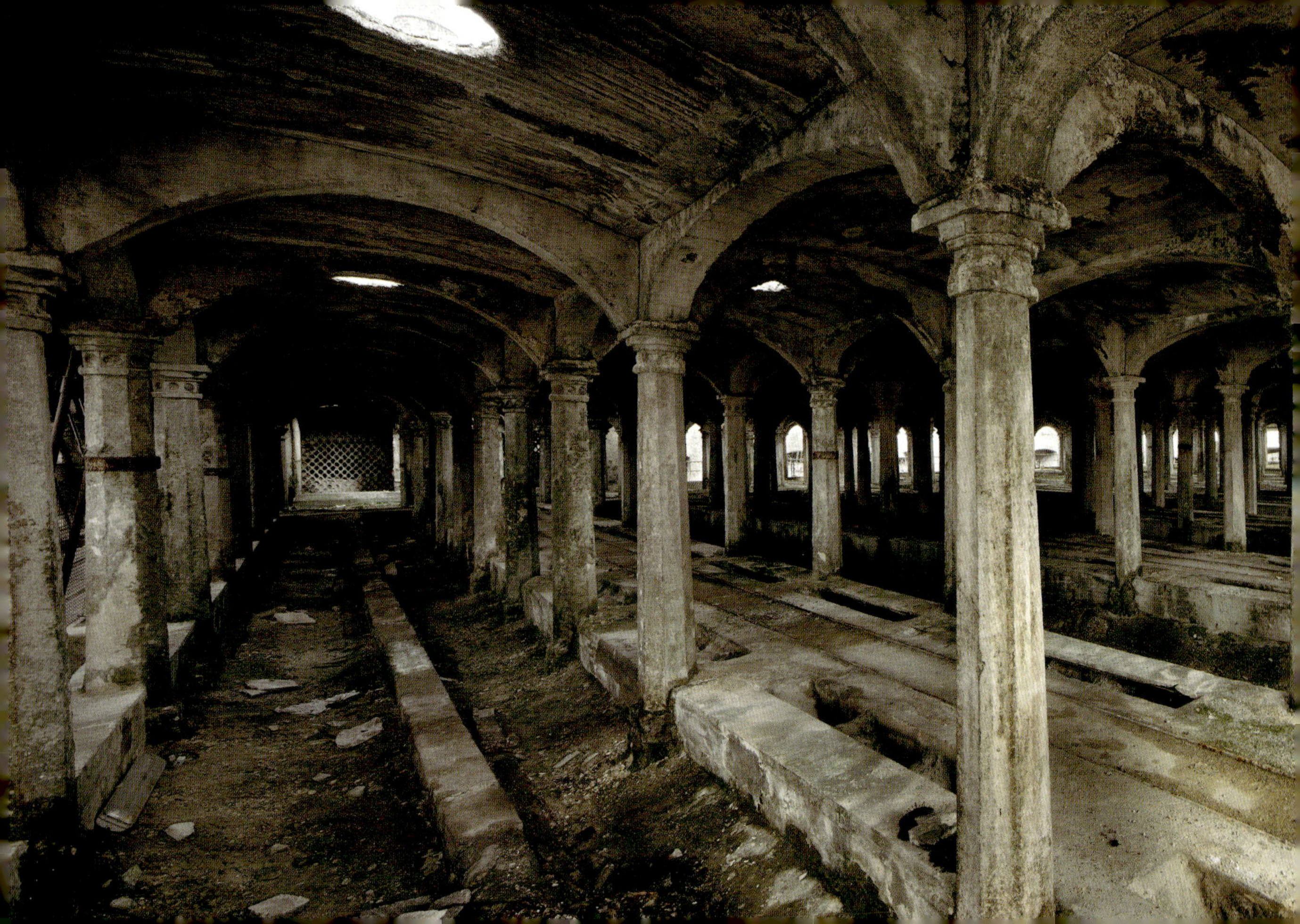

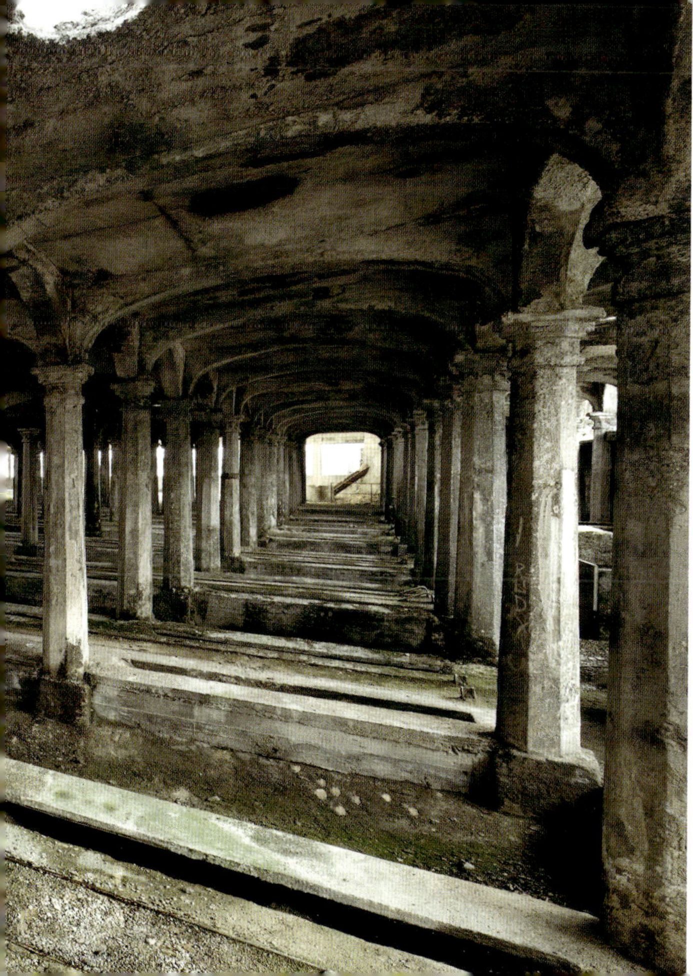

◁ **MAGNIFICEMENT**

ITALY, 2011

What genius dreamed up this mega cement factory? As monumental as a Greek temple, dark corridors like those leading to the tomb chambers of an Egyptian pyramid. And then that unmistakable copy of the Basilica Cistern in Istanbul.

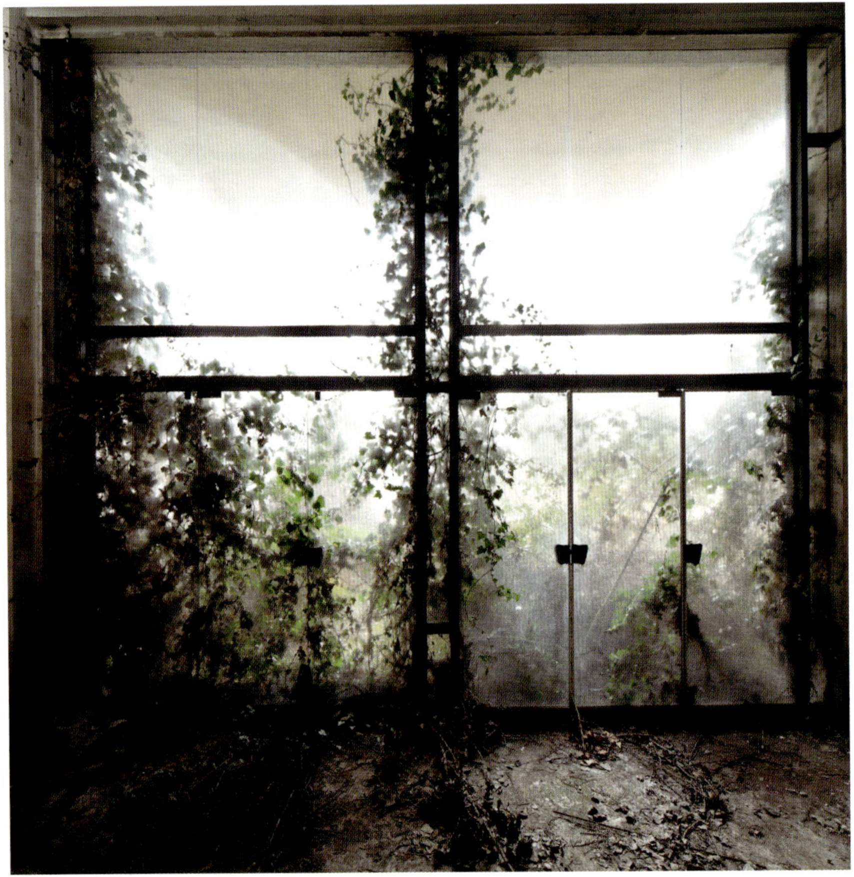

△ Let nature in!, Italy, 2011

▽ Ivy corridor, Belgium, 2009

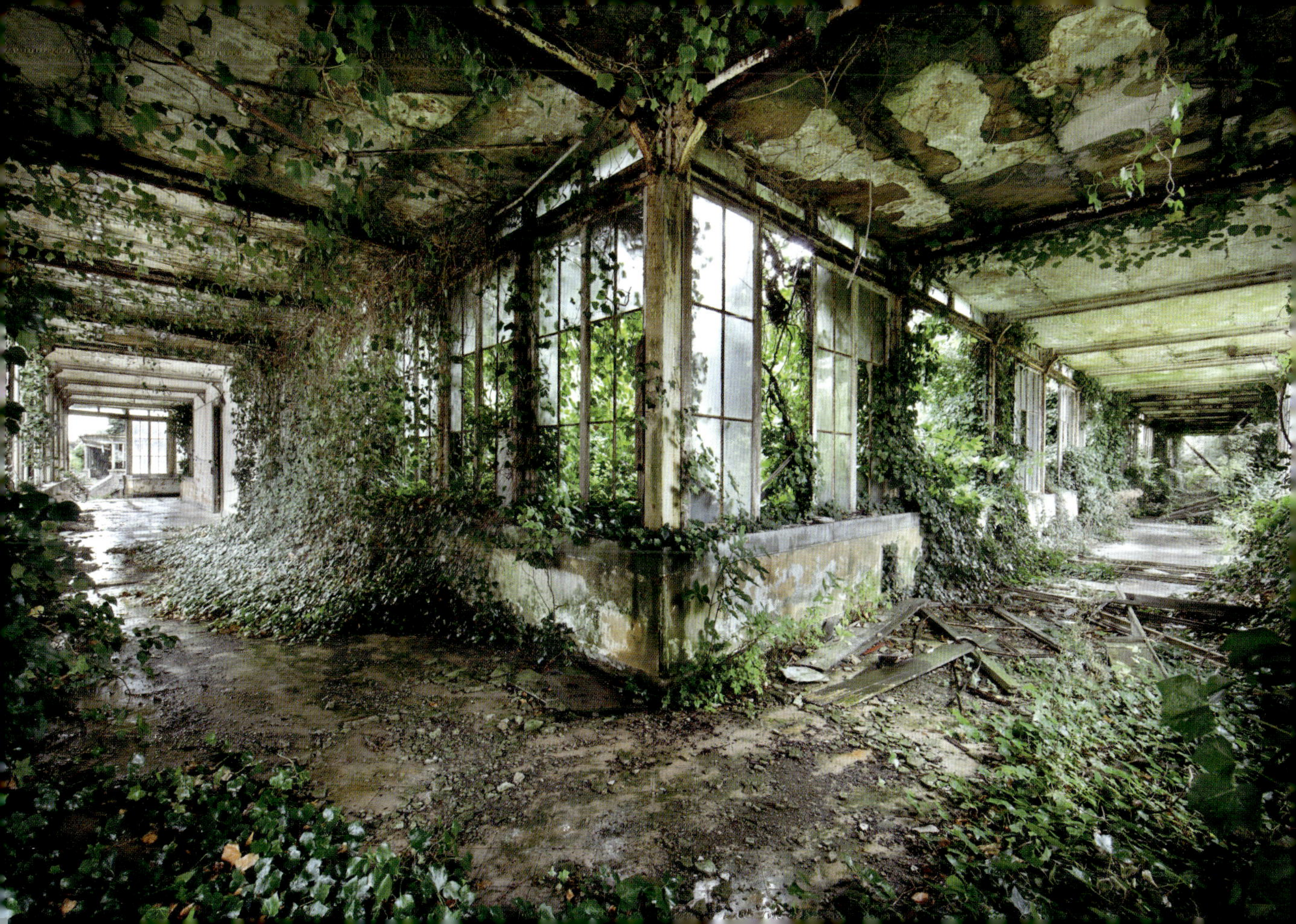

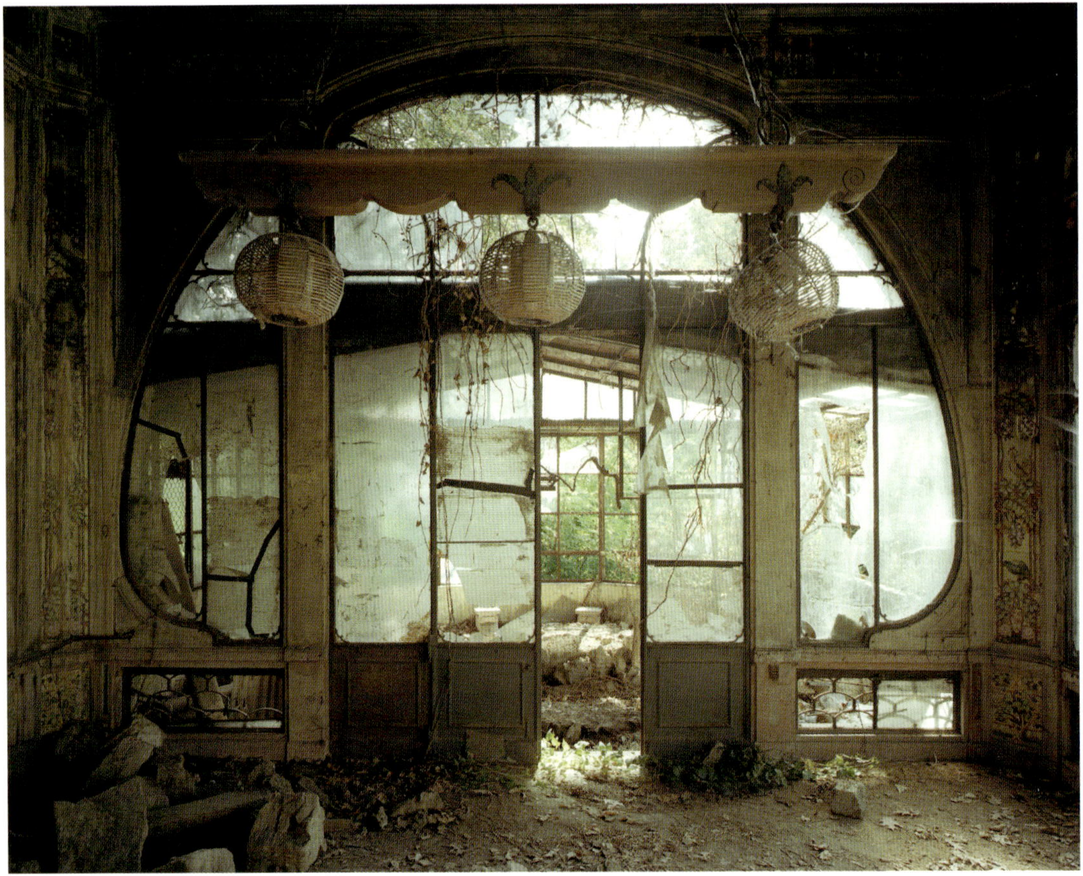

Winter Garden, Italy, 2016

Villa Sant'Andrea, Italy, 2016

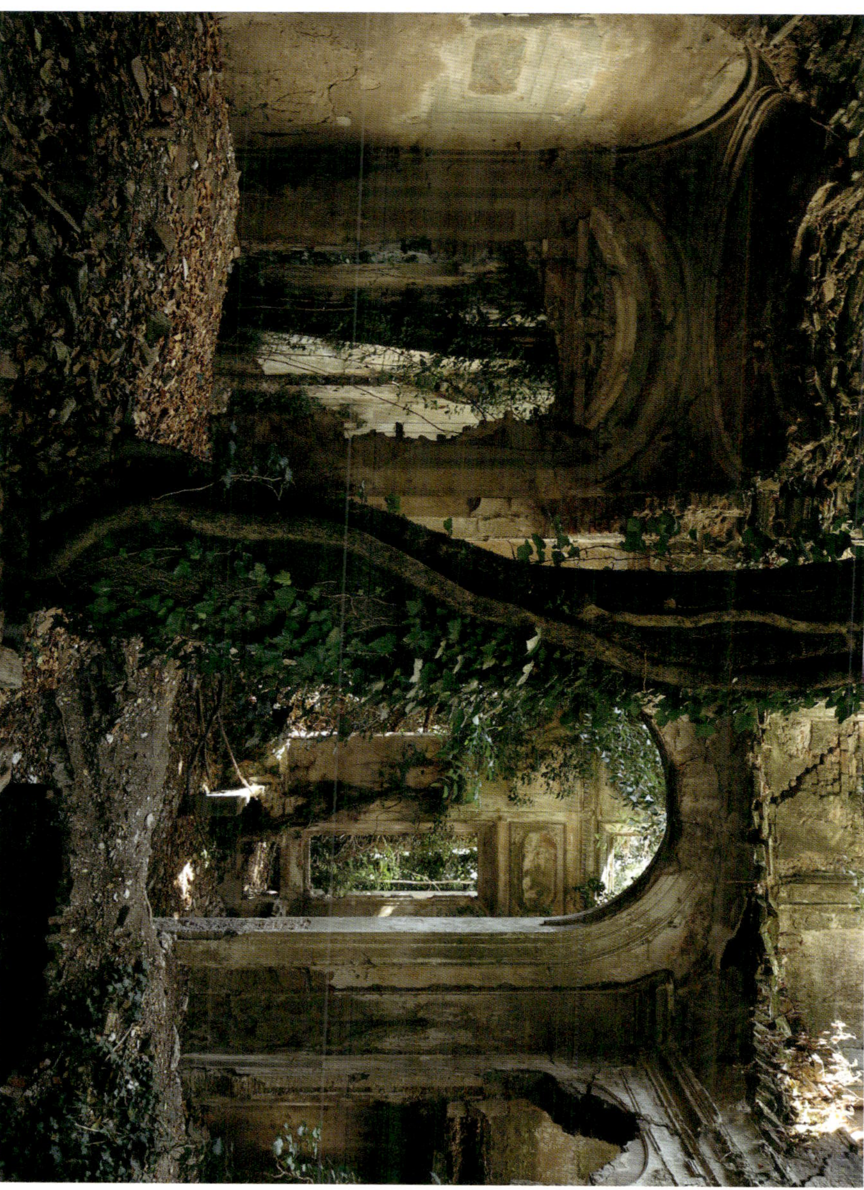

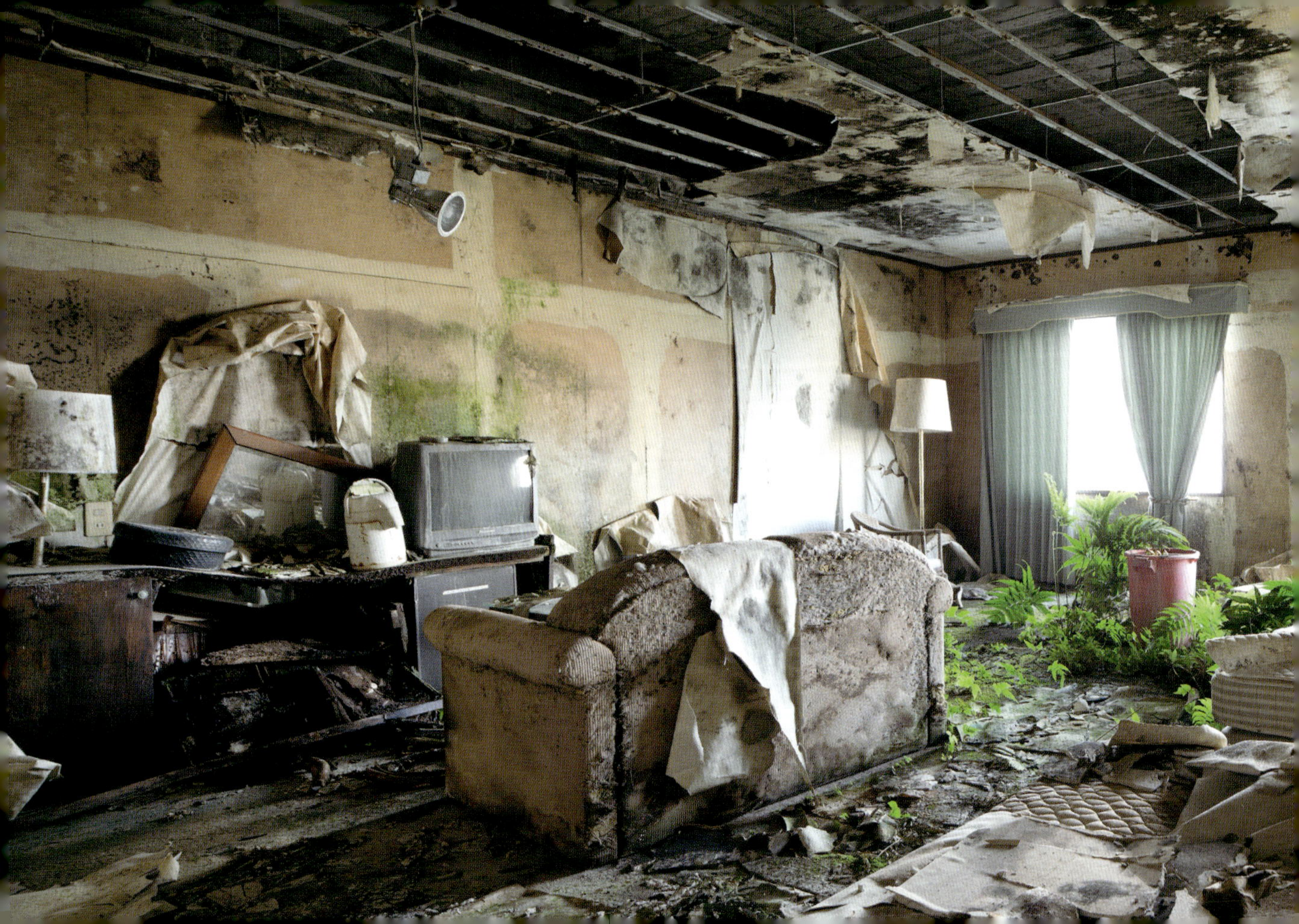

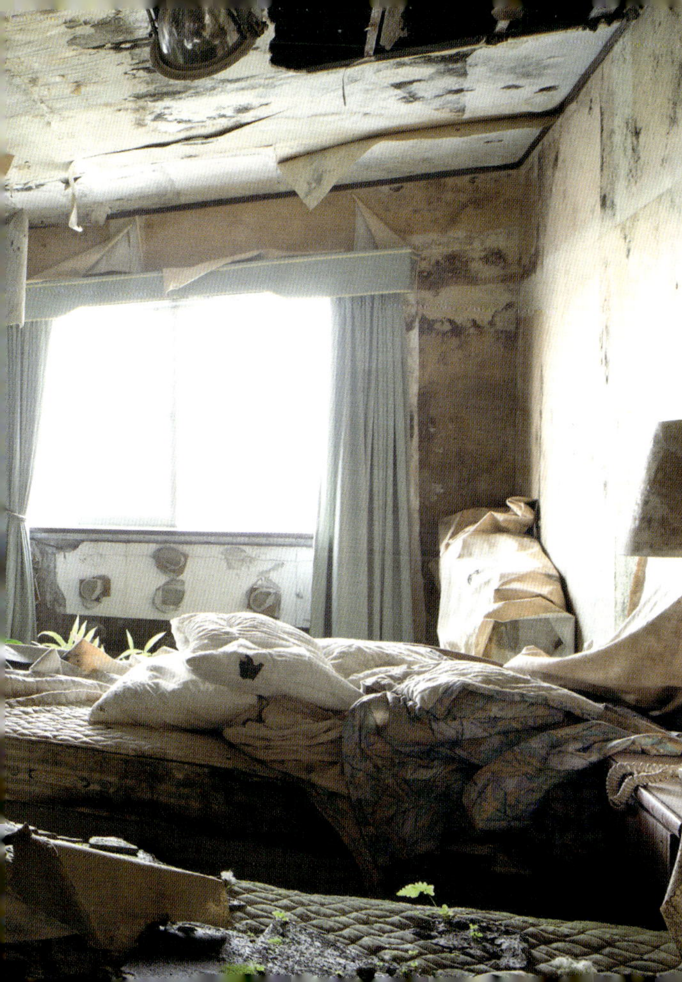

HAPPINESS ISLAND ▹

JAPAN, 2014

In earlier times, murderers, thieves, swindlers, gamblers, rapists and believers in forbidden religions were banished to this paradise-like island. It was practically impossible to escape from this Japanese version of Alcatraz.

In the 1960s, there were plans to remake the island into a Japanese version of Hawaii. The largest luxury hotel in Japan was built here in French baroque style, and it's not the only hotel on the island that stands empty. ◆

 △ Happiness Island, Japan, 2014 ▽ Happiness Island, Japan, 2014

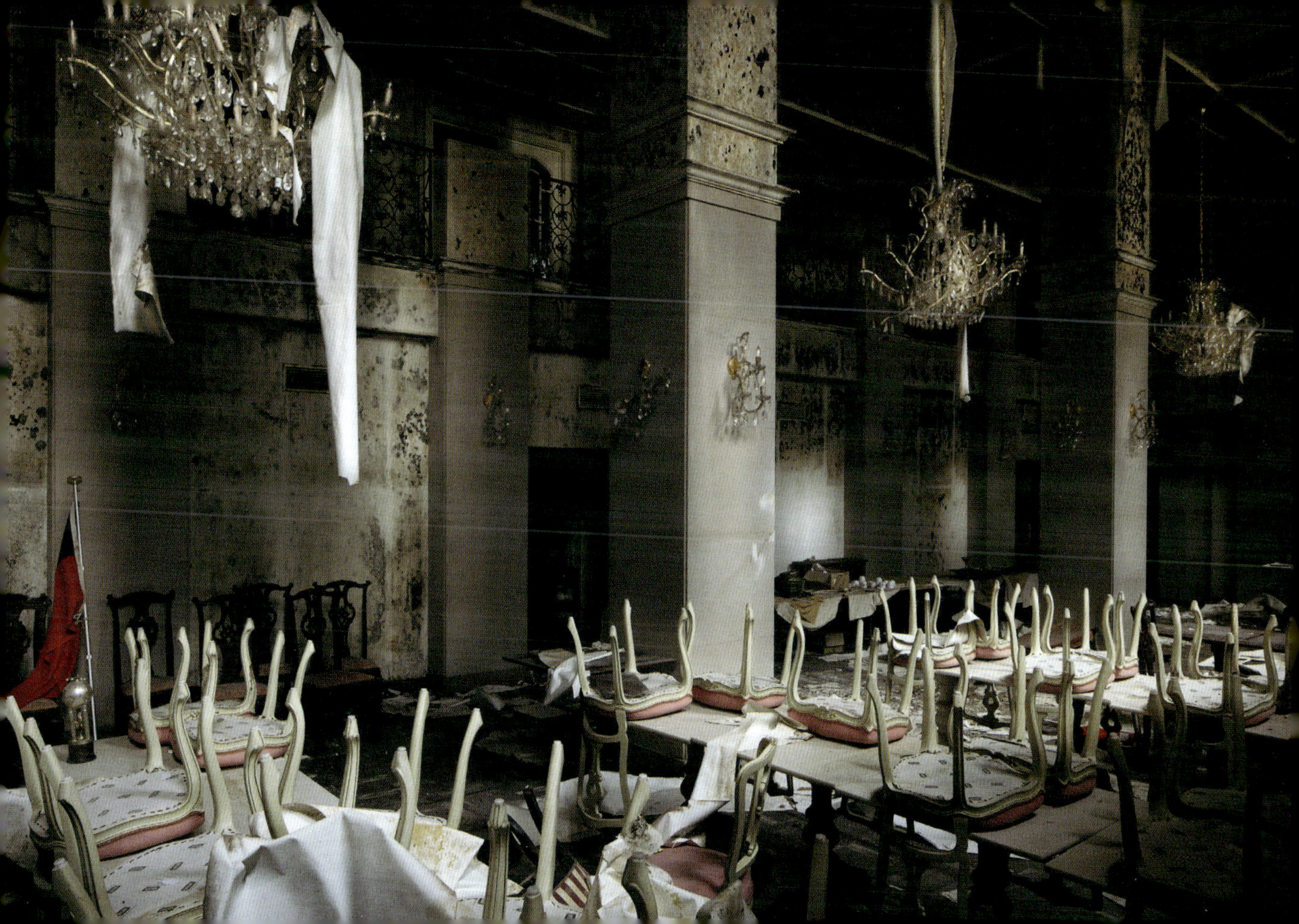

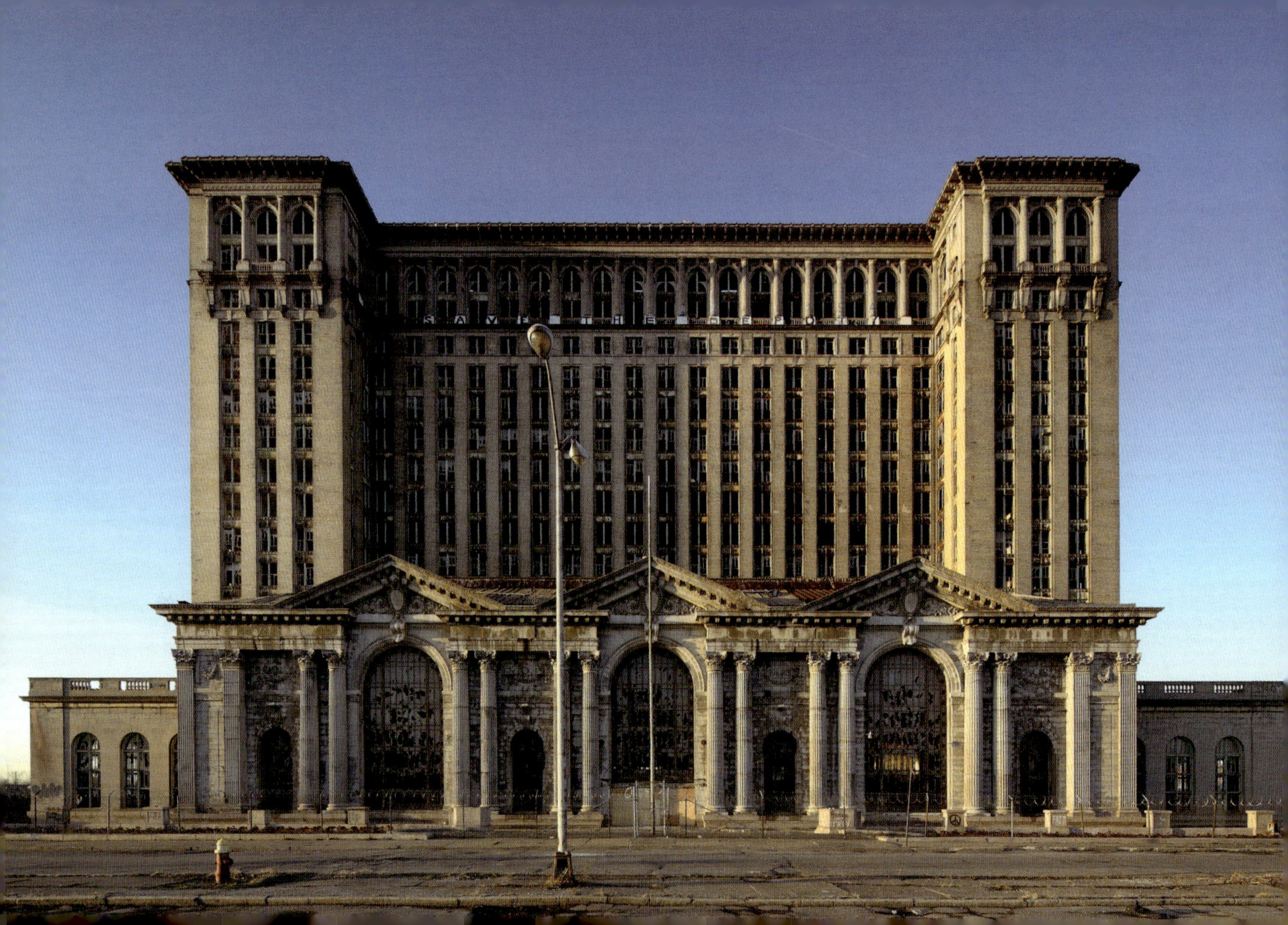
SAVE THE

◁ MICHIGAN CENTRAL STATION
DETROIT, USA, 2010

Detroit. The view through the broken windows from the top floor of the Broderick Tower is both breathtaking and uncanny. There is something strange about this city. There were hardly any cars driving on the wide, six-lane roads. Three cars were parked in the parking lot and the woman by the barrier was staring absently into space. On the pavement, a homeless person was wandering around aimlessly. The other skyscrapers around me stared at me with hollow eyes: most of the buildings are empty above the first floor, and you can sometimes see a curtain flapping out through an open window.

Is this the image of a metropolis after the Apocalypse? There is almost no one living in the city center and the surrounding districts any more. Many of the houses have been burnt out or look totally dilapidated. Over a third of the surface area is waste ground and nature is eagerly re-asserting itself.

In the distance, we saw the proud Michigan Central Station. Later on, I would be walking with Brett through its dark cellars, watching out for the Latino gangs that are rumored to hang around there doing shady deals (but in fact we encountered no one and had the monumental, graffiti-clad arrivals hall to ourselves).

Standing in the draughty corridors of the Packard Plant, in the basement swimming pool of Highland Park, or in Cass Tec High School's dining hall, I tried to comprehend the forces that had been at work here. The causes of Detroit's phenomenal rise and fall are well-known and well-documented, but observing it first hand is a different matter. ◆

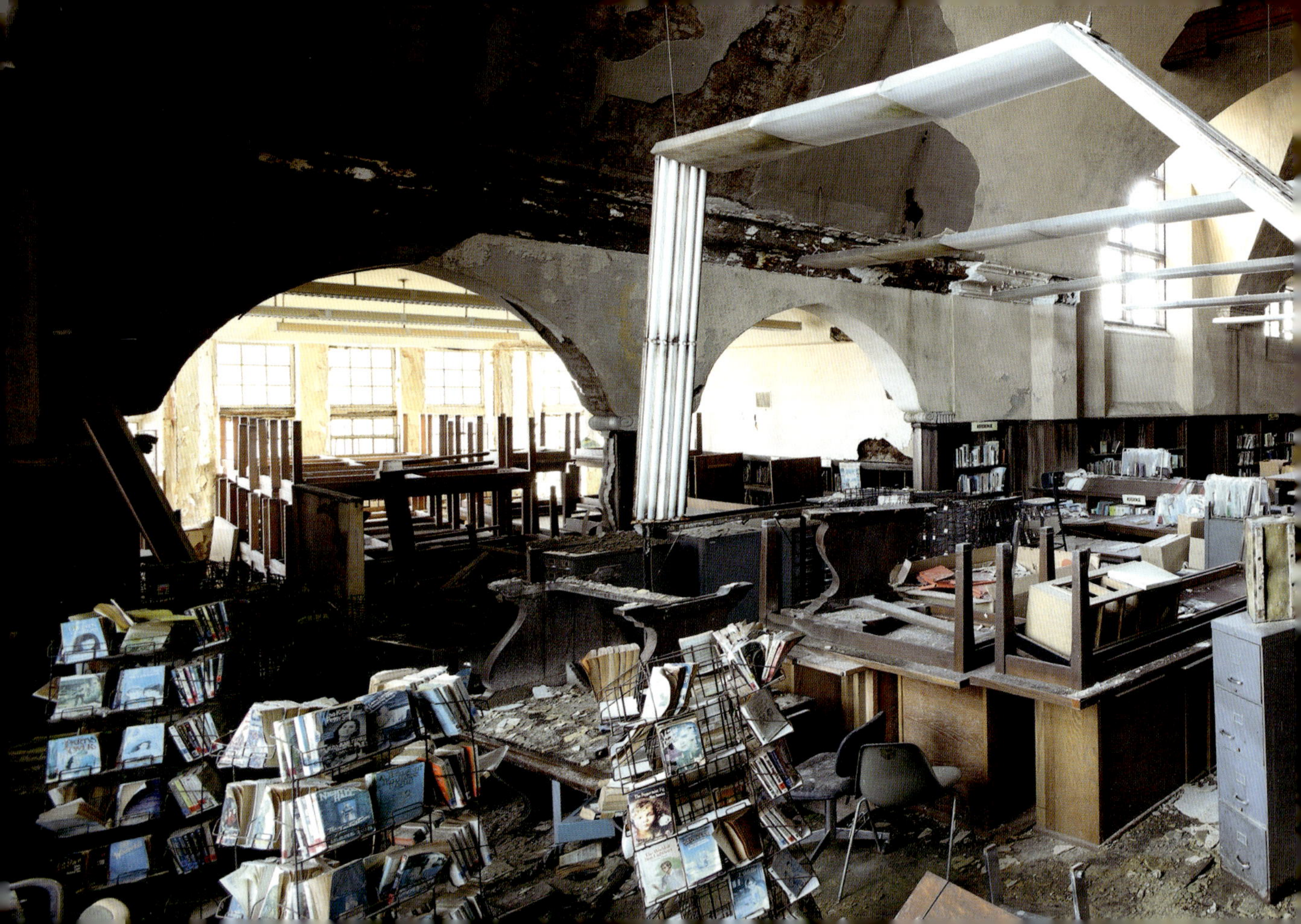

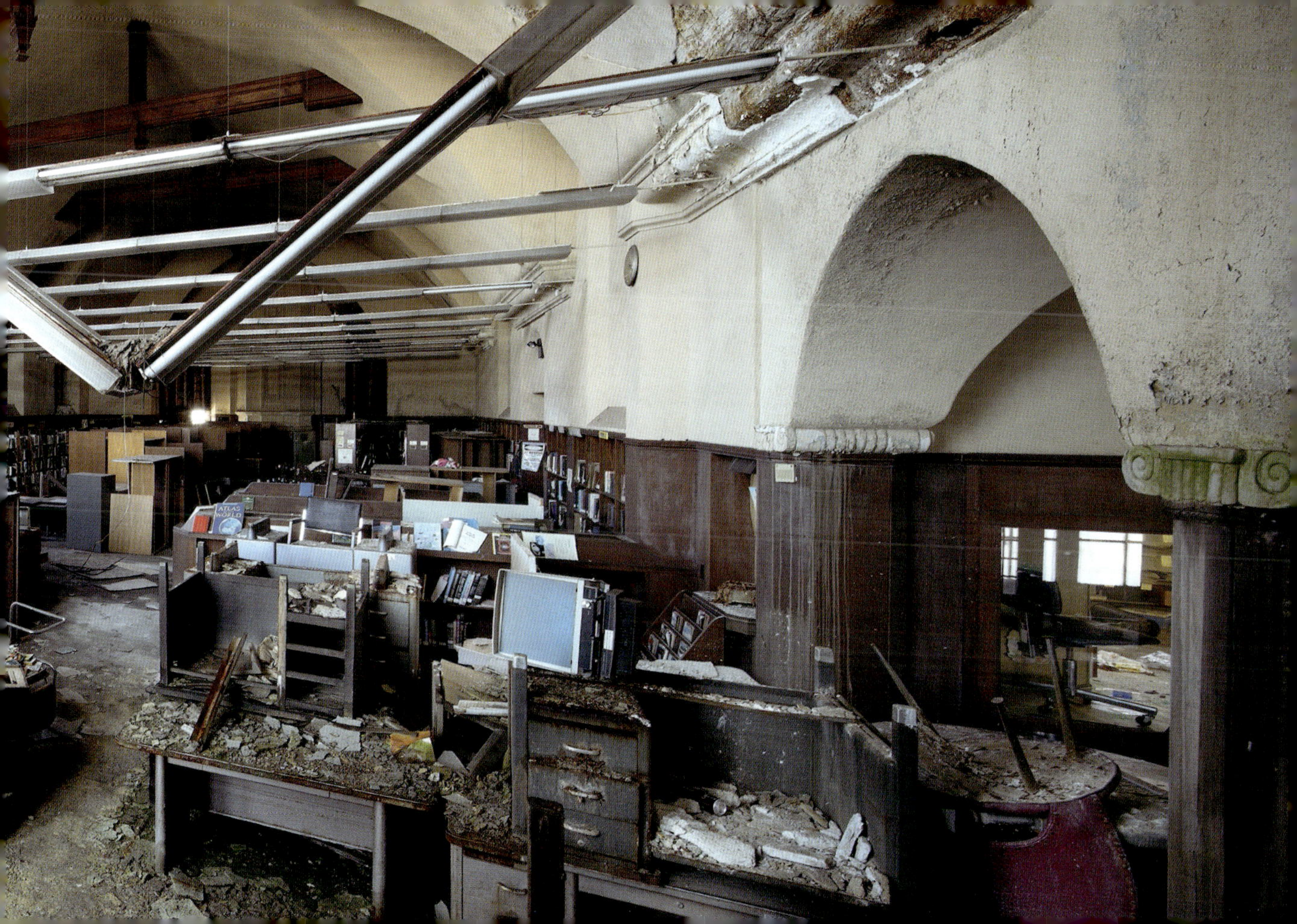
ATLAS
WORLD

Highland Park, Detroit, USA, 2012

P122–123: Marc Twain Library, Detroit, USA, 2010

Cass Tech High School, Detroit, USA, 2010

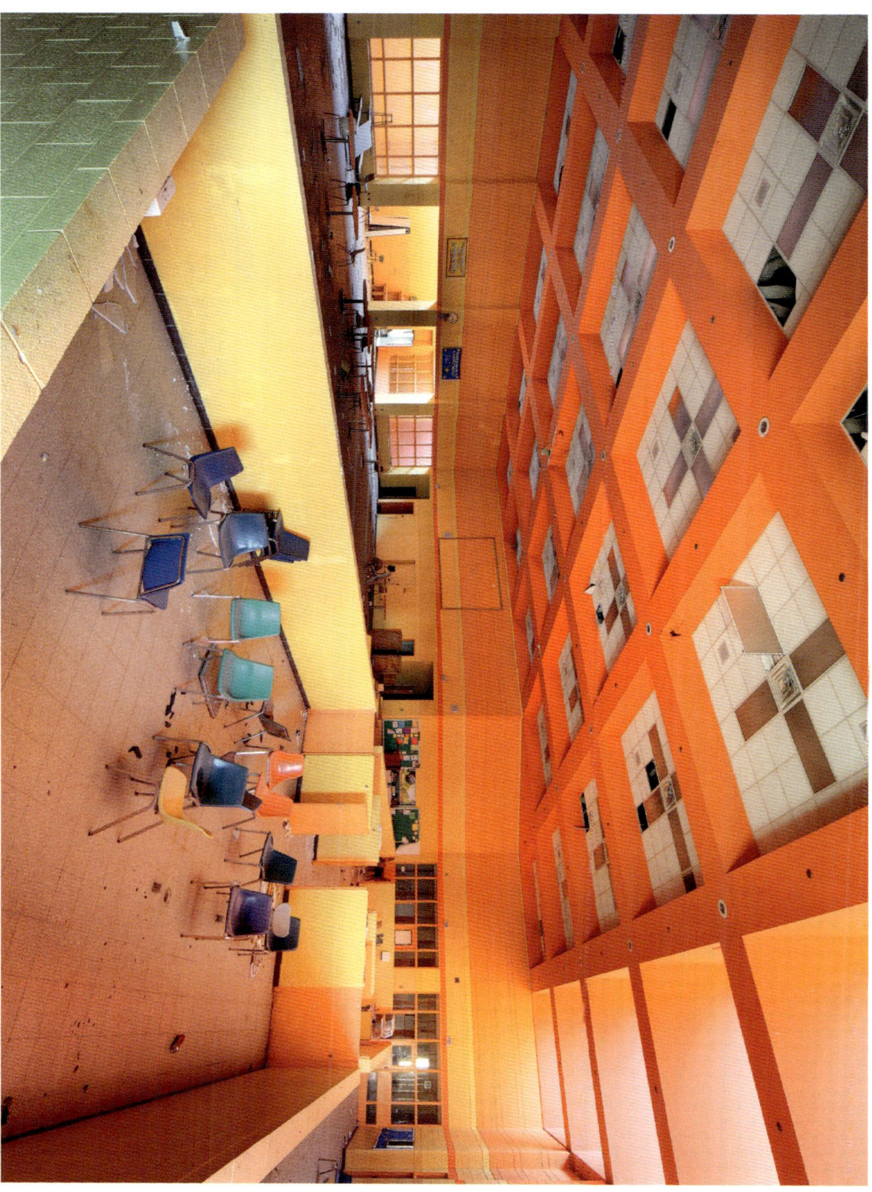

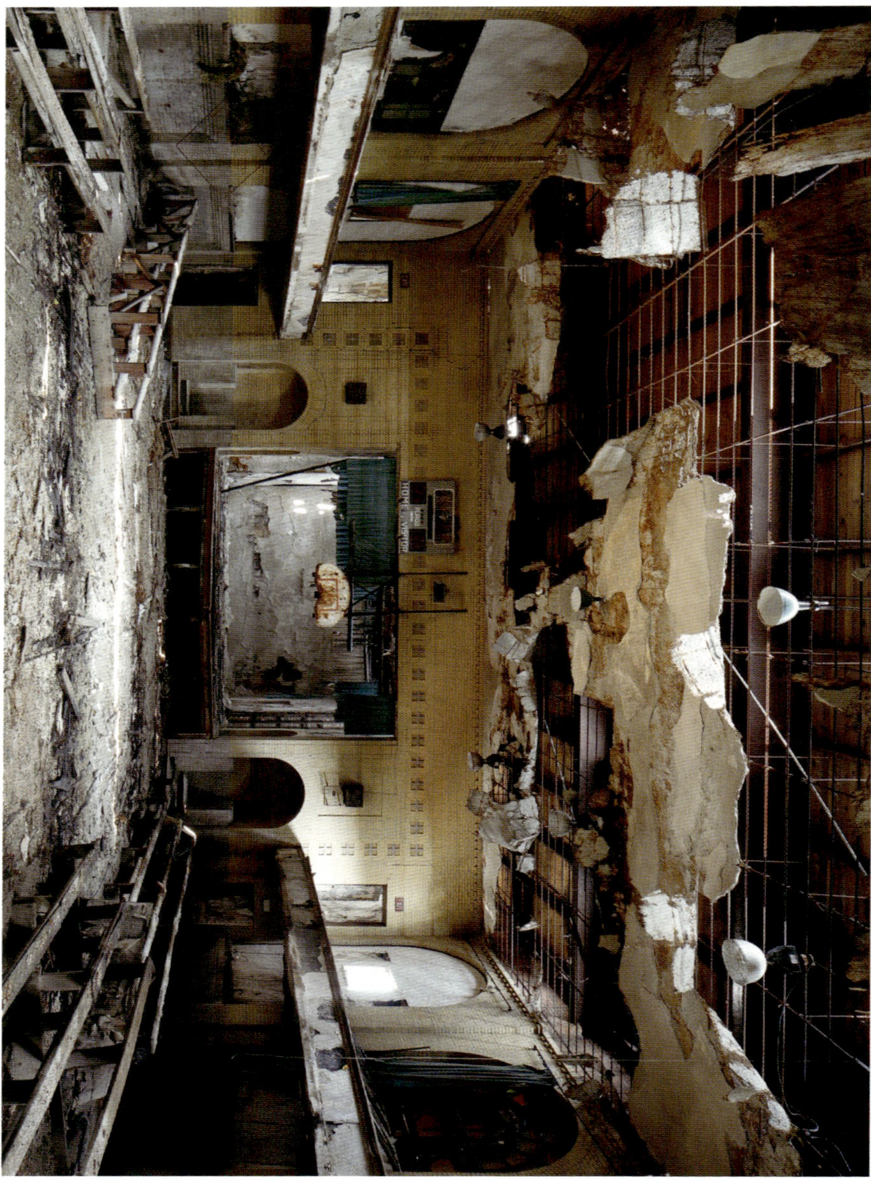

St. David School, Detroit, 2015

 DDR Basketball - Krampnitz, Germany, 2013

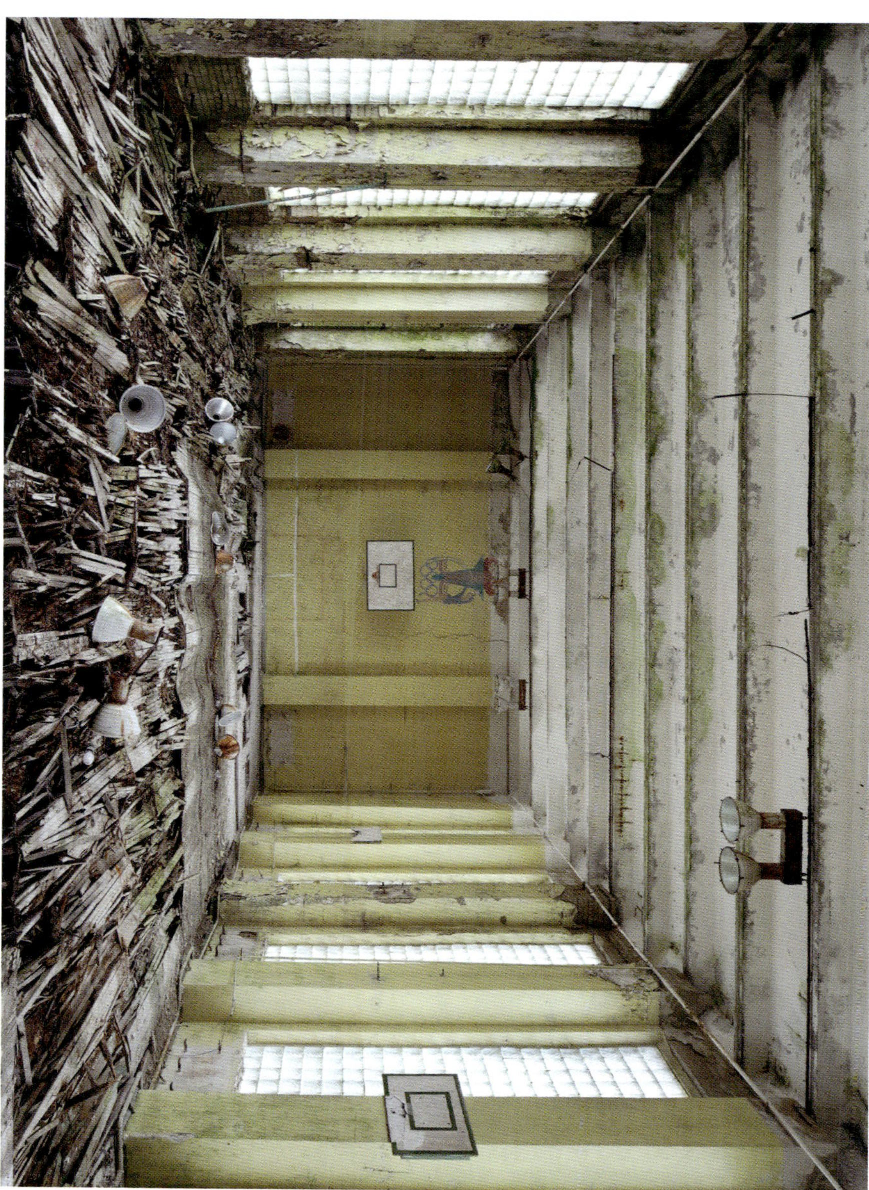

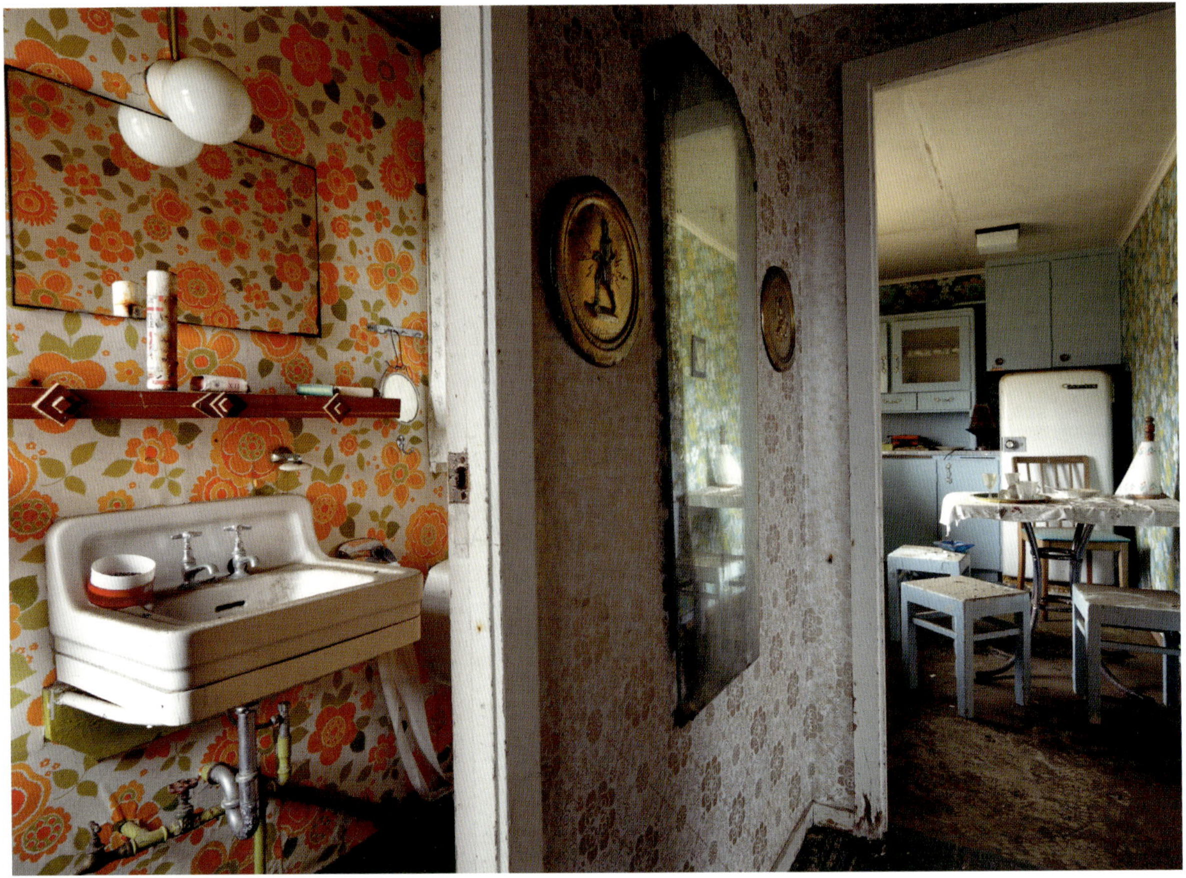

Vik, Iceland, 2011

 Apple Factory, Belgium, 2007

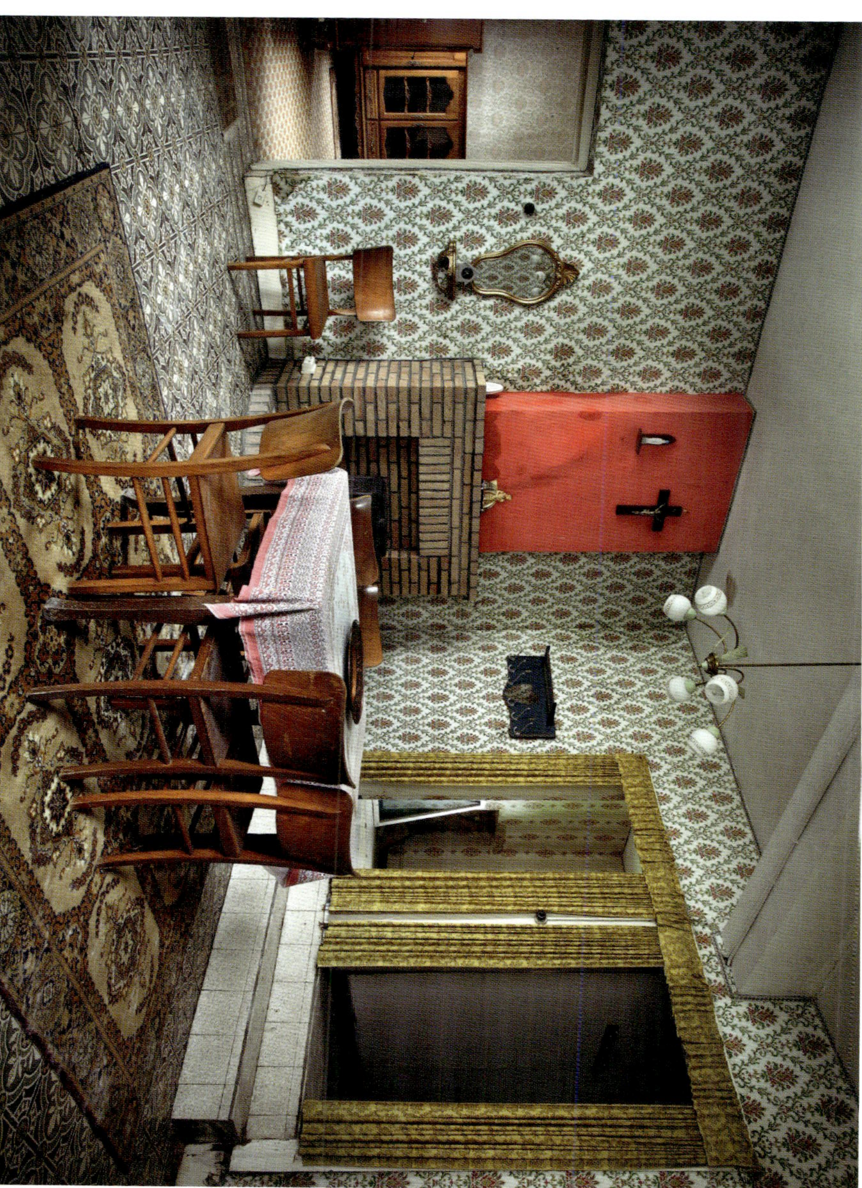

ABKHAZIA

ESHERA ▷

ABKHAZIA, 2018

Never before have I had the feeling of going somewhere and asking myself whether I would come back safe and sound.

During the previous decade, Abkhazia – with the help of Russia – fought a bloody war of independence with Georgia. Rocket and bullet holes can still be seen everywhere. The population was reduced by half and the country became extremely poor. Georgian influence was replaced by Russian influence. The east of the country is still not entirely safe. Weapons are everywhere, people are still traumatized from the war, and corruption and lawlessness are rampant.

Those who stayed behind rebuilt their homes from demolished materials. Anything that could be dismantled is gone. Some apartment buildings are inhabited by only one family. Clothes hang to dry on a single balcony. All the other apartments have been stripped of their windowsills, sanitary facilities, electrical wiring, tiles, staircase banisters, floors, ceilings and certainly furniture.

In the neighbourhood of the capital city is a gigantic dilapidated hotel with an Olympic size pool. No guests in the lobby; instead two horses and a colt. A surrealistic sight. I was standing on the roof when two vans arrived at high speed. I saw military uniforms and suddenly heard dogs barking everywhere. I had nowhere to go and decided to walk towards them before they let the dogs loose in the hotel. ◆

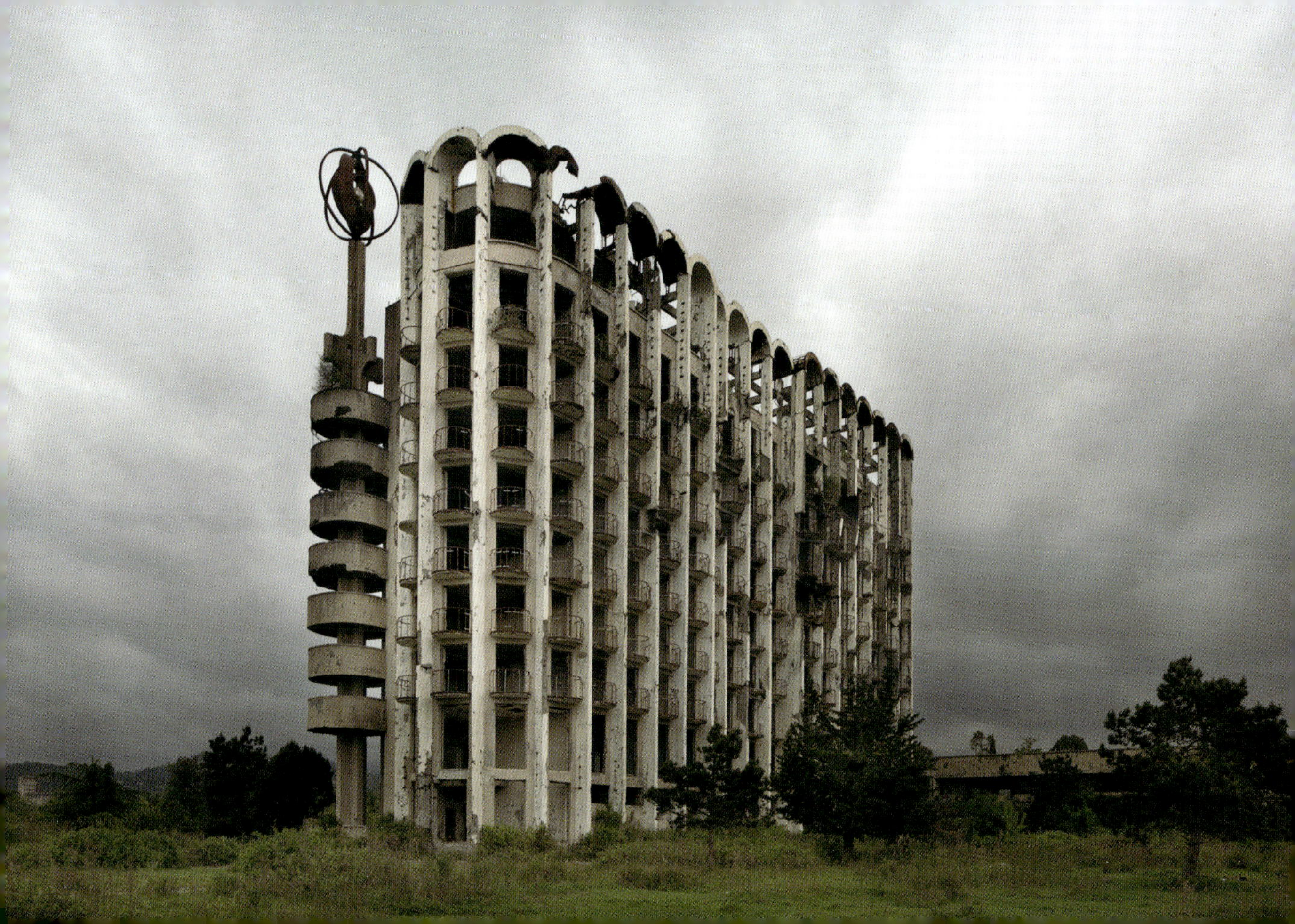

Tkvarcheli Power Plant, Abkhazia, 2018

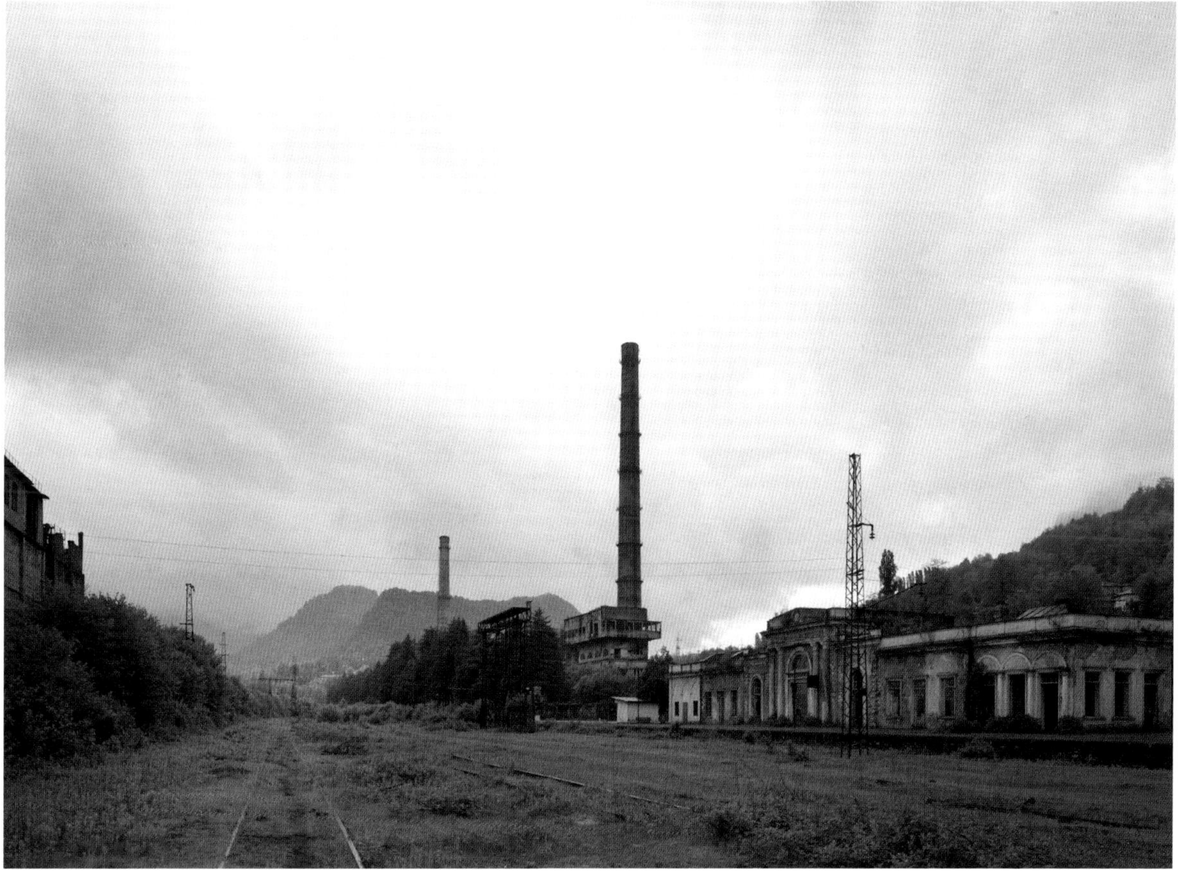

Tkvarcheli Railway Station, Abkhazia, 2018

AGHDARA ▹

ABKHAZIA, 2018

Driving into the old industrial city of Tkvarcheli is hallucinating. Giant empty factories stare at you in a hollow gaze. Like every other place, the train station is dilapidated. Large villas and apartment blocks are empty, the roads are full of potholes and the bridges that were meant to last forever are crumbling and no longer have railings.

I stayed in a small cottage in the mountains. Adam, the grandson of the woman who lived in the house, drove me there. He told me that during the war the entire family fled to Moscow. One day his father disappeared and never returned, but he was too young to remember. His grandparents had searched for his father for years, but there was absolutely no trace of him, he simply disappeared. Liquidation? An accident? No one knows. When we arrived at the house, the grandmother was waiting for us. A brave, stooped woman wearing clogs. We were hardly inside when she showed me a photo of her son...I didn't understand what she said, but I understood what she meant.

Cows, chickens, pigs, sheep and horses roam freely in all these empty buildings. I was standing in a former machinery hall taking photos, unaware that a few metres behind me, in a dark corner, a frightened cow was watching me. While I was focussing my camera, she panicked, and her loud moo scared me out of my wits. Soon after, I burst into a fit of laughter when she galloped on her scrawny legs over the slippery concrete floor out of the factory. ◆

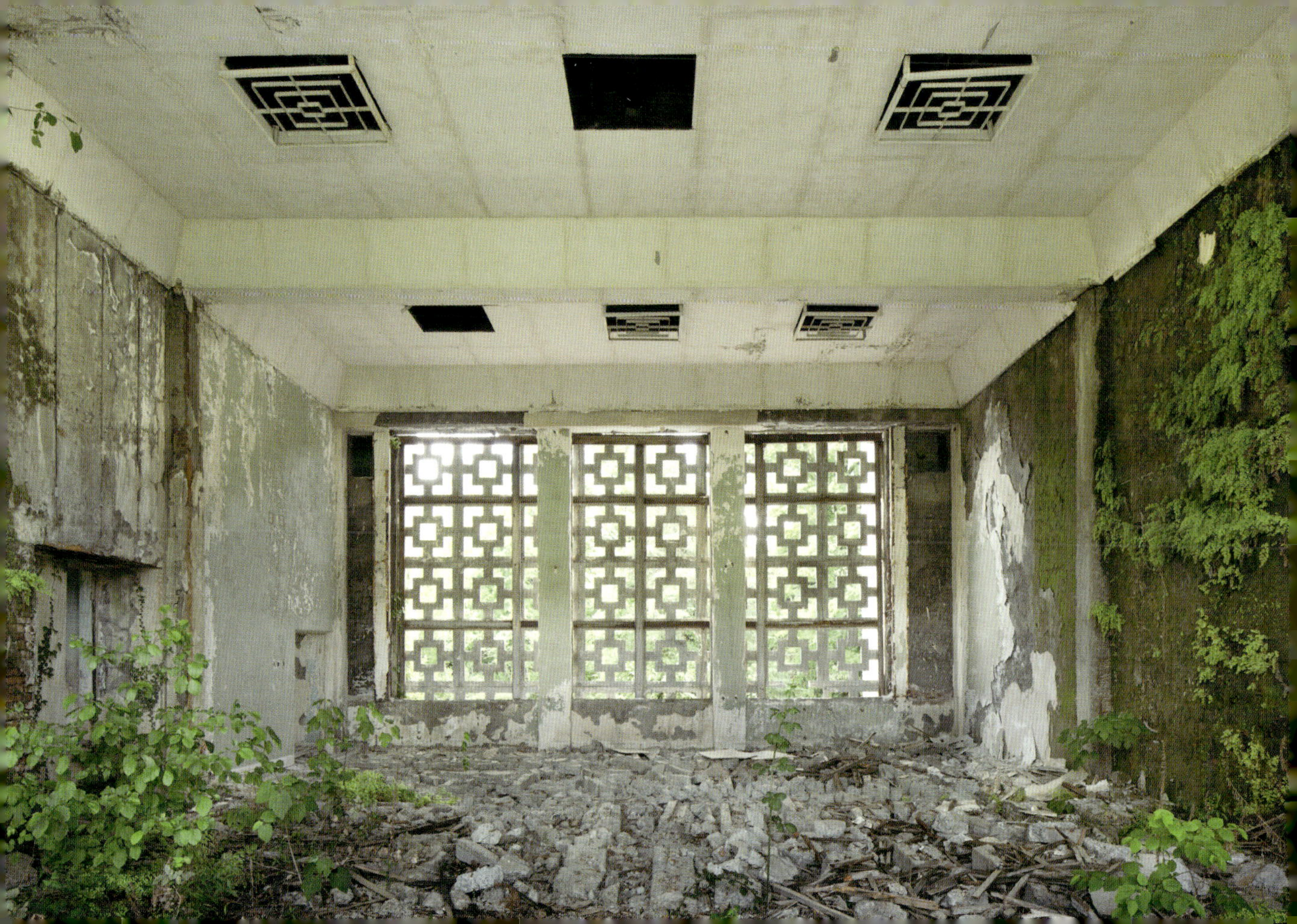

 ▵ Torpedo Factory, Abkhazia, 2018 ▿ Pergola Hotel, Abkhazia, 2018

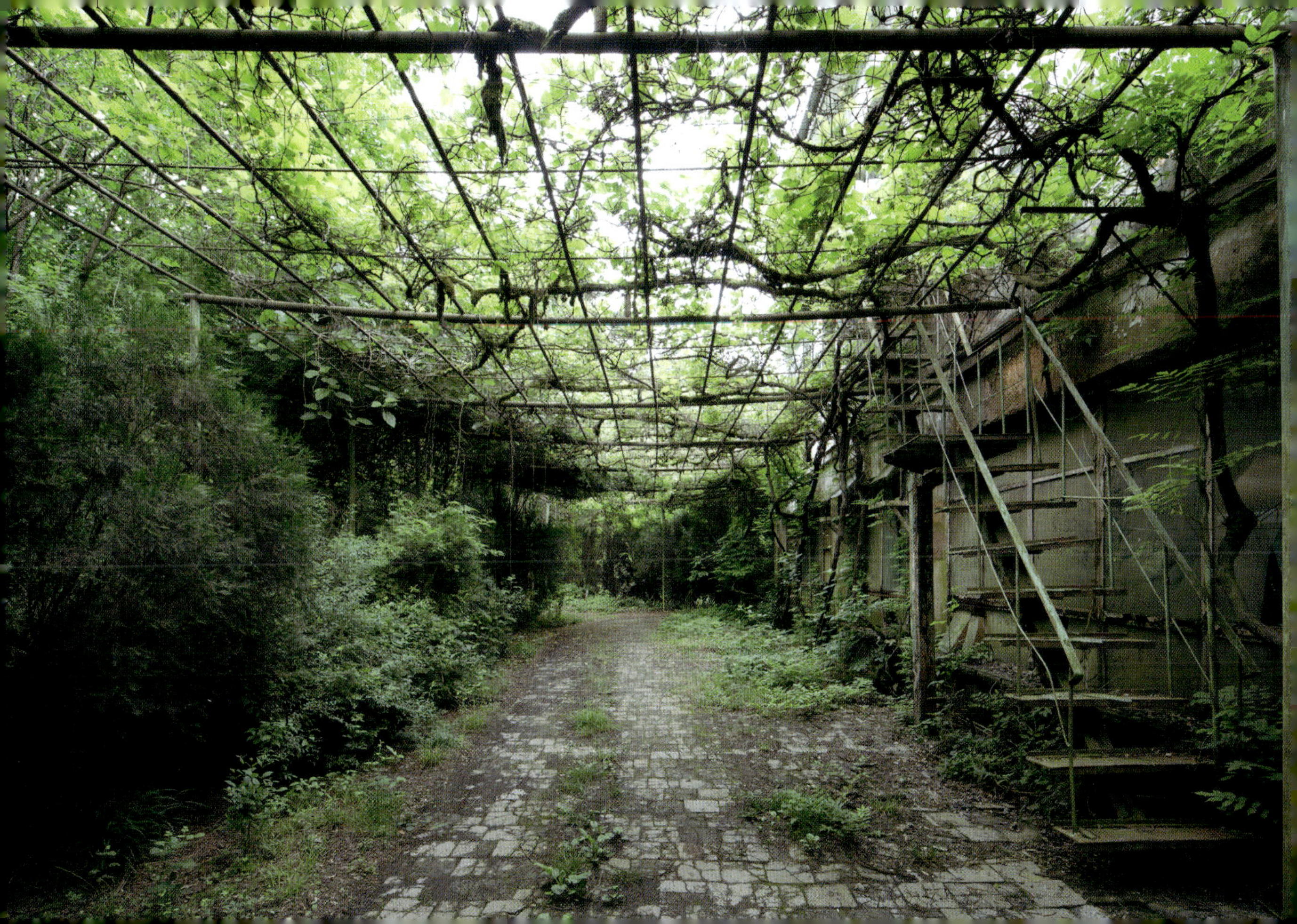

PARLIAMENT BUILDING ▷

ABKHAZIA, 2018

The parliament building in the centre of the capital city of Sukhumi is in total ruins, an open wound from the war. The imposing building is riddled with bullet holes and completely plundered. All that's left is the concrete shell.

Inside it is a public rubbish dump and a meeting place for youngsters. The ground is littered with injection needles, and taxi drivers come in here to relieve themselves between rides. Apparently, this is very fertile ground for trees that are growing metres high through the windows. This combination of jungle and lost glory is magical; the reality of this country is far less. ◆

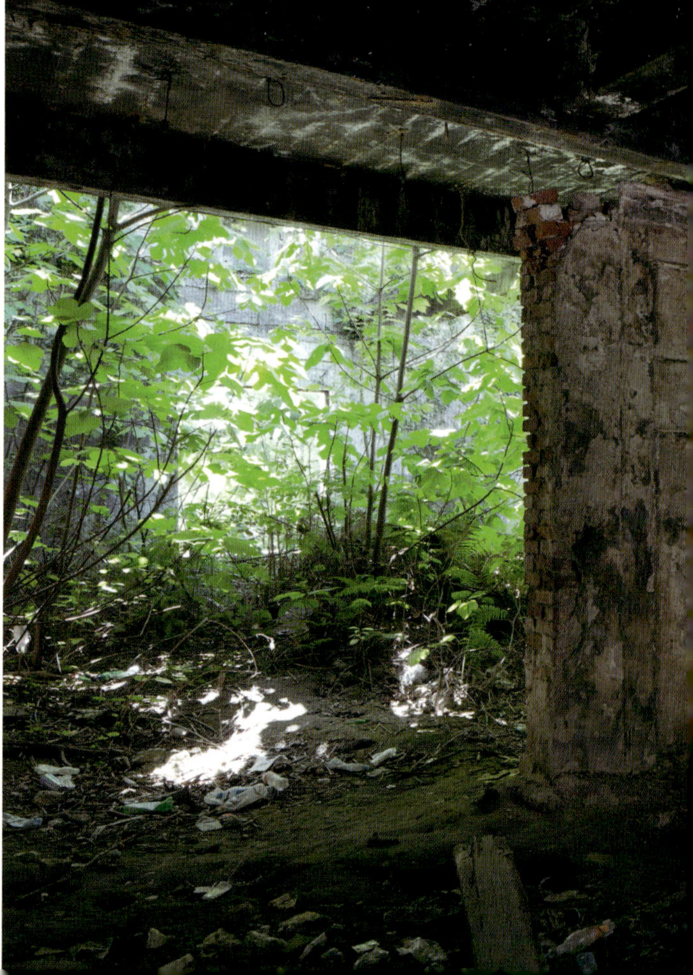

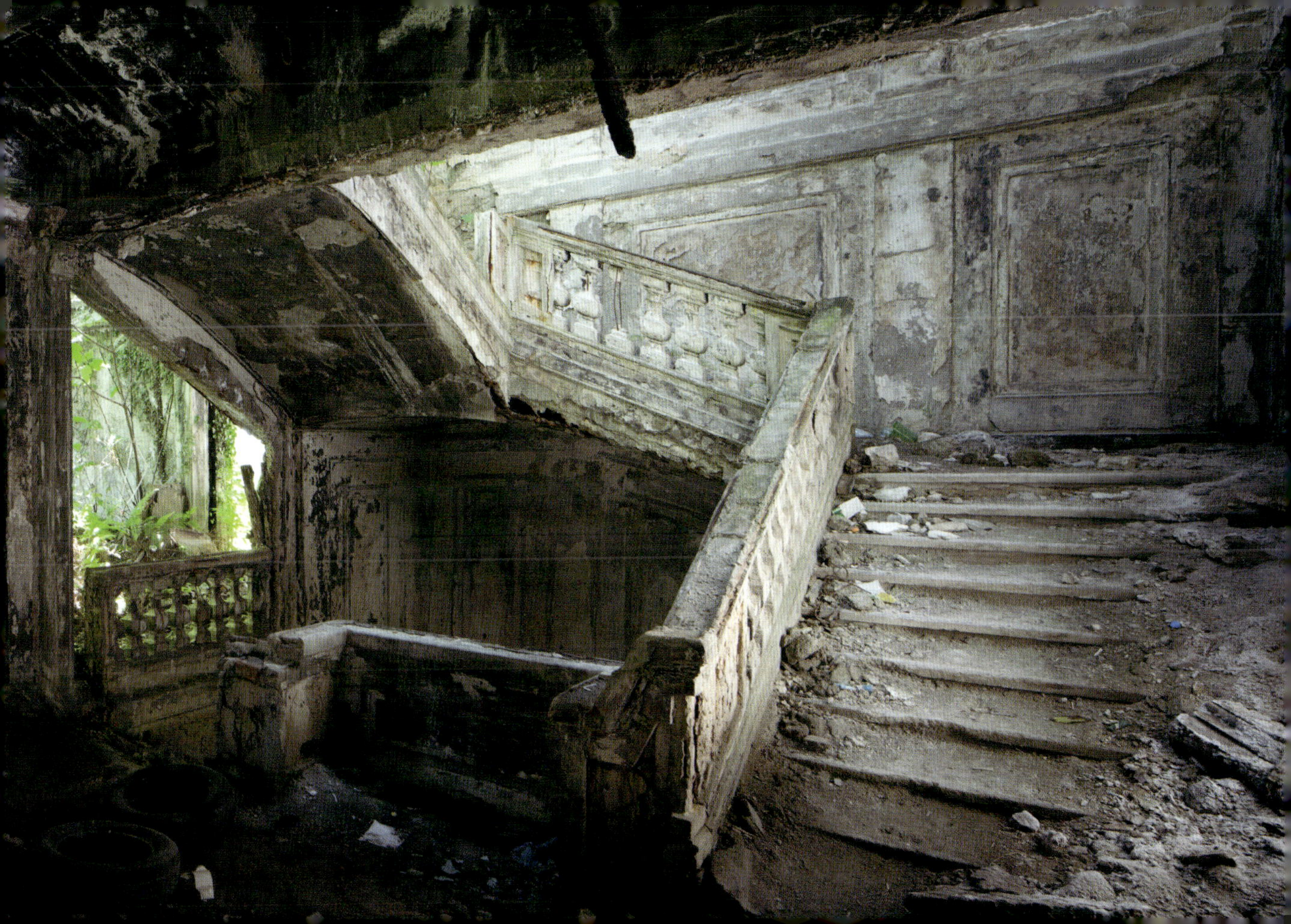

PRINCE SMETSKI SANATORIUM ▹

ABKHAZIA, 2018

You can't rent a car in Abkhazia. I found someone who knows someone who was willing to drive me around for two days. What I got was an escaped lunatic as a chauffeur. He lies flat on his seat, a cigarette dangling from the corner of his mouth and a mobile phone stuck to the front windshield with a suction cup. We communicate using Google translate, while he zigzags through the city, tailgating and honking a police car until the latter allows him to pass – giving him a guilt-ridden look. When we see a woman walking in the street, my chauffeur always has to get her attention by swerving around, tyres screeching, even if it means driving against the traffic. Yet somehow, we got through day 1 unscathed. On day 2, a friend of his joined us, providing a new car, because the previous evening, after he dropped me off, he managed to crash his own car. It was actually quite fun with these two fellows, because Google translate sometimes made the most hilarious translation errors and when the sun was setting, they made a campfire near an empty swimming pool.

In a beautiful, but extremely dilapidated sanatorium in the mountains, all the floors had rotted. Only the central stone staircase stood relatively firm. The building had four floors with the traditional cow-dung cakes on the ground floor, and to my great surprise, also on the fourth floor! The sanatorium was actually built against a steep cliff and from the top floor a bridge led to the outside where cows pastured during the day. ◆

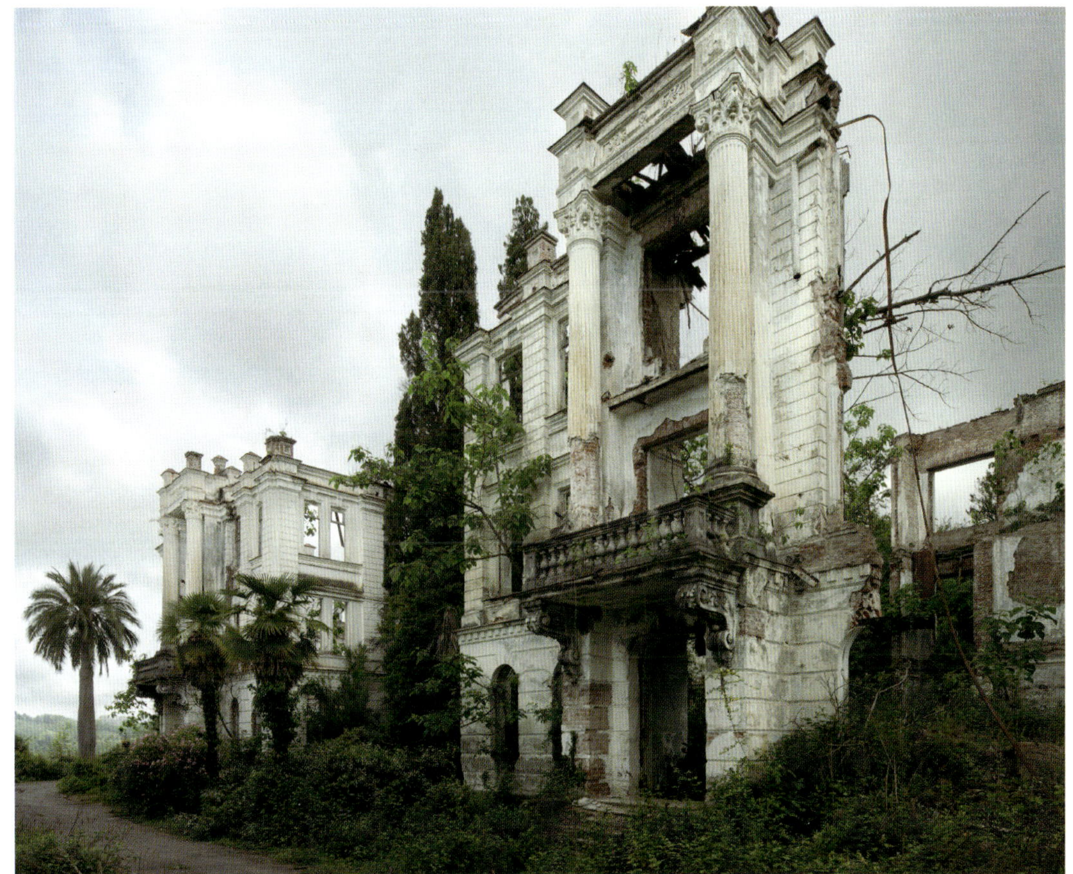

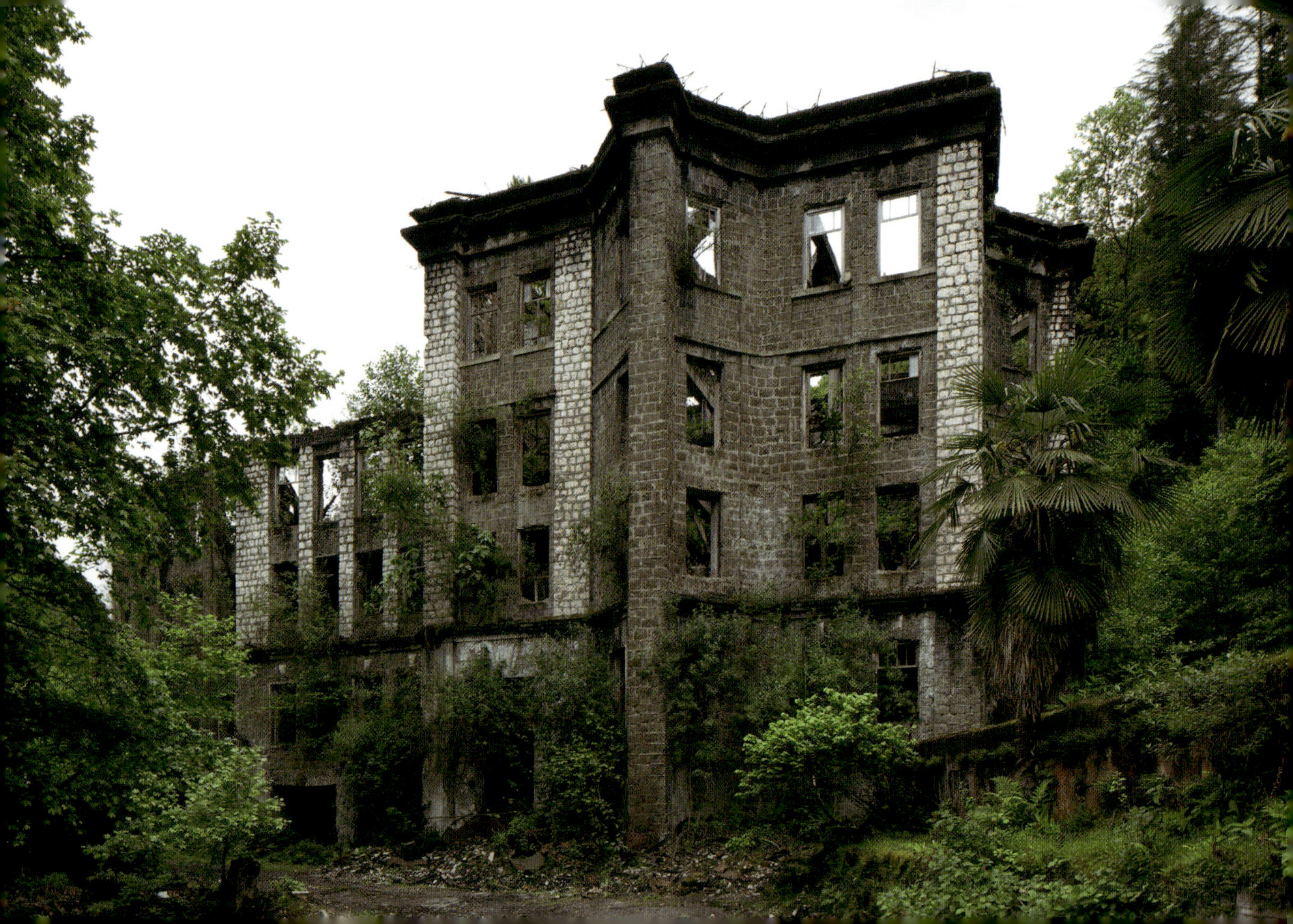

 △ Akarmara, Abkhazia, 2018 ▽ Akarmara, Abkhazia, 2018

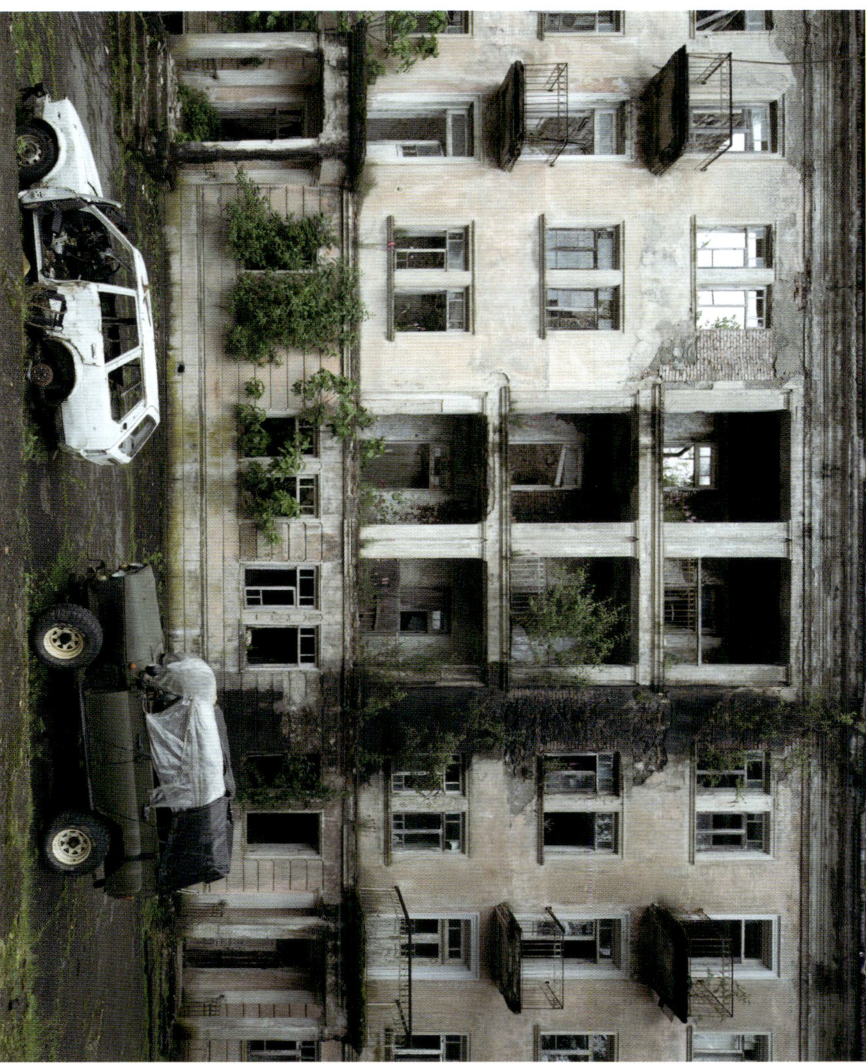

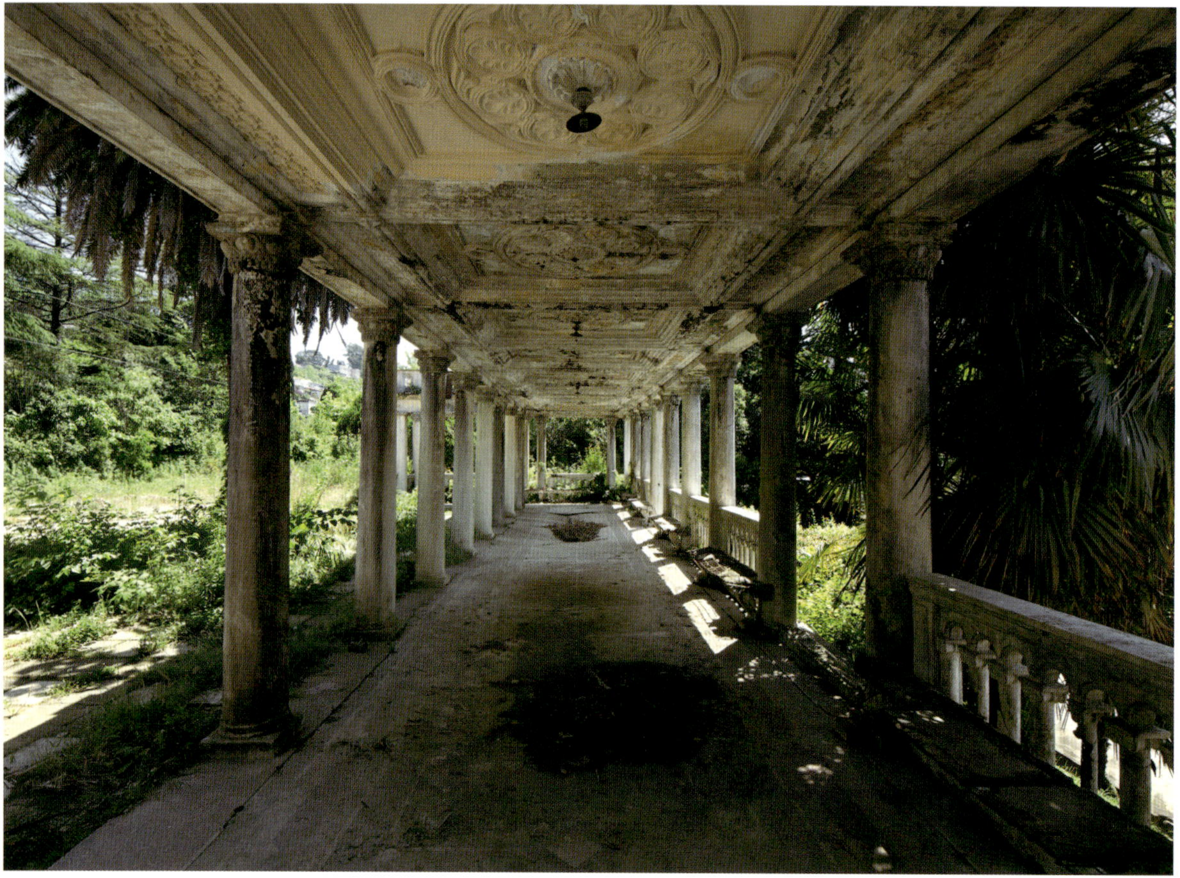

Gagra Railway Station, Abkhazia, 2018

 Prince Smetski Sanatorium, Abkhazia, 2018

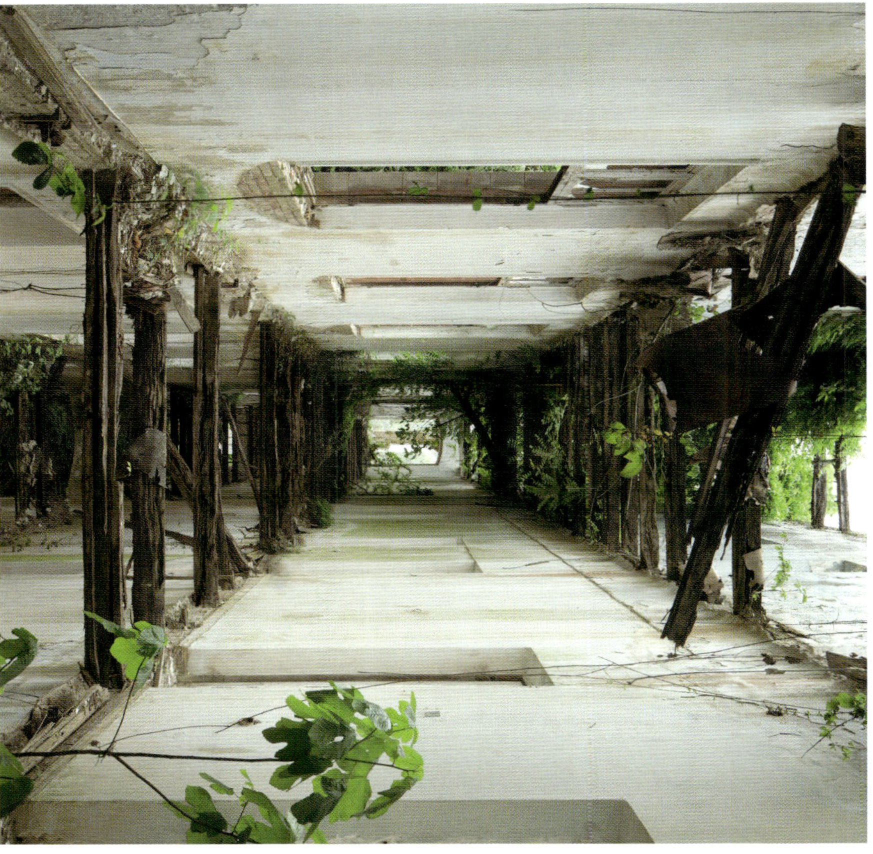

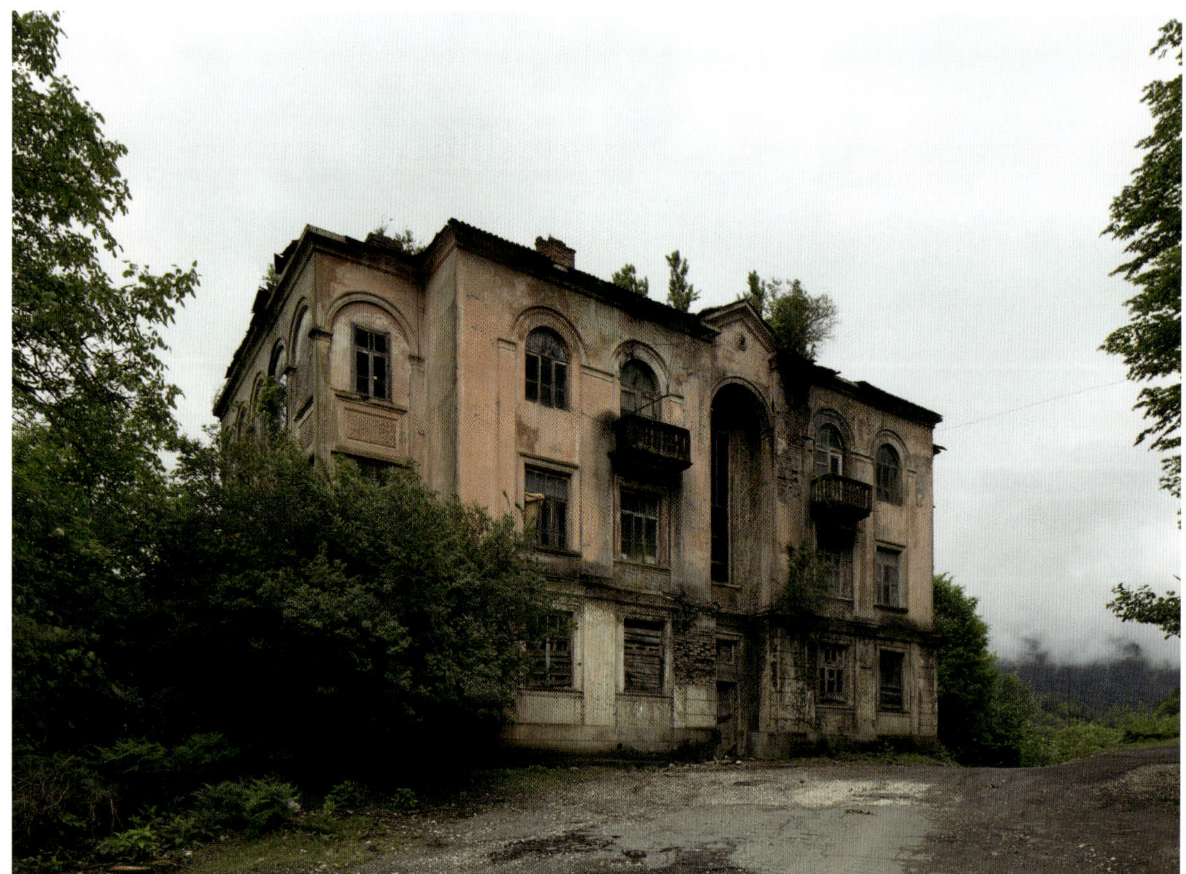

The Pink Villa, Abkhazia, 2018

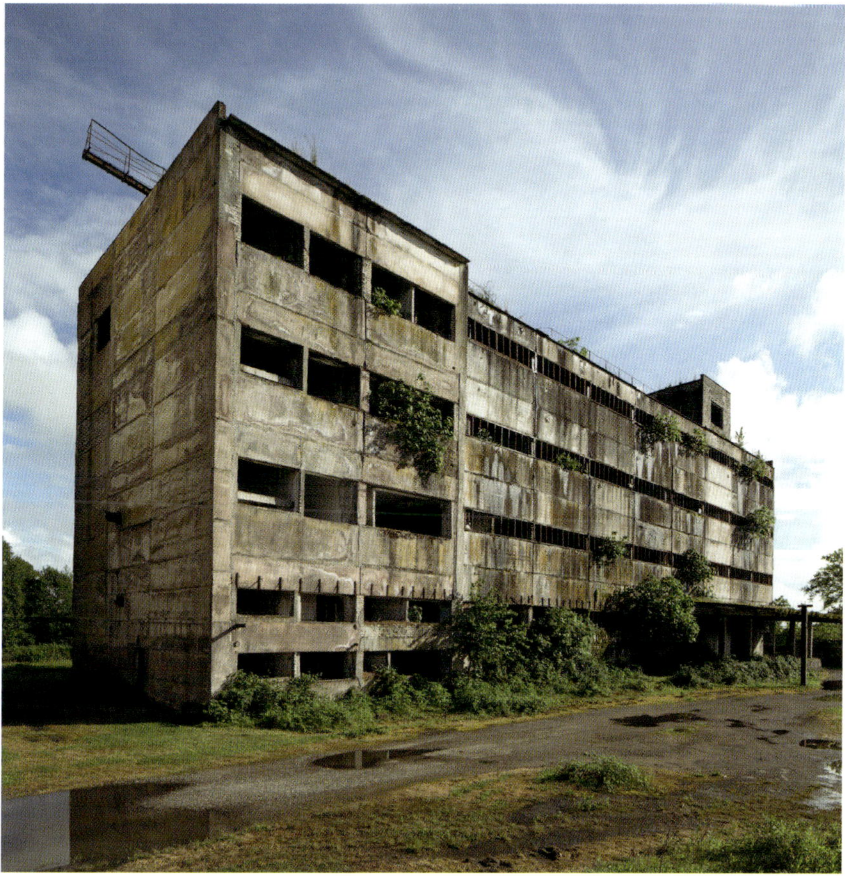

Promko, Abkhazia, 2018

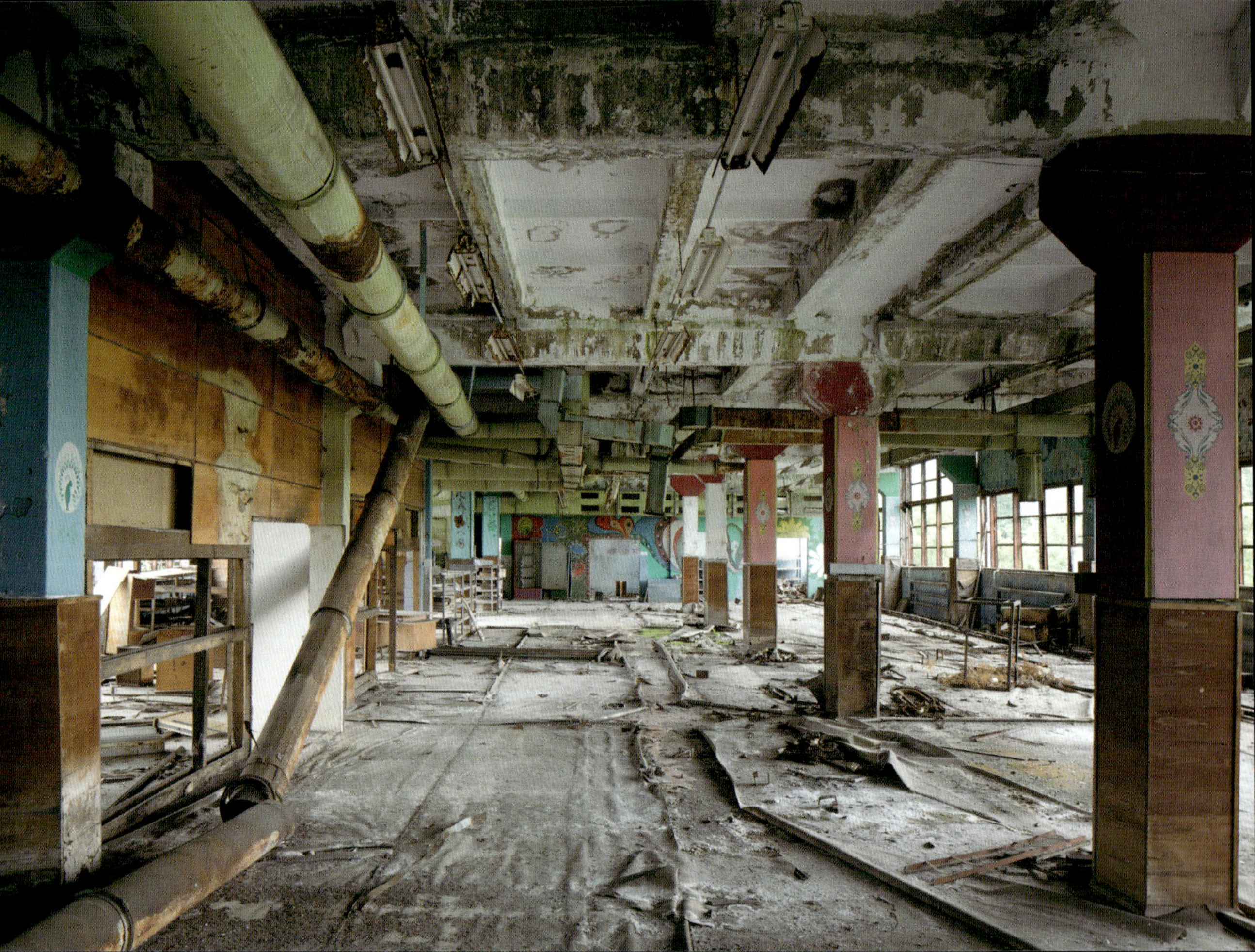

△ The Russian Factory, Abkhazia, 2018 ▿ Sukhumi Railway Station, Abkhazia, 2018

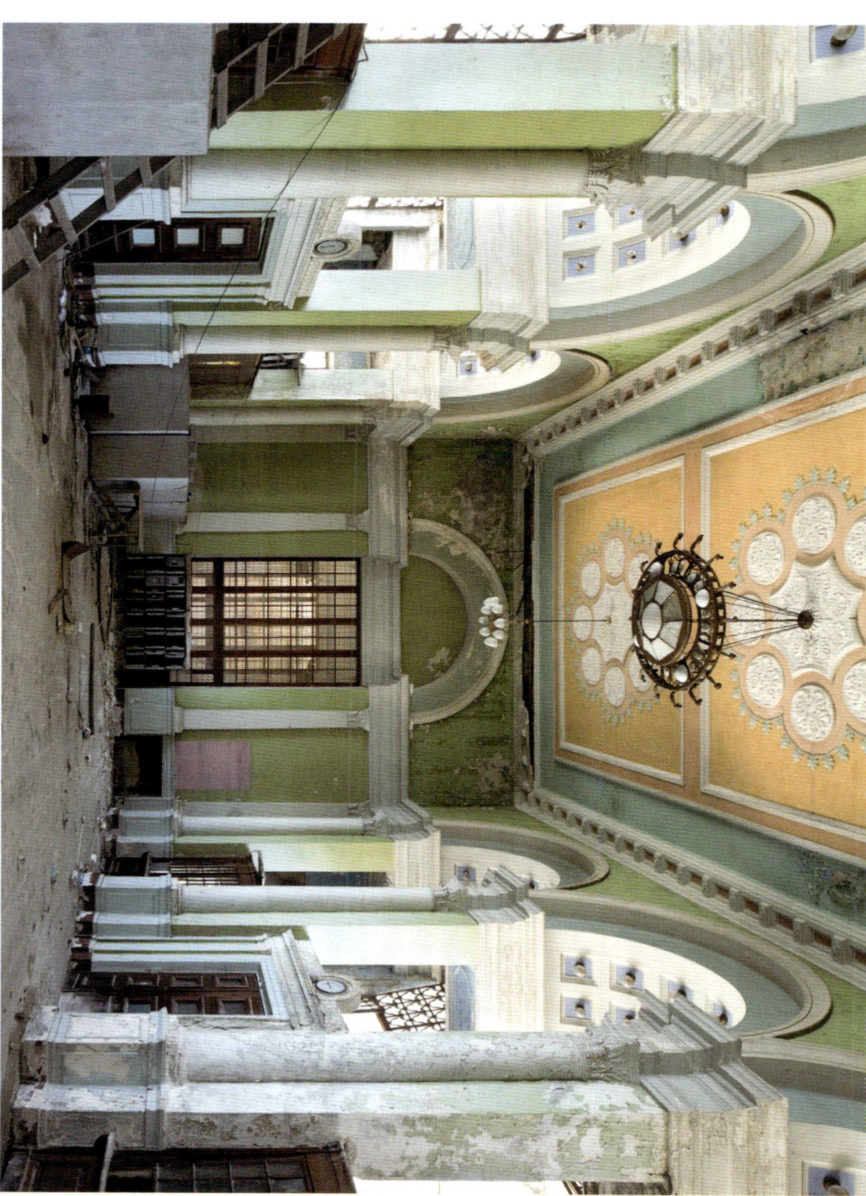

GAGRA WINTER THEATER ▷

ABKHAZIA, 2018

I wander around the sinister neighbourhood with its empty factories and stray dogs that force me to circumvent. Occasionally I see a shadow disappear behind a tree or around a street corner. I take side streets to avoid these characters, but I am hopelessly attracted to the buildings. At the end of a dead-end street, I see three men standing next to a white Land Rover. An unexpected scene: an expensive car in a godforsaken alley. Nevertheless, I decide to approach them. The men stare at me silently. They are Russians. They have an appointment with someone from the city to view an empty but closed factory. They want to buy the building, but they won't say why. The rear window of the car is smashed, there is glass everywhere. They briefly left the car to inspect the outside of the building and during those few minutes, someone saw his chance. It is a weird feeling to know that behind all these walls and bushes people are lurking and waiting for that moment. The Russians invite me in. This is the only time here that I've been in an empty building that was not completely looted. On the walls are communist-era slogans, the cheerful colours are somewhat reminiscent of Georgian culture. I lose track of time and before I know it, the Russians have disappeared. Outside it is getting dark and I'm locked up in a factory. I creep outside through a window, walk back past the dogs and weird characters. When back in town, the white Land Rover passes me and the Russians wave at me with apologetic faces. I give them the thumbs-up. ◆

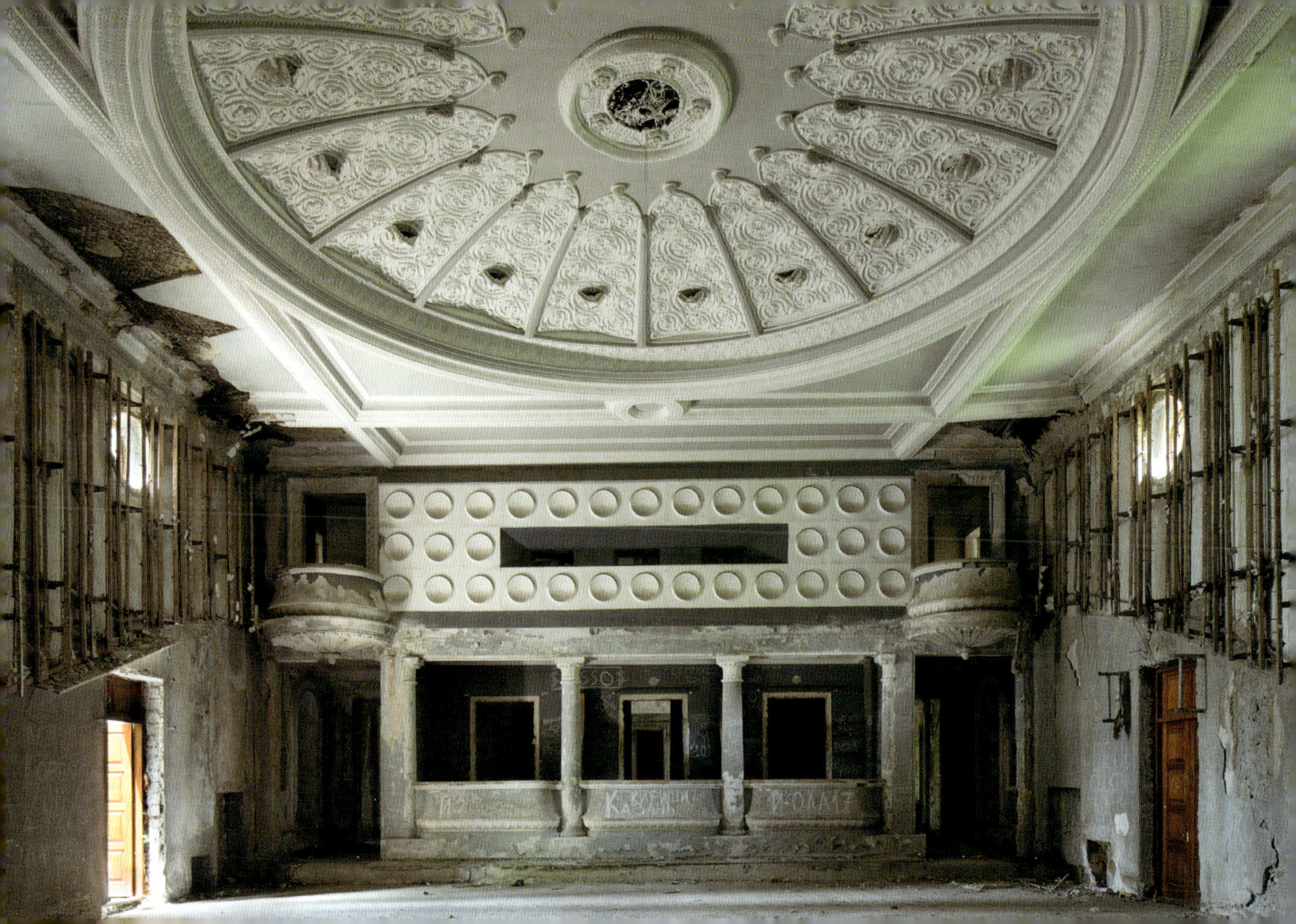

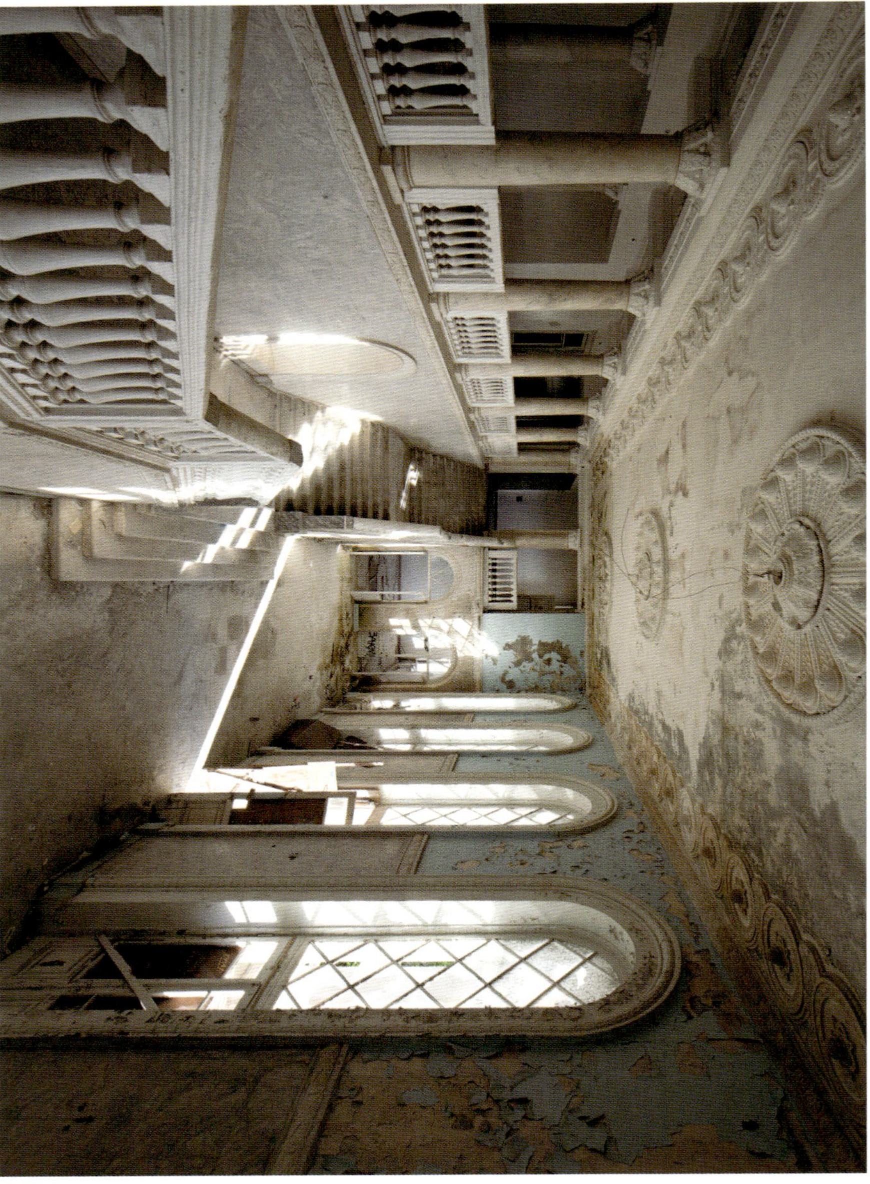

 Gagra Sanatorium Georgia, Abkhazia, 2018

 Gagra Sanatorium Georgia, Abkhazia, 2018

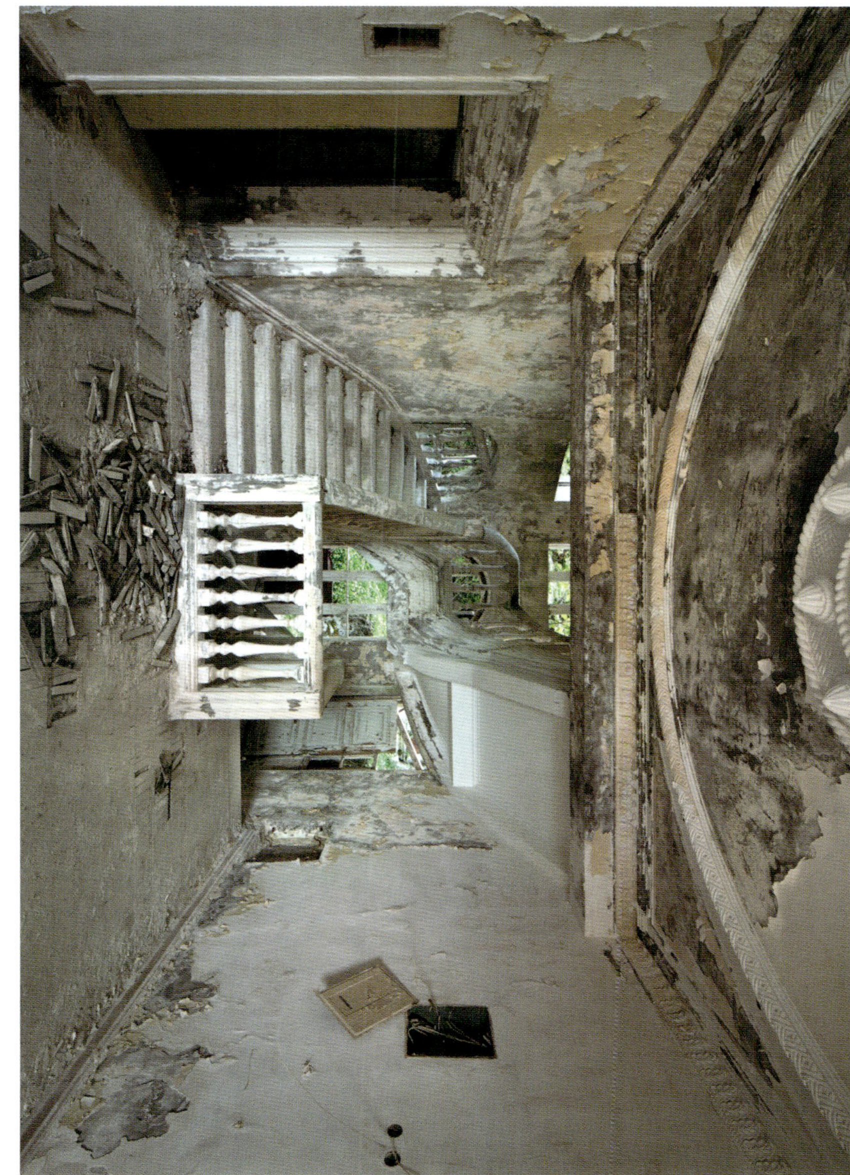

Prince of Oldenburg Gagra, Abkhazia, 2018

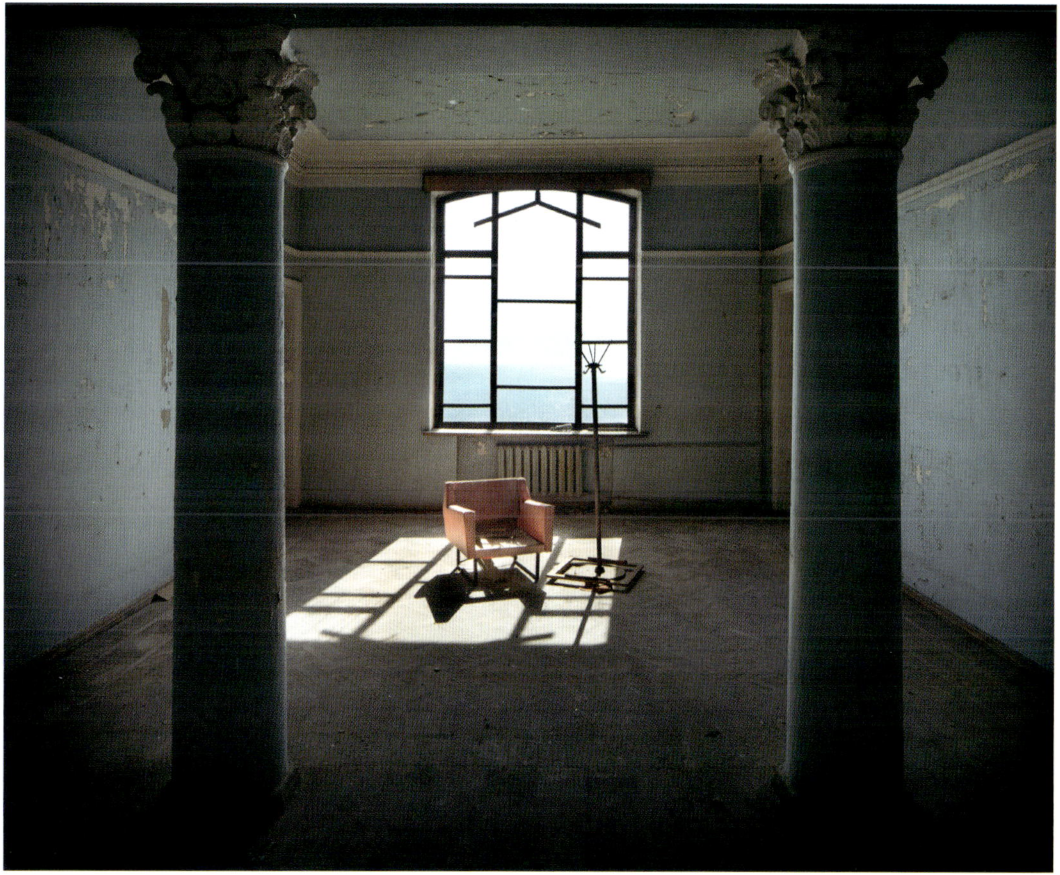

Gagra Sanatorium Georgia, Abkhazia, 2018

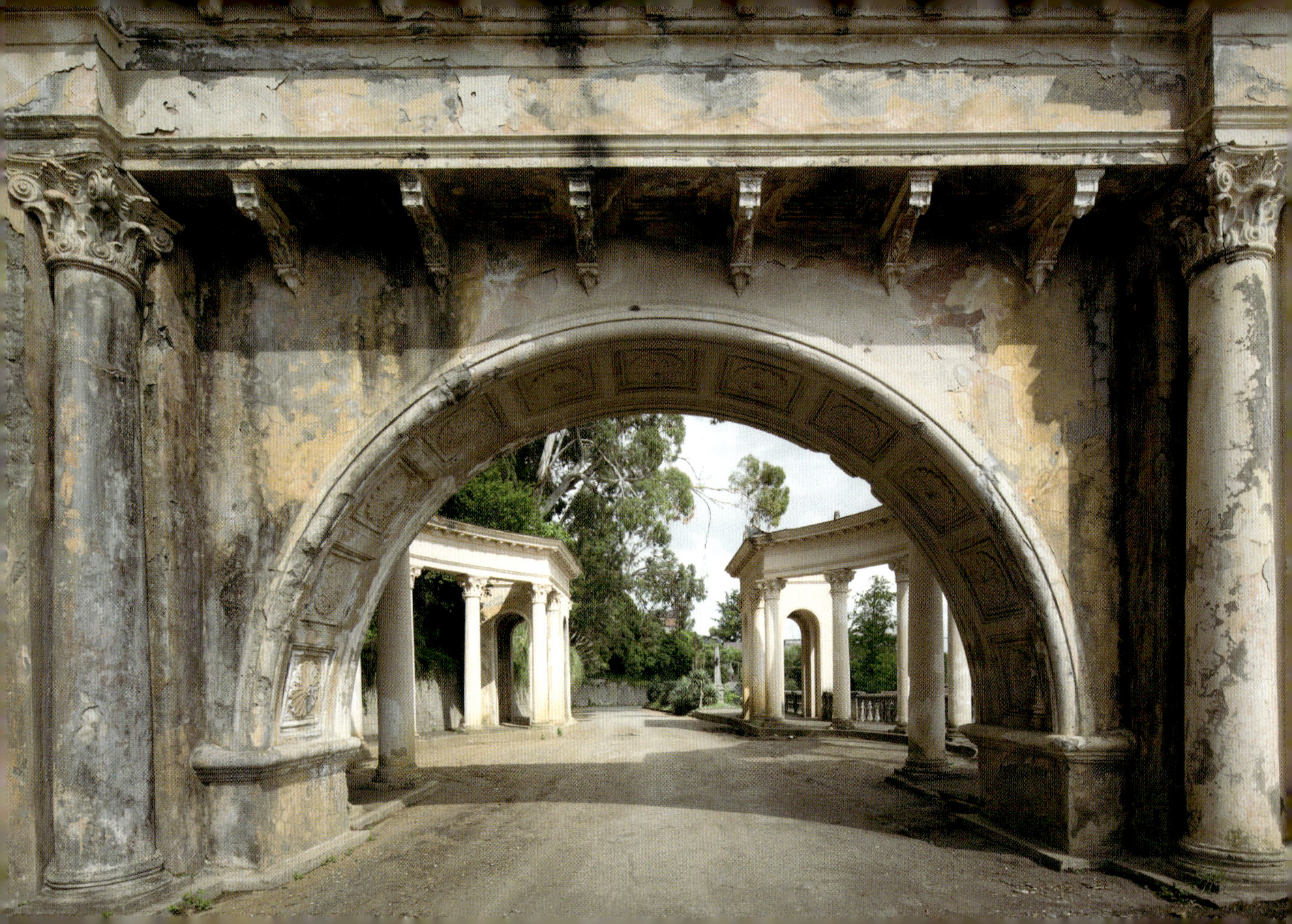

△ Nestor Lakoba, Abkhazia, 2018 ▽ Gagra Sanatorium Georgia, Abkhazia, 2018

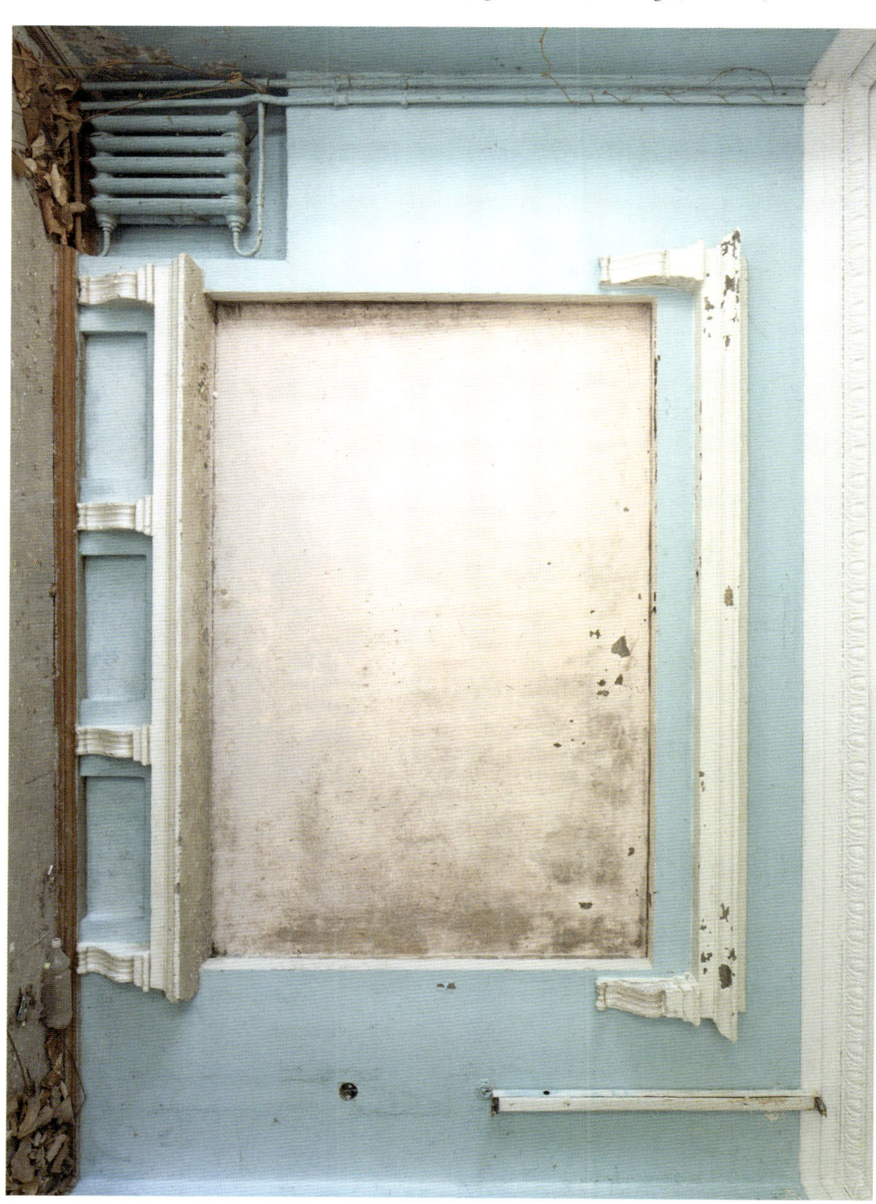

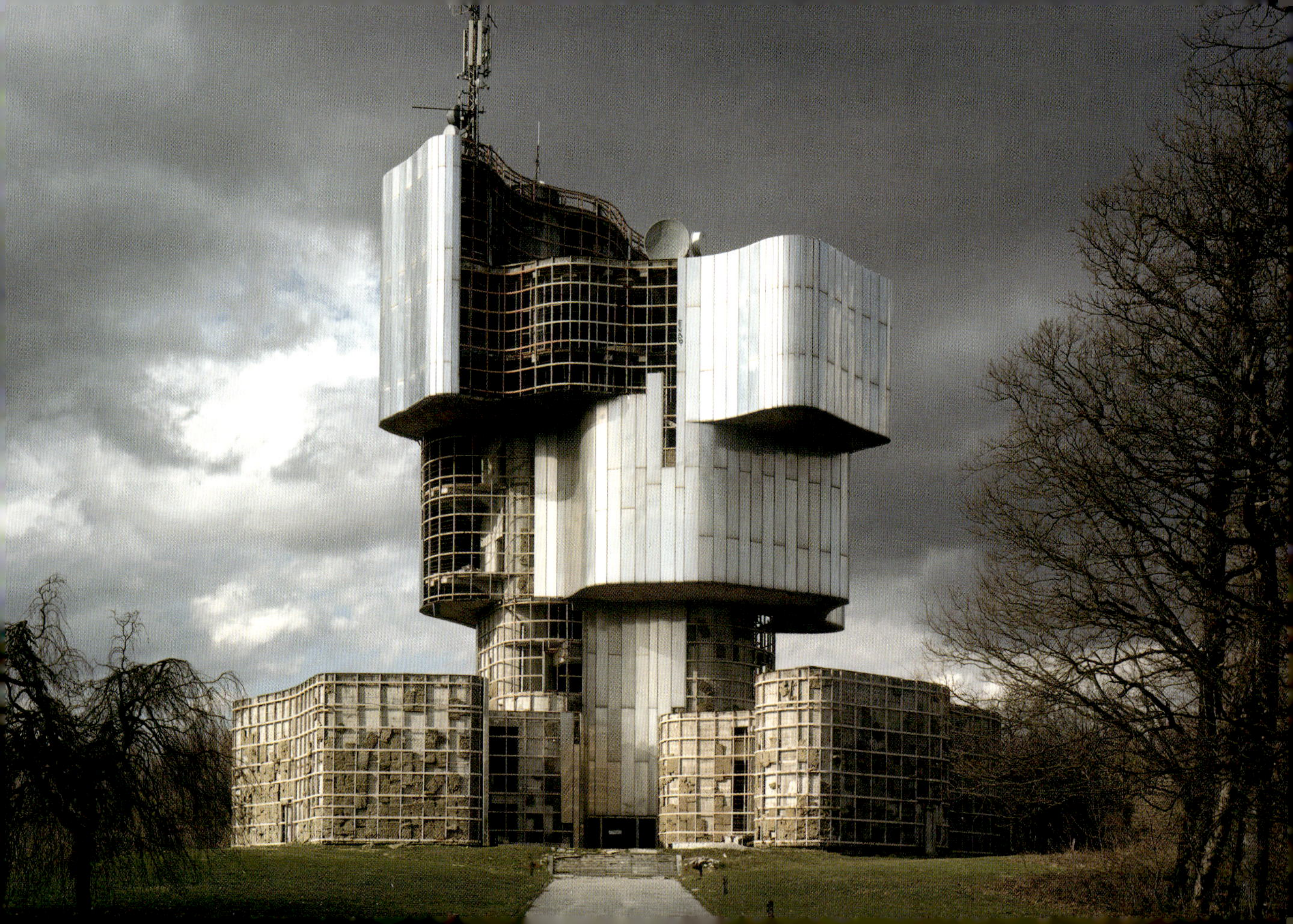

EPILOGUE

HENK VAN RENSBERGEN

It is an enormous privilege to visit an abandoned building.

Each time it feels like being invited. I come as a guest, with respect for these buildings that show their most sensitive side. Each has its story to tell. Some stories are short and concise, others long and hard to follow. But I never leave before hearing them. Occasionally, I have to search hard, but I always finally catch on. The silence says more than all the noise that was ever there.

Abandoned places touch a sensitive nerve. We are curious to know why these buildings were abandoned. Who lived there? What happened there? – the questions one asks when investigating a vanished civilization. My photos show our own forgotten civilization and what we have left behind. I observe our own crime scene. Not as a policeman but as a photographer. Not to establish the facts, but to reproduce the emotions of the moment. My photos, always detailed and seemingly objective, are open to interpretation and imagination. Ultimately, it is the spectator who rewrites the story of what took place: observation and imagination bring the buildings back to life.

What we see is often impressive, sometimes funny or endearing, recognizable or incomprehensible. Every visit is instructive, occasionally dangerous, and always exciting! ◆

Petrova Gora, Croatia, 2018

WWW.HENKVANRENSBERGEN.COM
WWW.ABANDONED-PLACES.COM

WWW.LANNOO.COM
Register on our website for our newsletter with new publications as well as exclusive offers.

TEXTS AND PHOTOGRAPHY:
Henk Van Rensbergen

TRANSLATION: Bracha de Man
COPY-EDITING: Melanie Shapiro
BOOK DESIGN: Jelle Maréchal, Evi Peeters

If you have any questions or remarks, please contact our editorial team: art@lannoo.com

D/2019/45/465 – NUR 640/653
ISBN: 9789401461511
Seventh print run